Prohibited Government Acts

Recent Titles in Reference Guides to the United States Constitution
Jack Stark, Series Editor

The Right to the Assistance of Counsel
James J. Tomkovicz

State Sovereign Immunity
Melvyn R. Durchslag

Consitutional Remedies
Michael Wells and Thomas A. Eaton

Prohibited Government Acts

A Reference Guide to the United States Constitution

Jack Stark

Foreword by Representative Tom Barrett

REFERENCE GUIDES TO THE
UNITED STATES CONSTITUTION, NUMBER 2
Jack Stark, *Series Editor*

PRAEGER

Westport, Connecticut
London

Library of Congress Cataloging in Publication Data

Stark, Jack, 1939-
Prohibited government acts: a reference guide to the United States Constitution / Jack Stark ; foreword by Tom Barrett.
p. cm. -- (Reference guides to the United States Constitution ; ISSN 1539-8986 no. 2)
Includes bibliographical references and index.
ISBN 0-313-31352-0 (alk. paper)
1. Constitutional law--United States. 2. Civil rights--United States. 3. Finance, Public--Law and legislation--United States. 4. Rule of law--United States. 5. Political questions and judicial power--United States. I. Title. II. Series.
KF45500 .S73 2002
342.73'02--dc21 2002067778
British Library Cataloguing in Publication Data is available.

Library of Congress Catalog Card Number: 2002067778
ISBN: 0-313-31352-0
ISSN: 1539-8986

First published in 2002

Greenwood Press, 88 Post Road West, Westport, CT 06881
An imprint of Greenwood Publishing Group, Inc.
www.greenwood.com

The paper used in this book complies with the Permanent Paper Standard issued by the National Information Standards Organization (Z39.48-1984).

10 9 8 7 6 5 4 3 2 1

In memory of Paul Sollie, a long-time friend

Contents

Series Foreword

JACK STARK

One can conceive of the United States Constitution in many ways. For example, noting the reverence in which it has been held, one can think of it as equivalent to a sacred text. Unfortunately, most of its devotees have had less knowledge and even less understanding of the document than they have had reverence for it. Sometimes it is treated as primarily a political document and on that basis has been subjected to analysis, such as Charles Beard's *An Economic Interpretation of the Constitution of the United States*. One can plausibly argue that the Constitution seems most astounding when seen in light of the intellectual effort that has been associated with it. Three brief but highly intense bursts of intellectual energy produced, and established as organic law, most of the Constitution as it now exists. Two of those efforts, sustained over a long period of time, have enabled us to better understand the document.

The first burst of energy occurred at the Constitutional Convention. Although some of the delegates' business, such as the struggle between populous and nonpopulous states about their representation in Congress, was political, much of it was about fundamental issues of political theory. A few of the delegates had or later achieved international eminence for their intellects. Among them were Benjamin Franklin, Alexander Hamilton, and James Madison. Others, although less well known, had first-rate minds. That group includes George Mason and George Wythe. Many of the delegates contributed intelligently. Although the Convention's records are less than satisfactory, they indicate clearly enough that the delegates worked mightily to constitute not merely a polity but a rational polity—that would rise to the standards envisioned by the delegates' intellectual ancestors. Their product, though brief, is amazing. William Gladstone called it "the most wonderful work ever struck off."

Despite the delegates' eminence and the Constitution's excellence as seen from our place in history, its ratification was far from certain. That state of affairs necessitated the second burst of intellectual energy associated with that document: the debate over ratification. Soon after the convention adjourned, articles and speeches—some supporting the Constitution and some attacking it—began to proliferate. A national debate commenced—not only about the document itself but also about the nature of the polity that ought to exist in this country. Both sides included many writers and speakers who were verbally adroit and steeped in the relevant political and philosophical literature. The result was an accumulation of material that is remarkable for both its quantity and its quality. At its apex is the *Federalist Papers*, a production of Alexander Hamilton, James Madison, and John Jay that deserves a place among the great books of Western culture.

Another burst, although not as impressive as the first two but highly respectable, occurred when the Bill of Rights was proposed. Some delegates to the Constitutional Convention had vigorously asserted that such guarantees should be included in the original document. George Mason, the principal drafter of the Virginia Declaration of Rights, so held, and he walked out of the convention when he failed to achieve his purpose. Even those who had argued that the rights in question were implicit recognized the value of adding protection of them to the Constitution. The debate was thus focused on the rights that were to be explicitly granted, not on whether any rights ought to be explicitly granted. Again many writers and speakers entered the fray, and again the debate was solidly grounded in theory and was conducted on a high intellectual level.

Thus, within a few years a statement of organic law and a vital coda to it had been produced. However, the meaning and effect of many of that document's provisions were far from certain; the debates on ratification of the Constitution and the Bill of Rights had demonstrated that. In addition, the document existed in a vacuum, because statutes and actions had not been assessed by its standards. The attempt to resolve these problems began after Chief Justice John Marshall, in Marbury v. Madison, asserted the right of the U.S. Supreme Court to interpret and apply the Constitution. Judicial interpretation and application of the Constitution, beginning with the first constitutional case and persisting until the most recent, is one of the sustained exertions of intellectual energy associated with the Constitution. The framers would be surprised by some of the results of these activities. References in the document to "due process," which seems to refer only to procedures, have been held also to have a substantive dimension. A right to privacy has been found lurking among the penumbras of various parts of the text. A requirement that states grant the same "privileges and immunities" to citizens of other states that they granted to their own citizens, which seemed to guarantee important rights, was not held to be particularly important. The corpus of judicial interpretations of the Constitution is now as voluminous as that document is terse.

As judicial interpretations multiplied, another layer—interpretations of interpretations—appeared, and also multiplied. This layer, the other sustained intellectual effort associated with the Constitution, consists of articles, most of them published in law reviews, and books on the Constitution. This material varies in quality and significance. Some of these works of scholarship result from meticulous examination and incisive thought. Others repeat earlier work, or apply a fine-tooth comb to matters that are too minute even for such a comb. Somewhere in that welter of tertiary material is the answer to almost every question that one could ask about constitutional law. The problem is finding the answer that one wants. The difficulty of locating useful guidance is exacerbated by the bifurcation of most constitutional scholarship into two kinds. In "Two Styles of Social Science Research," C. Wright Mills delineates macroscopic and molecular research. The former deals with huge issues, the latter with tiny issues. Virtually all of the scholarship on the Constitution is of one of those two types. Little of it is macroscopic, but that category does include some first-rate syntheses such as Jack Rakove's *Original Meanings*. Most constitutional scholarship is molecular and, again, some fine work is included in that category.

In his essay, Mills bemoans the inability of social scientists to combine the two kinds of research that he describes to create a third category that will be more generally useful. This series of books is an attempt to do for constitutional law the intellectual work that Mills proposed for social science. The author of each book has dealt carefully and at reasonable length with a topic that lies in the middle range of generality. Upon completion, this series will consist of thirty-seven books, each on a constitutional law topic. Some of the books, such as the book on freedom of the press, explicate one portion of the Constitution's text. Others, such as the volume on federalism, treat a topic that has several anchors in the Constitution. The books on constitutional history and constitutional interpretation range over the entire document, but each does so from a single perspective. Except for a very few of the books, the special circumstances of which dictate minor changes in format, each book includes the same components—a brief history of the topic, a lengthy and sophisticated analysis of the current state of the law on that topic, a bibliographical essay that organizes and evaluates scholarly material in order to facilitate further research, a table of cases, and an index. The books are intellectually rigorous—in fact, authorities have written them—but, due to their clarity and to brief definitions of terms that are unfamiliar to laypersons, each is comprehensible and useful to a wide audience, one that ranges from other experts on the book's subject to intelligent non-lawyers.

In short, this series provides an extremely valuable service to the legal community and to others who are interested in constitutional law, as every citizen should be. Each book is a map of part of the U.S. Constitution. When this series is complete, each book will be a third kind of scholarly work that combines the macroscopic and the molecular. Together they will explicate all of the important constitutional topics. Anyone who wants assistance in understanding either a topic in constitutional law or the Constitution as a whole can easily find it in these books.

Foreword

REPRESENTATIVE TOM BARRETT

When Jack Stark asked me to write the foreword for his historical analysis of Article 1, § 9, of the United States Constitution, I was proud to be asked and honored to serve. I was also not entirely surprised. You see, I recently had a close encounter with one of the provisions contained in this section.

I now serve on the U.S. House of Representatives' Committee on Commerce, but not too long ago, I served as a member of the House Committee on the Judiciary. My Judiciary Committee colleagues and I faced an unusual responsibility: an inquiry into the conduct of an individual criticized widely and loudly for violating the trust of family, friends and the American people, and charged by a special prosecutor with falsifying statements made under oath in connection with a civil suit. The subject of our inquiry, as you might have guessed, was William J. Clinton, and we were asked to recommend whether or not the House ought to impeach the President of the United States.

As our inquiry progressed, I and a number of my Judiciary colleagues advanced the notion that the case warranted a recommendation by the Committee that the House censure the president as an alternative to impeachment. Our censure idea was the subject of much discussion and debate in the public and the press, and the idea even drew some praise as a reasonable and appropriate alternative to impeachment. The notion did not, however, meet nearly so warm a reception in Congress, and in the end, the Committee voted along party lines to recommend impeaching the president. The House, of course, did so shortly thereafter.

An observant reader will note at this point that the House's authority and responsibility to consider questions of impeachment is vested in Article 1, § 2, and not in Article 1, § 9. How, then, does this experience relate to Jack's historical analysis of the constitutional section describing prohibited government actions?

One of the criticisms, indeed one of the more interesting ones, of our censure idea was that it proposed a bill of attainder unconstitutional under Clause 3 of Article 1, § 9. Since the censure option was never developed, we will never know if this criticism was sound, but the experience was an important and very personal reminder to me that the prohibitions contained in Article 1, § 9, remain active, vital elements of constitutional law.

Jack Stark's history of the Constitution's prohibited government action section opens with the case of Sir Thomas More. More's sacrifice of his life for his beliefs made him a martyr, but Jack offers the reminder that he might have lived to fight another day if England's unwritten constitution had at that time incorporated the protections of this section. As he reviews the case law pertaining to each of these clauses, we are reminded of just how important these protections have been in safeguarding our own personal liberties.

This volume offers invaluable lessons for those of us in the legislative business, meaning most directly myself and the other members of Congress, but also by analogy for our counterparts in state and local legislatures. As I read Jack's accounts of the mistakes of past Congresses and the very great harm that has in some cases resulted, I am reminded of the broad scope and heavy weight of the legislative power and the grave responsibility to use that power with discretion and foresight. I am also reminded that the legislative power is a fragile thing, dependent in large part on the sometimes murky reasoning of the courts.

Jack's discussion of the prohibition in Clause 6 against preference by the national government for the ports of one state over those of another provides an excellent example of the importance of the prohibited government actions section. This provision might at first seem remote from and unrelated to contemporary legislative issues, but as Jack's narrative points out, this is not at all so. An early decision pertaining to this clause offered the courts one of their first opportunities to test the force of the Constitution's Commerce Clause (in US Const, Art I, §8) against the force of competing or even potentially conflicting constitutional provisions. Had the United States Supreme Court ruled that national policy intended principally to promote interstate commerce was unconstitutional because it incidentally disadvantaged certain ports with respect to others, it would have set a precedent leading to dramatic erosion of the Congress' power to effectively regulate commerce. This in and of itself would have made today's federal government unrecognizable, but the effects would have encompassed much more than the regulation of commerce in its literal sense. The commerce power has provided a constitutional basis for assertive national action by Congress to address some of the great social ills of our time, including racial segregation and organized crime. This power also underpins very recent Congressional initiatives to fight violence against women and is the foundation for a current effort to expand the applicability of federal jurisdiction in the prosecution of hate crimes. As you can see, the development of case law under this ancient and fairly obscure provision in the Constitution's prohibited government actions section has played a critical role in the maintenance of an assertive, dynamic, and effective federal legislature.

Jack's work demonstrates that some of the more glamorous provisions of this section have played an even more vital role in the development of America's legislative tradition. The discussion in this book of the case law on Clause 3's prohibition against the enactment of ex post facto laws is illustrative. The rulings on this issue have not only served to correct Congress' misdeeds and to deter future transgressions. They have also changed the way we make the laws. Based largely on these decisions, we in the Congress business now work harder to ensure that the bills we draft, and in particular those imposing criminal penalties, provide regulation, not punishment, and have proactive, not retroactive, effect. Careful attention to the history of this section would make for more accurate, more responsible, and generally more effective legislation.

This book also offers interesting reading and valuable lessons for Americans who do not happen to be in the legislation business. When I talk to a constituent or almost any individual American about the Constitution (and as a consequence of my work, this happens more frequently than one might at first think), the conversation tends to focus on the Bill of Rights. This is certainly reasonable. The Bill of Rights was clearly intended as an easily identifiable guarantor of individual protection from unwarranted government intrusion. The Bill of Rights also gets more attention from mainstream educators and the media than do other constitutional provisions.

Though it is appropriate for individual Americans to focus on the Bill of Rights, this focus may encourage an unhealthy view of the Constitution's original text as little more than an organizational chart for the federal government. This book offers an important reminder that the original articles of the Constitution were all intended to define the expanses and limits of government power in terms of the rights and liberties of the governed.

The prohibitions in Article 1, § 9, serve as companions to the Bill of Rights. They are, as Jack writes, "a statement of rights that citizens have against encroachment by Congress." The protections in Clause 3 against the enactment of bills of attainder and ex post facto laws are perhaps the most obvious examples of this section's defense of individual liberty, and the case law history demonstrates that these prohibitions have shielded Americans from very troubling efforts by Congress to usurp the judicial process and take justice into its own hands. The explication of the case law on Clause 2, limiting suspension of the writ of habeas corpus, shows the delicate balance struck over time between the safeguard of individual liberty and the requirements of public safety and order.

His discussion of the prohibition in Clause 3 against the enactment of bills of attainder reminds us that these protections not only provide direct protections in and of themselves, but also reinforce other constitutional elements essential to the establishment and operation of a government respectful of the rights of its citizens. As but one example, Jack convincingly demonstrates that the case law has made the bills of attainder clause a pillar of support for the Constitution's separation of powers, as well as for the due process guarantees of the Fifth and Fourteenth Amendments.

When we first recall the provisions of the prohibited government actions section, we may think of them as distant relics of a more dangerous time, when abusive, arbitrary rulers meted out deadly punishment on a whim. We may think that these protections, though vitally necessary in their time, are simply no longer relevant in the modern age.

This is certainly true of the prohibition in Clause 1 against termination of the slave trade prior to 1808. However, as this book amply demonstrates, we would be wrong to regard the other prohibitions in this section as quaint antiques. The most recent case mentioned in the history of this section is only two years old. Though that case concerned the taxation of exports and may not be seen as directly relevant to the life of every American, the Court heard a 1994 case involving an ex post facto law, continuing a line of cases that protects every citizen from punishments for actions not proscribed at the time of their commission. This history is full of other very recent examples of cases that have challenged the courts to defend the rights of individual Americans against undue government encroachment. It also includes important reminders that, as was the case during the Cold War's "Red Scare," our otherwise generally reasonable government can be tempted to push or even erase the boundaries of personal freedom in instances of real or perceived emergency. These cases offer a chilling reminder that the protections of Article 1, § 9, will always be necessary.

The prohibition against ex post facto laws provides what may be the most contemporary illustration of the continuing relevance of this section. In describing its history, Jack observes that the Court in one case struck down an ex post facto law based in part on the framers' intent in including this provision. The Court in that case recalled that, as Jack paraphrases, "requiring notice promotes fundamental fairness, which is one of the glues that holds together just societies." In the year 2000, writing just weeks after the Supreme Court heard arguments in a case (Dickerson v. United States) seeking to overturn the landmark decision in Miranda v. Richardson that requires law enforcement officers to give suspects notice of their right to refrain from self-incrimination, I must conclude that these issues are all too relevant today.

I commend you for taking up this volume and exploring the rich history of the fundamental limitations on the power of America's national government. This book offers an important opportunity to recall that the relationship between the American government and the governed has occasionally been a very troubled one and to prepare for active participation in a political process that can help to ensure a more harmonious future. For a citizen in a free democracy, there can be no more important or rewarding responsibility.

Introduction

Article 1, § 9 of the U.S. Constitution consists of eight clauses, seven of which are discussed in this book. Clause 4, the provision on direct taxation, is covered in the volume in this series on the taxing power of Congress. This book covers provisions that prohibit specific acts of the federal government. Clause 1 prohibits discontinuing the slave trade before 1808; Clause 2 prohibits the suspension of the privilege of the writ of habeas corpus except in cases of emergency; Clause 3 prohibits the passage of bills of attainder and ex post facto laws; Clause 5 prohibits the imposition of taxes on exports from any state; Clause 6 prohibits giving preference to the ports of any state; Clause 7 prohibits drawing money from the treasury except by means of an appropriation; and Clause 8 prohibits the granting of titles of nobility and accepting gifts from foreign monarchs or nations. All of those provisions apply to the federal government.

Section 9 of Article 1 may seem insignificant when compared to other better known parts of the Constitution such as the First and Sixth Amendments, the commerce clause and the requirement of due process of law. Moreover, the obscure terms in § 9 probably induce some readers to scan it impatiently. However, not taking it seriously is a mistake. Moreover, § 9's importance has become obvious, especially during crises in the nation's history such as the Civil War, the Cold War, and the Vietnam War.

Part I of this book presents a brief history of the clauses in § 9 (except Clause 4), beginning with some background in English common law. Part II explains the current state of the law on these provisions and describes various important cases related to each of the clauses.

PART I

A HISTORY OF PROHIBITED GOVERNMENT ACTS

English Common Law

Although the Constitutional Convention is the obvious point to begin a history of the clauses in Section 9, the significance of the more important of these provisions will be more clear if the history begins earlier.

On April 13, 1534, a man, his son-in-law and a few of his servants descended into a small boat at Chelsea in England and rowed down the Thames to Lambeth Palace. The man never returned to his home. At the palace he was interrogated by two powerful governmental officials, including the Lord Chancellor, and two powerful ecclesiastical figures. The man refused their request to swear an oath affirming that the succession to the crown of England would extend through the children of Ann Boleyn (Catherine of Aragon's marriage to Henry VIII having been voided). He was taken into custody and eventually confined in the Tower of London. A short time later, he was indicted for treason under the Treason Act that was enacted shortly before he was taken to Lambeth Palace, tried by a special commission, convicted, and beheaded (being spared disembowlment because of his previous service to the king). By now it should be clear that the man was Thomas More.[1]

More's fate might have been different if provisions similar to Clauses 2, 3, and 7 of Article 1, § 9 of the U.S. Constitution had been incorporated into England's unwritten constitution when More began to defy Henry VIII and if the courts had enforced them. Despite his own persecution of "heretics" during his tenure as Lord Chancellor, More is a sympathetic figure. In addition, his case is a paradigm of a citizen enduring punishment, including capital punishment, for sincerely held beliefs that did not pose a serious threat to the polity.

In the sixteenth century, English common law included a fairly weak writ of habeas corpus (an order issued by a court to an official who is holding a person in custody to produce this person before the court so the court can inquire into the legitimacy of the custody).[2] English courts had used the writ since 1305 but it did not become an effective remedy until the seventeenth century. Article 3 of the U.S. Constitution grants general judicial power to the court system, implicitly including the authority to perform traditional judicial functions and, in particular, to issue writs of habeas corpus. If the writ of habeas corpus had been stronger in the sixteenth century and if a court had had the temerity to issue one in More's case, no doubt Henry VIII would have declared the religious tumult of the time an emergency. The king would have suspended the privilege of that writ and ordered his officials not to respond to writs of habeas corpus. The inclusion in the English constitution of a prohibition like Clause 2 against suspending the writ except in times of emergency would have allowed More to obtain that writ and to litigate whether there was an emergency or whether the king had violated the constitution by suspending the privilege. That is, More might not have had to languish in the Tower of London until the king and his officers decided to try him.

The connection between Clause 3 and More's fate does not depend on imagining the existence of a strong writ of habeas corpus. Clause 3 prohibits bills of attainder and ex post facto laws. Parliament passed legislation specifically directed at More that was explicitly a bill of attainder (a legislative act that imposes punishment without a judicial trial). The act proclaimed that he was "intending to sow sedition" by refusing to take the Oath of Succession, and it imposed punishment for this act. This legislation ordered the forfeiture of More's manors and estates to the crown (that is, "attainted" him), thereby impoverishing his family. If a provision prohibiting bills of attainder had been in the English constitution and if a court had been willing to rule on the merits alone, More would easily have won a challenge to the bill. In fact, if there had been a prohibition against bills of attainder, Parliament perhaps would not have passed the bill in the first place.

A court might also have ruled that the bill of attainder was also an ex post facto law (a law that makes a crime of an act that was not a crime when it was committed) if a prohibition like Clause 3 had been part of the English constitution. The Act of Succession had certainly already been passed when More refused to take the oath that it required, but it was the bill of attainder that made the refusal seditious.

If the prohibition against ex post facto laws had been part of the English constitution, then violation of the Treason Act, which led to More's execution, was a violation of an ex post facto law and, in effect, not a violation of a valid law. The Treason Act, which was passed at about the same time as the bill of attainder against More, made certain offenses such as claiming that the king was a schismatic punishable by death. More had already been incarcerated for, among other things, stating that the king had usurped papal authority by annulling his marriage to Catherine of Aragon and, implicitly, was a schismatic. The government might have sought stronger evidence than More's ambiguous conversation with Richard Rich, who was one of the king's more powerful officials, as grounds for prosecution and therefore prosecuted him for his earlier statements on the religious authority of Henry VIII, which would have made possible the argument that the application of the Treason Act to his assertion of that position was making him the victim of an unconstitutional ex post facto law.

Clause 7, the prohibition against drawing money from the treasury without an appropriation, if part of the English constitution, might also have helped More's case. Indeed, if Parliament had opposed Henry VIII instead of becoming his tool in his annulment of his marriage, his alteration of the succession to the crown and, underlying both, his reformation of English religion; it could have attached to an appropriation to the crown a rider (a condition directing or limiting the ways in which appropriated money is to be spent) that forbade use of any of the appropriated money to hold and try anyone for opposing the king.

In short, some of the clauses in Article 1, § 9 of the U.S. Constitution provide, or at least potentially provide, substantial protections that were not available to Sir Thomas More. That is true even though they appear on their faces to be at best only moderately important. On further examination, most of even the most apparently banal portions of the U.S. Constitution are significant. These clauses also might seem fairly trivial because they have not been at issue in very many cases. In addition, courts have disagreed about their significance and scope. Nevertheless, the clauses stand ready to be used as bulwarks by litigants who invoke them and by courts who take them seriously. At the very least, they are well worth further study.

The best source for the actual state of English common law at the time the U.S. Constitution was framed is William Blackstone's treatise[3] on that subject. Because this work was well known in colonial America, it is also the best guide to the framers' conception of English common law. This treatise, therefore, is also evidence about the framers' intent when they placed these provisions in the Constitution.

After telling of Roman emperor Caligula's practice of having laws written in very small characters on the tops of pillars, Blackstone remarks:

> [t]here is still a more unreasonable method than this, which is called making of laws ex post facto; when after an action (indifferent in itself) is committed, the legislator then for the first time declares it to have been a crime, and inflicts a punishment upon the person who has committed it. Here it is impossible that the party could foresee that an action, innocent when it was done, should be afterwards converted to guilt by a subsequent law; he had therefore no cause to abstain from it; and all punishment for not abstaining must of consequence be cruel and unjust. All laws should be therefore made to commence in future.[4]

The most important thing to be learned from that passage is that Blackstone believed that only criminal laws could be ex post facto. As Part II of this book indicates, courts have not always agreed with this position.

On bills of attainder, Blackstone wrote, "[w]hen sentence of death, the most terrible and highest judgment in the laws of England, is pronounced, the immediate inseparable consequence by the common law is attainder."[5] He continued, "upon judgment of outlawry, or of death, for treason or felony, a man shall be said to be attainted." The consequences of attainder are forfeiture of property and corruption of blood (denying the person the right to transfer property after death, which deprives the victim's family of his or her property). Blackstone's reference to "treason or felony" indicates his belief that bills of attainder apply only in criminal cases. Blackstone's conception of ex post facto laws and understanding of bills of attainder was sometimes accepted by courts in this country and sometimes not accepted.

Blackstone's comments on the writ of habeas corpus foreshadowed the U.S. Constitution's provision on this subject:

> confinement of the person, by secretly hurrying him to jail, where his sufferings are unknown or forgotten, is a less public, a less striking, and therefore, a more dangerous engine of arbitrary government. Yet, sometimes, when the state is in real danger, even this may be a necessary measure.[6]

Blackstone recognized both the substantial protection of individual liberty that the writ provides and that the needs of the state may sometimes require suspension of the writ. Alexander Hamilton, in the *Federalist Papers* number 84, included the first sentence of the quotation from Blackstone, but not the second, to support his argument that some of the provisions in Article 1, § 9 are a bill of rights.

The Constitutional Convention

The debates at the Constitutional Convention provide important clues about the beliefs that some of the delegates had about the seven provisions discussed in this book. Judges and commentators vary in their opinion on the weight that should be given to these debates. Those who believe that the "original intent," the views of the Framers and their contemporaries, is the most important guidance for constitutional provisions therefore ascribe great importance to those debates.

The amount of attention that the delegates gave to these different provisions varied considerably. Nothing of substance was said on Clause 6 (preferences to ports), Clause 7 (appropriations), and Clause 8 (titles and gifts). Indeed, the absence of debate on the appropriation clause is surprising. There was considerable debate on Clause 1 (slave trade). Although this provision has been a dead letter for a long time, the debate was extremely important at the time. The Constitution's treatment of slavery and the slave trade had to satisfy both Northern and Southern states or the Constitutional Convention would not have adopted the Constitution. The debate on the slave trade and the underlying sectional differences presaged the turmoil that would eventually erupt into the Civil War. For these reasons, treatment of Clause 1 during the convention and the debate on its ratification bears further examination.

The version of Clause 1 of Article I, § 9 that the Constitutional Convention passed follows:

> [t]he migration or importation of such persons as any of the states now existing shall think proper to admit, shall not be prohibited by the Congress prior to the year 1808, but a tax or duty may be imposed on such importation, not exceeding 10 dollars for each person.

The generic wording might make some readers think that Clause 1 is about immigration because the delegates avoided using the phrase slave trade. Clause 1 is one of three clauses in the unammended version of the Constitution that deal with slavery. Article 1, § 2, Clause 3 provides that the number of representatives to Congress and the amount of direct taxes will be divided among the states according to their population. In computing population, § 2, Clause 3 directs that "other persons" will be counted as three-fifths of a person. Again, the delegates avoided a direct reference to slaves, but certainly meant them. Another provision is Article 4, § 2, Clause 3, which provides that

> [n]o person held to service or labour in one state, under the laws thereof, escaping into another, shall, in consequence of any law or regulation therein, be discharged from such service or labour, but shall be delivered up on claim of the party to whom such service or labour may be due.

The phrasing of this provision is not quite so oblique as that of the others, although the delegates declined to refer explicitly to fugitive slaves.

Some delegates objected on pragmatic grounds to guaranteeing that the slave trade would not be curtailed for a specified term of years. Rufus King of Massachusetts discerned the connection between temporarily allowing the slave trade to continue and the prohibition against taxing exports.[7] He believed that importing slaves would increase the risk of danger for the slave states—that is, would make an insurrection more likely—which would require assistance from Northern states at the same time the prohibition against taxing exports would decrease the ability of the Northern states to assist the slave states. He also argued that if slaves were allowed to be imported, the goods slaves helped to produce should be taxable upon export. No doubt, King was thinking primarily of cotton. Gouverneur Morris of Pennsylvania made almost the same argument, although he was more concerned that the presence of slaves in the Southern states would increase the chance of insurrection.[8]

Other delegates opposed the moratorium on ethical grounds. Roger Sherman of Connecticut called the slave trade "iniquitous."[9] However, Sherman said later that despite his disapproval of the slave trade, he would retain the moratorium that applied to federal legislation to end it because the public good was not threatened by that trade, and he wished to minimize objections to the Constitution.[10] George Mason, a delegate from Virginia who had been the principal drafter of that state's noble *Declaration of Rights*, began an impassioned plea to delete the moratorium from the Constitution's text by stating "[t]his infernal trade originated in the avarice of British Merchants.[11] He continued with an attack that in essence foretold the turmoil that would lead to the Civil War and that cataclysm itself:

> Slavery discourages arts and manufactures. The poor despise labor when performed by slaves. They prevent the immigration of Whites, who really enrich and strengthen a Country. They produce the most pernicious effect on manners. Every master of slaves is born a petty tyrant. They bring the judgment of heaven on a Country. As nations cannot be rewarded or punished in the next world they must be in this. By an inevitable chain of causes and effects providence punishes national sins, by national calamities.

Those words are reminiscent of the anguished meditations of some of the characters in William Faulkner's novels, who are convinced that slavery has placed a curse upon their region, except that Mason, who is one of the neglected heroes of American history, spoke them before the "curse" led to civil war.

The defenders of the moratorium also made both pragmatic and ethical arguments. Rather than framing a prudential argument based on military danger or the sapping of the financial resources that the North could call upon to aid the South in the event of an attack on it, Hugh Williamson argued, practically, that failing to include the moratorium would cost votes on the Constitution, putting at risk its chance of being passed by the convention.[12] Williamson made his point a bit more delicately, referring to the choice between keeping the moratorium in the Constitution and excluding South Carolina and Georgia from the union. In contemporary parlance, Williamson in effect said what many others knew: that the moratorium was a bottom line of many Southern delegates. Charles Pinckney of South Carolina made an argument that was tantamount to an ethical argument, pointing out that slavery is "justified by the example of all the world."[13] He said that slavery had been entrenched in Greece and Rome and that France, England, Holland, and other modern states had sanctioned the practice.

Williamson correctly appraised the situation: to ensure the votes of at least two Southern states (Georgia and South Carolina) for ratification of the Constitution, it was necessary to include Clause 1. The way in which the Northern and Southern states consummated this issue became clear after the convention. Luther Martin of Maryland informed his state legislature that a committee consisting of one delegate from each state had been elected and charged with the responsibility of dealing with the issue of the clause on the slave trade and another clause: "[n]o navigation act shall be passed without the assent of two thirds of the members present in each House [of Congress]."[14] The Southern states wanted a temporary prohibition against Congress ending the slave trade, and they also wanted the provision on navigation acts to remain in the Constitution in order to protect themselves against control of their shipping by Northern states. Many of the delegates from the Northern and middle states would have preferred to end the slave trade immediately by including a provision to that effect in the Constitution or at least including a provision that allowed Congress to do so, but they approved of the provision on navigation. As one would predict, the committee split the difference, retaining the moratorium on the slave trade and deleting the provision on navigation acts. George Mason of Virginia confirmed Martin's description of the political arrangement.[15]

The first reference in the records of the Constitutional Convention to the writ of habeas corpus appears in a description of a number of "propositions" that were submitted to a subcommittee. One of these propositions was "[t]he privileges and benefit of the writ of habeas corpus shall be enjoyed in this government in the most expeditious and ample manner: and shall not be suspended by the Legislature except upon the most urgent and pressing occasions, and for a limited time not exceeding months."[16] The convention was to specify the time period later. This early version differs from the final one in two important ways. First, the early version required that the writ be made available; whereas, the final version dealt only with the suspension of the privilege, which only implied that there must be writs of habeas corpus. Second, although the earlier version forbade the legislative branch from suspending the writ; the final version stated in general that the privilege of the writ may not be suspended. One might interpret the later deletion of the reference to the legislature as an implicit authorization of suspension by other entities, most likely the President.

The delegates did not debate the provision about bills of attainder, but Edmund Randolph made a comment on them during the debate on another subject.[17] He assumed that bills of attainder applied only to criminal matters and inferred that ex post facto laws did also because the provisions on those two matters appeared in the same clause. This is a slender reed on which to base an argument that the prohibition against bills of attainder should be applied only to bills that impose criminal penalties. As we shall see in Part II, the courts have sometimes limited the prohibition in that way and sometimes have held that the prohibition applies also to civil penalties.

The debate on the prohibition against ex post facto laws was more substantial. Several delegates argued that the prohibition ought not to be placed in the Constitution because that kind of law was invalid and that prohibiting it would demonstrate that the delegates did not know the principles of legislation.[18] Others pointed out that state legislatures had passed ex post facto laws, in some instances despite a prohibition against them in their own constitutions, and that adding the prohibition would give judges a means to invalidate that kind of law.[19] The more important part of the debate on ex post facto laws consisted of statements that the term applied only to laws that imposed criminal penalties. As we have seen, that was Edmund Randolph's understanding. John Dickinson agreed, citing Blackstone's *Commentaries* as an authority for his position.[20] George Mason moved to delete the provision because it did not explicitly apply only to laws that imposed criminal penalties. Mason was concerned that it was necessary to make some civil laws apply retroactively. In short, there is a fair amount of evidence that the Framers, like Mason, conceived of ex post facto laws as being only criminal laws.[21] However, we will see in Part II that courts sometimes have disagreed.

The prohibition against imposing export taxes on goods that were exported from a state was a regional issue. Charles Pinckney of South Carolina warned the delegates that if the Southern states were not protected by including a prohibition against export taxes and a provision that forbade the emancipation of slaves he would vote against the Constitution.[22] He did not clarify whether he wanted a provision that applied to the federal government only or a prohibition against states imposing such taxes. Although the protection against emancipation of slaves was not afforded—the closest provisions to it are Clause 1, Article 1, § 9 and the one about fugitive slaves—he did vote for the Constitution. Pinckney, like many Southerners, feared the imposition of export duties on Southern goods, such as cotton. Rufus King saw the regional implications of Clause 1 very differently. Early in his speech on the clause, he appeared to be talking about another clause in the next section that prohibits states from taxing both imports to and exports from other states. However, King later and very bluntly made a point that appears to apply to this clause: "[i]f slaves are to be imported shall not the exports produced by their labor, supply a revenue the better to enable the Genl. Govt. to defend their Masters?"[23]

At the Constitutional Convention, the debate on whether to include a bill of rights was among the more important. Some delegates believed that basic rights were implicitly part of the document. Others were convinced that omitting explicit grants of them was a serious mistake. A member of the latter group was George Mason, the principal drafter of the Virginia *Declaration of Rights*. Mason not only declined to sign the Constitution but also left the convention when it became clear that the document would not include an explicit bills of rights. During the debates on ratification, this argument about the need to include explicit grants of rights in the Constitution became related to the debate on this section.

The Ratification Debates

It is not surprising that an important issue in the debates about ratification of the U.S. Constitution was the absence of an explicit bill of rights. It is surprising, however, that § 9 was implicated in that debate. In the *Federalist Papers* number 84, Alexander Hamilton argued that a number of provisions in the U.S. Constitution amount to the same thing as a bill of rights. Among those that he cited are § 9's Clause 2 (prohibition against the suspension of the privilege of the writ of habeas corpus), Clause 3 (prohibiting bills of attainder and ex post facto laws), and Clause 8 (prohibitions against the granting of titles of nobility and the acceptance of gifts from other countries). Writing in the *Freeman's Journal* of Philadelphia, "Centinel" (Samuel Bryan) conceded that the habeas corpus clause and the guarantee of a trial by jury for all crimes except impeachment (Article 3, § 2) were rights that the Constitution granted.[24] However, he argued that a long list of rights that ought to have been guaranteed were not. Among these were many rights that were later added by amendment. Similarly, in a letter to James Madison about the Constitution, Thomas Jefferson wrote,

> I will now add what I do not like. First the omission of a bill of rights providing clearly & without the aid of sophisms for freedom of religion, freedom of the press, protection against standing armies, restriction against monopolies, the eternal & unremitting force of the habeas corpus laws, and trials by jury in all matters of fact triable by the laws of the land & not by the law of Nations.[25]

A main argument of those who defended the Framers' decision not to add a conventional, explicit, and strong bill of rights was that if rights were listed the logical inference would be that only the specific rights listed were protected. At the Pennsylvania Convention, Robert Whitehill countered that the rights to habeas corpus and jury trials were listed and turned the argument around by asking whether that meant that the Constitution protected no other rights.[26]

It is not surprising that, during the debate on ratification, the reaction of the Northern and middle states to Clause 1 (the slave trade) was diverse. At one end of the spectrum was Luther Martin of Maryland.[27] He was pessimistic that the slave trade would be ended only after the moratorium ran its course. He would have preferred an immediate end:

> [w]hen our own liberties were at stake, we warmly felt for the common rights of men. The danger being thought to be past, which threatened ourselves, we are daily growing more insensible to those rights. In those States which have restrained or prohibited the importation of slaves, it is only done by legislative acts, which may be repealed. When those states find, that they must, in their national character and connexion, suffer in disgrace, and share in the inconvenience attendant upon that detestable and iniquitous traffic, they may be desirous also to share in the benefits arising from it; and the odium attending it will be greatly effaced by the sanction which is given to it in the general government.

Others from these regions took a more conciliatory position, expressing dislike for the slave trade but accepting the clause on practical grounds. For example, James Iredell, who assumed the pseudonym "Marcus" for the purpose, wrote that although the slave trade "has already continued too long for the honor and humanity of those concerned in it, states that had profited from slave labor ought not to forbid Georgia and South Carolina from doing so as well."[28] James Wilson of Pennsylvania admitted that he would have wished the slave trade to be curtailed sooner but believed that the delayed curtailment was "laying the foundation for banishing slavery out of this country."[29] Similarly, James Madison, in the *Federalist Papers* number 42, wrote that the slave trade "has so long and so loudly upbraided the barbarism of modern policy" but that the eventual end to the prohibition against abolishing it would at some point result in the end of that traffic.

The contrast between the two dominant reactions of non-Southerners to Clause 1 is sharply drawn, and the two sides are ably represented, in an exchange between James Madison and George Mason at the Virginia convention.[30] Mason opposed the slave trade both because of its practical effect on the country and because of its immorality: "[t]he augmentation of slaves weakens the States; and such a trade is diabolical in itself, and disgraceful to mankind," and he thought that the provision was "fatal" and that it "created more dangers than any other." Oddly, however, he also objected that the Constitution allowed a tax to be imposed on slaves, which might result in their owners being forced to free them. Madison countered that the situation in regard to the slave trade had improved because the Articles of Confederation had allowed the slave trade to continue indefinitely and that Clause 1 was necessary to make it possible to ratify the Constitution. He dismissed the argument that a confiscatory tax would be imposed on slaves and pointed out that the Constitution included a clause protecting the owners of fugitive slaves. Thus, even Mason and Madison were solicitous of slave owners.

Like Northerners, Southerners argued that the slave trade clause was needed, both on its merits and on the pragmatic grounds that without it the Constitution would not be ratified. Charles Cotesworth Pinckney of South Carolina argued that slaves were needed in order to cultivate his state's land—specifically, that slaves from Africa were needed because of the climate and swampy terrain—and that the Southern states had facilitated the creation of the union without giving away too much because the slave trade would not necessarily be curtailed when the protection of it elapsed.[31] Rawlins Lowndes of South Carolina declared that the slave trade "could be justified on the principles of religion, humanity and justice; for certainly to translate a set of human beings from a bad country to a better, was fulfilling every part of these principles."[32] David Ramsay, also of South Carolina, writing as "Civis," asserted that there must be a union, so that the Constitution, with the slave trade clause, should be ratified. Also, Ramsay thought that after the moratorium, the trade would not be abolished because by using slaves his state could produce more rice for the middle and Northern states to ship. This economic advantage[33] would encourage them to allow the trade to continue.

Thus, a wide range of positions on slavery became evident during the debates at the Constitutional Convention and these debates about ratification. Persons such as Luther Martin who abhorred slavery were at one end; at the other were persons such as Rawlins Lowndes who thought that it was moral. Ranging between them were many persons who could live with the slave trade clause, differed about whether the trade would eventually be abolished and were not zealously opposed to slavery itself. As the years passed persons who occupied positions in the middle of this spectrum were forced toward one end or the other. In hindsight, one can see in these debates the inevitability of a civil war during which the ethical status of slavery would be a major issue.

As one would expect, some persons objected to Clause 2 (habeas corpus) because they did not want the Constitution to bestow any right to suspend that writ. It is surprising that some persons also objected to the clause because of their concern for states' rights. Luther Martin of Maryland was among the latter.[34] He told the Maryland House of Representatives that the power to suspend the privilege of the writ would give the central government "a power over Citizens of particular States who should oppose their encroachments" and that the states were capable of deciding when the privilege ought to be suspended. Later he made the same point to the same body but in more overblown language:

> whenever a State should oppose its views, however arbitrary and unconstitutional, and refuse submission to them, the general government may declare it to be an act of rebellion, and suspending the habeas corpus act, may seize upon the persons of those advocates of freedom...and may imprison them during its pleasure in the remotest part of the union.

The facet of the debate on the habeas corpus clause that is most relevant to the case law is the comments that reveal the entity that persons at the time thought had the authority to suspend the privilege. Although Luther Martin had located the power to suspend the privilege in the "general government,"[35] the prevailing view was that Congress had that power. Noah Webster was among those who took that position.[36] Similarly, "Brutus" wrote that "[t]his clause limits the power of the legislature."[37] Edmund Randolph agreed, arguing that each clause in § 9 creates an exception to a specific, not a general, power that is granted elsewhere in the Constitution.[38] In regard to the clause on habeas corpus, the specific power, he believed, was "the power given to Congress to regulate courts." As we shall see, presidents, not Congress, have suspended the privilege.

The states' debates on ratification of the Constitution repeated the debate at the convention on the nature of bills of attainder and the importance of forbidding them. At the Constitutional Convention, the most common view was that bills of attainder imposed criminal, not civil, penalties. This view was also the most commonly held opinion in the debates on ratification. Edmund Randolph, for example, stated that "[w]e know well that attainders, and ex post facto laws, have always been the engines of criminal jurisprudence."[39] In the *Federalist Papers* number 44, James Madison called bills of attainder "contrary to the first principles of the social compact." This indicates the importance of Clause 3 that limits the suspension of the privilege of that writ.

At first glance, discussing arguments that the Constitution should not prohibit ex post facto laws seems irrelevant, because this prohibition remains in the Constitution. However, a belief that ex post facto laws are occasionally useful might be one reason why courts have sometimes interpreted the prohibition very narrowly. Samuel Bryan wrote that the prohibition against ex post facto laws would have the unfortunate effect of protecting persons who had incurred debts to the federal government before the Constitution took effect.[40] George Mason believed that "there never was nor can be a Legislature but must and will make such laws, when necessity and the public safety require them."[41] Patrick Henry, using his characteristic fiery rhetoric, defended ex post facto laws: "[a] pirate, an out-law, or a common enemy to all mankind, may be put to death at any time. It is justified by the laws of nature and nations."[42] Naturally, there were also many supporters of the prohibition. One of the more forceful was James Iredell.[43] Of that kind of law he wrote,

> they have been the instrument of some of the grossest acts of tyranny that were ever exercised, and have this never failing consequence, to put the minority in the power of a passionate and unprincipled majority....This very clause, I think, is worth ten thousand Declaration of Rights, if this the most essential right of all is omitted in them.

The opinion of those who debated the ratification of the Constitution and who addressed the issue of whether ex post facto laws included laws that inflicted civil penalties is more obviously relevant to the case law. A few persons believed that the term was that broad. George Mason,[44] for example, considered the prohibition's effect on disputes about title to land, and Samuel Bryan[45] worried that people who owed debts to the country would be protected, presumably from civil proceedings, by this prohibition. However, most people at that time appear to have believed that "ex post facto" should be used to describe only laws that imposed criminal penalties. These persons included Edmund Randolph[46] and the delegates to the New York ratification convention.[47]

During the debate on ratification, there was some disagreement about the force and effectiveness of Clause 6 that prohibits giving preference to the ports of a particular state or states. Hugh Williamson of North Carolina believed that the provision prevented Congress from favoring one part of the country at the expense of other parts.[48] Specifically, he meant favoring the North at the expense of the South. Luther Martin of Maryland was more pessimistic about the clause's effectiveness.[49] He conceded that the Maryland delegation had introduced the provision because it recognized the possibility that the federal government could require all vessels entering Chesapeake Bay to enter and clear at a port in Virginia, which would disadvantage Maryland. Despite the prohibition, Martin recognized that the federal government still could indirectly favor ports in certain states, for example, by specifying that shipping into a state might be accomplished only by using a specified, inconveniently located port. Martin was prescient in that the pertinent facts in the cases on this clause turned out to be quite complex, and the clause therefore turned out to be something other than a simple, completely general prohibition.

At the Constitutional Convention, James McHenry gave a convincing statement of the purpose of Clause 7 (appropriations): "the People who give their Money ought to know in what manner it is expended."[50] As Part II shows, neither the courts nor the executive branch of government has always kept this purpose in mind. The courts, for example, have accepted as appropriations legislation that most persons would not characterize that way. The executive branch, often with the acquiescence of Congress, has hidden or mischaracterized some of its spending. Other considerations have prevailed over the taxpayers' right to know the ways in which the revenue that they have supplied to the government has been used.

Before the Civil War

The remainder of the history of this section consists mainly of brief accounts of the more important cases on prohibited government acts. The rest of Part I describes acts the executive and legislative branches took in relation to the prohibition against withdrawing money from the treasury without an appropriation and to the most important scholarly debates on Clause 6. These three topics will be dealt with in chronological order. The rest of Part I is a history also because, whenever it is possible, a case or other development will be placed in its historical context. Some of the cases arose from historically significant events or conditions or reflect concerns that were characteristic of particular eras. This part of the history will also show that interpretation of the clauses in § 9 by the U.S. Supreme Court has changed over time, and this part will illuminate the current state of the law on the section.

The first case (Calder v. Bull, 1798) that significantly illuminated Clause 3, the ex post facto clause, is actually on the analogue of that clause in Section 10 (Clause 1), which applies to actions by state legislatures. As we have seen, near the end of the eighteenth century, the prevailing opinion in this country was that only laws imposing criminal penalties could be ex post facto. Calder v. Bull involved state legislation that changed title to property, which was certainly retroactive. The Court listed some legislative acts that it considered to be repugnant to the social compact: "[the legislature] cannot change innocence into guilt; or punish innocence as a crime; or violate the right of antecedent lawful contract; or the right of private property." The first two acts imposed retroactive criminal sanctions, but the last two were non-criminal retroactive legislative acts. However, the Court later listed kinds of law that were specifically ex post facto and thus violated this section:

> 1st. [e]very law that makes an action, done before the passing of the law, and which was innocent when done, criminal; and punishes such action. 2nd. Every law that aggravates a crime, or makes it greater than it was, when committed. 3rd. Every law that changes the punishment, and inflicts a greater punishment, than the law annexed to the crime, when committed. 4th. Every law that alters the legal rules of evidence, and receives less, or

different testimony, than the law required at the time of the commission of the offence, in order to convict the offender.

In short, the Court followed the most commonly held view at the time the Constitution was framed and ratified: that only laws that imposed criminal penalties could be ex post facto.

Clause 7, which requires an appropriation in order for money to be drawn from the federal treasury, has been interpreted by courts with varying degrees of rigor. In an early case (Reeside v. Walker, 1850), the Court was rigorous. A widow litigated to obtain money under a court judgment that her dead spouse had won in a case that was brought against the Post Office Department. It is difficult to imagine a more sympathetic plaintiff or a more clear-cut instance of a debt. Many courts would have been tempted to find a way, notwithstanding the constitutional requirement of an appropriation, to order that money be drawn from the Treasury to pay the widow. However, the Court declined to do so, noting that "any other course would give the fiscal officers a most dangerous discretion." The Court, however, was not totally unresponsive. It wrote that the widow, instead of litigating, should have made a claim against Congress, which could have appropriated the sum needed to satisfy the debt. This tactic could have resulted in—and perhaps later did result in—the widow receiving the money that most persons would agree she deserved without doing violence to the constitutional provision that was at issue.

In a case (Pennsylvania v. Wheeling & Belmont Bridge Co., 1855) that set the direction for the interpretation of Clause 6 prohibiting giving preferences to ports, like the Court in Calder v. Bull, took account of the intent of the Framers as revealed in the debate at the Constitutional Convention. That Court denied a petition for an injunction to stop the building of a bridge that would diminish the flow of river traffic to some ports in West Virginia. The Court noted that the Framers were primarily concerned about legislation or governmental decisions that would directly force commerce to move through, or not move through, certain ports. The construction of the bridge was primarily an exercise of the commerce power and its effects on ports were only incidental. To rule that this construction violated Clause 6 would have been a serious diminution of the commerce power and a misinterpretation of this clause's intent. The Court also pointed out that Clause 6 refers to prohibiting preferences for all the ports of a particular state, not to preferences for one port in a particular state. This case established the principle that this clause is to be interpreted narrowly so as not seriously to impair Congress' power over commerce.

The Civil War Era

A much more famous case, the *Dred Scott* case (Dred Scott v. Sandford, 1856), was decided in the next year. Scott had been the slave of an army surgeon, who took him along from post to post before the surgeon died. During his travels Scott had resided for two years in Illinois, a free state, and in an area that is now part of Minnesota, which was in the Louisiana Territory and thus apparently was free. Beginning in a Missouri court and ending in the U.S. Supreme Court, Scott argued that his residence on free soil had made him a free man.

The Supreme Court, Chief Justice Roger Taney writing the majority opinion, ruled against Scott. The Court held that African-Americans were not citizens and thus did not have the constitutional rights that citizens had, that residence in a free state did not make Scott free, and that the Missouri Compromise, principally because it outlawed slavery in the territories, was unconstitutional. On the first issue, Taney noted that the Preamble of the Constitution did refer to formation of the nation by the people, which seemed to include all the people in the country, and that it did declare securing the blessings of liberty to be one of its goals. However, Taney wrote, the Constitution "does not define what description of persons are intended to be included under these terms [people and citizen]." Looking elsewhere in the Constitution for clues to those terms' meaning, Taney asserted that "there are two clauses in the Constitution which point directly and specifically to the negro race as a separate class of persons, and show clearly that they were not regarded as a portion of the people or citizens of the Government then formed." One clause was Clause 1 in § 9 which forbade discontinuation of the slave trade until 1808. Taney concluded that Scott had no constitutional rights, including no right to litigate this case. Thus, Clause 1, which appeared to be a dead letter after 1808, played a role in one of the more famous U.S. Supreme Court decisions.

The Dred Scott case's first effect was to delight most Southerners. However, its long-term results were quite the opposite. Eventually it made more severe the differences between Northern Democrats and Southern Democrats, which eventually aided the newly formed Republican Party. Dred Scott provided substance for the debates between Stephen Douglas and Abraham Lincoln that occurred a few years later and that began propelling Lincoln toward the White House. The decision energized the anti-slavery forces, particularly when persons realized that a majority of the Court were Southerners. Also, persons began to suspect that President Buchanan had interfered in the Court's deliberations. In short, the decision was a cause of the Civil War, which, in turn, has influenced the history of this country even until the present. Chief Justice Taney had other arguments to support his decision, but it is somewhat ironic that one he used was based on a clause in this section that, because the year specified in it had occurred, appeared to have become irrelevant.

An important question about Clause 2, the habeas corpus clause, regarding who has the authority to suspend the privilege, was an issue in a Civil War era case (Ex Parte Merryman, 1861). On April 27, 1861, President Lincoln, recognizing the danger of pro-Confederacy activity in Maryland, suspended the privilege in parts of that state.[51] John Merryman, a leader of the activity that led to the suspension, was arrested. After Merryman's petition for a writ of habeas corpus was rebuffed by a local court, he appealed to a federal district court. Supreme Court Justice Roger Taney was presiding over the court, as was the custom for Supreme Court justices at the time, when it considered the petition. Taney held that only Congress could suspend the privilege of habeas corpus. But rather than issuing an injunction or taking another action that would precipitate a constitutional crisis, Taney sent Lincoln a strongly worded letter advising him to follow the law (as Taney saw it).

Attorney General Bates and others responded with written arguments that Lincoln had acted within his authority. The importance of this case is not its decision but the absence of enforcement of it. The law might be that only Congress may suspend the privilege of the writ, but the reality is that Presidents also do so and courts are highly unlikely to impede their actions. The sanctions that they confront are, rather, political, and, indeed, during the 1862 congressional campaigns, the Democrats, who at the time were badly cast as civil libertarians, vilified the Republicans for suspending the privilege of the writ.

In addition to Ex Parte Merryman, another case (Ex Parte Milligan, 1866) from the Civil War era clarified the statement in Clause 2 that prohibits the suspension of the writ of habeas corpus except during emergencies. First, this case identified the action that could be suspended during an emergency. That action was a response to a writ of habeas corpus by a governmental official who was holding someone in custody; it was not the issuance of such a writ. That is, not even an emergency would justify ordering courts to stop issuing the writ. To allow such an order would be to allow the branch of government that declared the emergency to usurp some of the power of the judicial branch. Second, the Supreme Court in Ex Parte Milligan clarified the relation between suspension of the writ and declarations of martial law. After stating that martial law may be declared only under certain circumstances, which do not include the mere threat of an invasion, the Court decreed that even if citizens cannot avail themselves of the writ because its privilege has been suspended they must be tried by civil, not military, courts: "[m]artial rule can never exist where the courts are open." In other words, the Court in this case resisted the temptation to overreact to the emergency that was effected by the Civil War. In this landmark case, it established boundaries beyond which military authorities could not go in order to abridge the rights of citizens and the prerogatives of courts.

The Civil War also gave rise to important cases on Clause 3 in § 9. In two companion cases (Cummings v. Missouri, 1867, and Ex Parte Garland, 1867), the Supreme Court expanded the meaning of both bills of attainder and ex post facto laws. (The former involved the analogous prohibition in the next section, which applies to the states.) *Cummings* involved a provision in Missouri's constitution, and *Garland* involved a federal law; both required oaths that were intended to make it impossible for persons who had supported the Confederacy in certain ways from practicing certain professions and engaging in certain occupations. As the strongly worded dissent in each case argued, the decisions changed the law on both doctrines. That occurred because the punishments were not criminal. Both the former view of these two doctrines and the view that informs *Cummings* and *Garland* persisted, and there are two lines of cases on these issues.

Another Civil War era case further delineated Clause 7, which prohibits payments of money from the federal treasury except by means of an appropriation (Knote v. United States, 1877). Under a law that was designed to punish former supporters of the Confederacy, the plaintiff's property had been seized and sold and the proceeds of the sale deposited into the federal treasury. After President Andrew Johnson pardoned him, the plaintiff litigated in an attempt to reclaim the proceeds of the sale. The Court held that the President's constitutional power to pardon did not take precedence over the constitutional restriction on drawing funds from the treasury without an appropriation. That is, those constitutional provisions must, rather, be harmonized. That result should have made it clear that Presidents cannot convincingly invoke the powers that the Constitution grants to them in order to circumvent this clause by spending federal funds without an appropriation that authorizes that expenditure. Presidents, abetted by others, continued to argue that they could do so, and they in fact did do so, although a recent case (OPM v. Richmond, 1990) should lay that argument to rest.

Between the Civil War and 1950

A later Court (Burgess v. Salmon, 1878) agreed with the majority opinions in *Cummings* and *Garland* that Clause 3, the prohibition against ex post facto laws, applied to civil punishments as well as to criminal punishments. At issue was an additional tax and a penalty that were imposed retroactively on a shipment of tobacco even though the tax that was in effect at the time of the taxable event had been paid in full. The Court held that the statute was an ex post facto law because it imposed a retroactive tax, and thus led to the penalty. The Court arrived at that result by using a broader definition of ex post facto law than the one propounded by the court in the first important ex post facto case (Calder v. Bull, 1798). The Court in Burgess wrote that "[a]n ex post facto law is one which imposes a punishment for an act which was not punishable at the time it was committed, or a punishment in addition to that then prescribed." The tax and the penalty were forms of punishment.

Early this century, the scope of Clause 5 (prohibition against taxing exports) started to become clearer (Fairbank v. United States, 1901). At issue was the interplay between two laws. One required that carriers issue a bill of lading or a similar document to shippers and consignors. Another law required internal revenue stamps to be affixed to all bills of lading. The second law set the price of a stamp at one cent for goods that were not going to be exported and at seventy cents for goods that were going to be exported. The Court responded that "a stamp tax on a bill of lading is in substance and effect equivalent to a tax on the articles included in that bill of lading and therefore a tax or duty on exports," meaning that the tax violated the export clause. The logical inference is that Clause 5 applies not only to export taxes per se but also to a number of other governmental charges that fall on exporters. The ensuing problem was to determine which charges were related intimately enough to exportation to be governed by the export clause.

A fairly long line of cases on one aspect of Clause 3 began in 1912 (Johannessen v. United States, 1912). The Court interpreted this clause narrowly, as applying only to laws that impose criminal penalties, although, inconsistently, it recognized that the laws litigated in *Cummings* and *Garland* did not impose criminal penalties. In

Johannessen, the plaintiff had obtained citizenship fraudulently and argued that deportation after he had become a citizen punished him retroactively. The Court held that the government was merely taking away something that he had never rightfully held. The line of cases beginning with this one concern not fraudulent acts but deportation. The Court has consistently held that Clause 3 does not apply to deportation proceedings.

Although the amount of exports from this country has increased apace, the effect of Clause 5 has remained less than totally clear for some time. The Court in *Fairbank* had held that the prohibition applied to more than taxes that were imposed directly on exported goods; for example, Clause 5 applied to taxes on stamps that must be affixed to goods that were to be exported. However, it took a while for courts to discover an analytical tool that would help them distinguish between exactions that violated this clause and those that did not violate it. By deciding that this clause actually forbade taxing the process of exportation, not merely taxing exports per se, courts also discovered that in cases that were brought on this clause they were dealing with a process that unfolded over time.

In the next movement forward the courts recognized that the law on this clause would become considerably clearer if they could "fix a point at which, in view of the purpose of the Constitution, the export must be said to begin" (A.G. Spalding & Bros. v. Edwards, 1923). In this case, a transfer of goods to a carrier and the acquisition at that time of a bill of lading indicated that the goods were surely destined for export, even though several other steps remained before the goods were loaded on the ship that was to take them abroad. Later courts benefited greatly from this temporal analysis.

A Court in an earlier case (William E. Peck & Co. v. Lowe, 1918) had identified another point (the imposition of an income tax on a corporation that derived only some of its income from exporting goods) that occurred too long after exportation to be subject to the prohibition on taxing exports. This Court, however, had not thought in temporal terms but had labeled the tax as indirect and only remotely connected to exportation. Thus, the Court in *Spalding* not only pointed the way to a temporal analysis of the cases on the export clause, but also made it possible for other courts to see that there was a continuum that had three parts. The earliest part consisted of events that preceded exportation; the middle part consisted of events that were part of the export process even though some of them occurred well before the loading of goods that were to be exported; and the last part consisted of events that occurred after exportation was completed. This clause forbade taxing only events that occurred during the second part of the continuum.

Sometimes courts have taken Clause 7, the appropriations clause, seriously, but sometimes courts have adopted a *laissez faire* attitude toward it. The latter reaction is well illustrated by a taxation case that was decided during the Depression (Cincinnati Soap Co. v. United States, 1937). A statute that imposed a tax on coconut oil specified that all the proceeds from the tax that were attributable to coconut oil that was produced in the Philippine Islands were to be turned over to the government of that dependency. Despite that provision, there was no appropriation that directed the withdrawal of these funds from the U.S. Treasury and their transfer to the Philippines. The Court held that the possibility of enacting an appropriation in the future to accomplish this transfer was enough to satisfy the appropriation clause's requirements. The Court also was swayed by the "high moral obligation" that the United States owed to its dependencies. The decision is replete with non sequitors, and if it were always followed, the appropriations clause would be a virtual nullity.

A case (United States v. Lovett, 1946) from the Cold War era is doubly interesting. It exhibits the interaction between Clauses 3 and 7 in § 9. *Lovett* also exhibits the disturbing political forces that were let loose at that time and a court's willingness to stand resolutely against them. Congress, as part of its relentless pursuit of "subversives," had passed an appropriation for operating the federal government but had added to it a proviso that forbade use of the money to pay the salaries of three specified federal employees. The government argued that the law was an ordinary appropriation. By this time Congress had been taking advantage of the appropriations clause by inserting riders (statutory statements of specific, unrelated conditions) into appropriations bills in order more effectively to control the executive branch's spending. The Supreme Court, looking directly at the reality of the situation, held that the rider denied employment to the three specified persons, thereby punishing them for their political activities. Congress had added this rider without a full-blown judicial proceeding but only after its own proceedings, which resembled those of the Star Chamber. Therefore, the Court held that the legislation was a bill of attainder and was unconstitutional under § 9, Clause 3. In other words, the Court stood firm, attributing great significance to the pertinent constitutional provision, although at the time the politically popular result would have been to allow the cold warriors to run roughshod over their victims.

However, a few years later the court did make a politically expedient decision by attributing only minimal effect to Clause 3 (Communications Ass'n v. Douds, 1950). *Lovett* and *Douds* provide an interesting contrast, illustrate the political currents that flowed during the Cold War, and indicate the two threads in the case law on Clause 3. At issue in *Douds* were the portions of the National Labor Relations Act that denied certain benefits to, and placed certain restrictions on, labor unions if their officers had not filed affidavits that they had not been Communists. The Court acknowledged that Ex Parte Garland and Cummings v. Missouri were about placing restrictions on individuals "according to belief and loyalty." However, in their decision, they tried to distinguish those earlier cases on the grounds that they involved only past actions; "whereas[,] in this case [individuals] are subject to possible loss of position only because there is substantial ground for the congressional judgment that their beliefs and loyalties will be transformed into future conduct." However, in the next sentence, the Court gave away the secret that the distinction between the facts in *Douds* as compared to those in Ex Parte Garland and Cummings v. Missouri was not nearly as sharp as it claimed: "[o]f course, the history of the past conduct is the foundation for the judgment as to what the future conduct is likely to be."

The Current Era

Ironically, in 1960, when the pursuit of "subversives" had abated somewhat, the Court indicated its willingness to allow their punishment, in the process taking a narrow view of Clause 3 (the prohibition against bills of attainder) (Flemming v. Nestor, 1960). The government had stopped making social security payments to a person who had been deported to Bulgaria because he had, decades earlier, been a member of the Communist Party. The Court held that the decision was not punitive because it was directed at the person's activities, not at the person himself. However, a distinction between a person and his or her activities seems to be exceedingly difficult to draw. The Court also held that the government needed flexibility in administering the social security system and that denial of government benefits was not punishment. The dissent argued that Nestor had paid into the system hoping later to get benefits, not flexibility, that the payments might be necessary to keep him alive, and that the decision ignored the competing line of cases, including *Lovett*, in which the Court had taken very seriously the prohibition against bills of attainder.

A later case is an example of a more expansive interpretation of Clause 3 (United States v. Brown, 1965). In fact, a detailed majority opinion by Chief Justice Warren and a detailed dissent by Justice White allow a reader to see the main arguments for both an expansive and a narrow reading as well as to obtain a review of the history of the concept and the earlier case law. *Brown* concerns a law that made it a crime for anyone who had been a member of the Communist Party to hold office in a labor union. Thus, as late as 1965 the Court was still hearing cases based on the hunt for "subversives." Chief Justice Warren thought of Clause 3 as a way to implement the concept of separation of powers. He noted that the statute under which the person had been convicted identified the Communist Party as a dangerous organization rather than generally identifying the characteristics that Congress considered dangerous and then leaving it to the courts to decide whether the party exhibited those characteristics. To use his terms, he distinguished specification from rule-making. He also argued that the actions taken against Brown were punishment and he concluded that the act was a bill of attainder. Justice White asserted that the majority opinion reversed some of the case law and called into question many regulatory statutes. His main point was that the statute evinced no punitive purpose and was purely regulatory. He concluded that for those reasons it was not a bill of attainder.

By 1970 the battles over the appropriation clause were being fought primarily not in the courts but in the executive branch and Congress. Presidents had begun to expend federal funds while obscuring or totally hiding their use, sometimes with the tacit or even explicit authorization of Congress or at least of some members of Congress. Meanwhile, Congress had frequently used Clause 7 to add force to conditions that it attached to appropriations and had begun to pass legislation opposing particular instances of the executive branch's covert spending. These practices occurred at the same time as a spirited debate in law reviews and at symposiums about the relative power of the two branches to control the ways in which federal money was spent.

The Vietnam War was the occasion for some of the more important and interesting developments of this debate. Congress took its first step in that direction in 1969, when it added to an appropriations bill a rider that restricted military action in Laos and Thailand.[52] Two years later, Congress added to a military appropriations act a statement that it was "the policy of the United States to terminate at the earliest practicable date all military operations of the United States in Indochina."[53] In 1973, when the war in Southeast Asia appeared to be ending, President Richard Nixon began a bombing campaign in Cambodia and Laos. Congress responded by adding a rider to an appropriations bill for military actions in Southeast Asia that required cessation of all military action in Southeast Asia by August 15, 1973.[54] Congress, reacting to yet more covert funding by the executive branch of military activities, took similar measures against the executive branch's funding of the Contras in Nicaragua.[55]

A few years later, Richard Nixon, by that time out of office, again appeared on the scene in the context of the US Constitution Article I § 9, when he argued that a statute that imposed restrictions on his presidential papers was a bill of attainder (Nixon v. Administrator of General Services, 1976). The case was difficult to resolve. Nixon argued that the restrictions were punishment. The majority opinion of the Court pointed out that, if any burden that a legislative act placed on only some persons was a punishment and the legislative act was therefore a bill of attainder, the prohibition against this kind of legislation would hamstring Congress, particularly its ability to regulate conduct in order to protect the health, welfare, and safety of citizens. The Court held that the act was not a bill of attainder because it did not impose a kind of punishment that was traditionally imposed by that kind of statute because the act's function was to preserve the papers, not to punish, and because Congress' motive, as evidenced by the debate on the bill, was not to punish. A dissenting justice argued vigorously that the act's application to only one person, the universal understanding before the case that a former president's papers were private property and Congress' desire to punish the plaintiff made the statute a bill of attainder. The facts of the case, which became even more highly charged because of the plaintiff's prominence, were one reason why the case was difficult to resolve. Another reason for the difficulty is that the Court had not, and still has not, found and consistently used a single rational test to determine whether a statutorily imposed burden was a punishment.

As they have in cases on the prohibition against bills of attainder, courts in cases on the prohibition against ex post facto laws have struggled with cases that involved burdens that were unlike those that are imposed in criminal trials. The objects of their struggles are, first, to decide whether this kind of burden can be a punishment for purposes of those prohibitions and, second, if so, to devise a test that will divide those burdens into two categories: those that inflict punishment and those that do not. In fact, nearly all ex post facto cases are about these issues.

However, there are a few ex post facto cases that arise from the criminal law. The definition of ex post facto law as it applies to criminal cases has been accepted since an eighteenth century case (Calder v. Bull, 1798), which is described earlier. According to that case, ex post facto laws make criminal an action that was innocent when it was done, that aggravate a crime after it was committed, that change the punishment of a crime after it was committed, or that alter the rules of evidence after a crime was allegedly committed. Despite this definition's clarity, some criminal ex post facto cases present difficulties, as a more recent case (Portley v. Grossman, 1980) illustrates. A person who had been convicted of a crime argued that his eligibility for parole should be determined under the rules that were in effect when he was sentenced, not those in effect when he became eligible for parole. Although using the more recent rules seems to be retroactively increasing a penalty because the rules for parole were part of the sentence, the Court held that the act was not a bill of attainder.

Legislation that was enacted during the Vietnam era led to an important case on Clause 3 (bills of attainder) (Selective Service v. Minn. Public Int. Res. Gp., 1984). This legislation denied financial aid to college students who had not registered for the draft. Another law required registration and imposed penalties for failing to do so. The Court assumed that a law imposing a non-criminal sanction could be a bill of attainder, but it held that the legislation in question was not such a bill. It reasoned, not quite convincingly, that the law allowed late registration, which distinguished it from the laws in *Cummings* and *Garland* (Cummings v. Missouri, 1867; Ex Parte Garland, 1867), both of which punished actions that could not be reversed. Moreover, the Court wrote that the statute merely denied a "non-contractual governmental benefit" and had none of the earmarks of punitive legislation. This case certainly is part of the line of cases that narrowly interprets the bill of attainder clause.

By far the most significant scholarly debate about Article 1, § 9 is the one that was generally about the effect of Clause 7 (the prohibition against drawing money from the treasury without an appropriation) and specifically about whether that clause authorizes Congress to limit the President's power. The debate began in earnest after many years of struggle between the two branches, which occurred most frequently not in the courts but by means of Congress' passing of legislation that limited the executive's spending authority and by means of the executive branch's attempts to circumvent that kind of limit.

Kate Stith was the first major voice in the debate.[56] Stith included a good deal of useful background information, such as a description of Congress' budget process and of major legislation that limits the spending authority of the executive branch. Her main concern, however, was to argue that Congress, not the executive branch, has the right under the Constitution to control spending. Stith argued that this followed from two basic principles. The principle of the public fisc is that all funds received from any source by the federal government are public. The principle of appropriations control is that legislative authority is required for the expenditure of public funds and applies to both the executive branch and to Congress. She argued that this principle derived from the "necessary and proper clause": Clause 17 of Article 1, § 8 which bestows on Congress the right "to make all laws which shall be necessary and proper for carrying into execution the foregoing powers [those granted earlier in Section 8], and all other powers vested by this constitution in the government of the United States, or in any department or officer thereof."

The principle means that the executive branch may not spend without prior Congressional authorization, and it means that Congress has a duty to control spending. Congress' duty, she remarked, requires monitoring expenditures even to the point of refraining from creating appropriations that are not limited in both time and amount. Although Stith did concede that Congress' power over spending is limited by other constitutional provisions, she was vague about that point, which is a crucial issue. She cited as an example a case in which the Court held that the power to appropriate did not trump the prohibition against bills of attainder (United States v. Lovett, 1946). As Part II will indicate, she conceded too much. For example, Congress is explicitly forbidden by the Constitution to pass bills of attainder. To generalize from Lovett that the whole Constitution limits Congress' power to control spending is to open the door to claims that, say, powers granted to the President by the Constitution also override Congress' authority over spending.

That argument is precisely the one that J. Gregory Sidak soon made.[57] Like Stith, Sidak provided a good deal of historical material, but he, too, was most concerned with attempting to strengthen the hand of one of the branches of government, in his case the executive branch. He founded his argument on the principle of separation of powers. From that principle, he argued, derived the conception of the "unitary executive." According to Sidak, the President and, in general, the executive branch, are entitled to exercise their rights and perform their duties, both as specified by the Constitution, unimpeded by either of the other two branches and, most importantly, by Congress. An example of the executive branch's duties is to execute the laws.

By this point, several problems have occurred in Sidak's argument. One is that the link between the doctrine of separation of powers and a "unitary executive" is not substantiated. Another is that if the "unitary" nature of the executive branch follows from the doctrine of separation of powers, then it seems that the "unitary" nature of the legislative branch would also follow. If it does follow, then the executive branch may not foil the rights and duties that the Constitution bestows on Congress, including its right; under Article 1, § 9; to control, by means of appropriations, the flow of money from the treasury. Also, if one of the President's duties is to execute the laws, one can argue, as Sidak did, that the appropriations power cannot impede that duty. But one can also argue that the appropriations that are at issue are also laws and that the President's duty to execute the laws also applies to them. Sidak found support for his position in the same case as Stith (United States v. Lovett, 1946), which is about using an appropriation rider to deny federal jobs to three persons. However, that case's holding is much more narrow: that Congress may not pass bills of attainder, which is clear from the text of Clause 3 of this section.

According to Sidak, Clause 7, the appropriations clause, functions merely to mandate efficient use of federal money and to provide notice about the ways in which it is spent. He also argues that the reference to "by law" in Section 9 refers to more than the enactment of statutory law. It follows from that, he asserted, that other entities, including, of course, the executive branch, may "appropriate" federal money. Therefore, the executive branch may spend without a Congressional appropriation money that it has obtained by means of another appropriation, by gift or by any other means. The problem here is that in Section 9 "by law" modifies "appropriation" and only Congress may "appropriate," in the ordinary meaning of the word. Sidak did propose two kinds of limits on the executive branch's spending without, or in opposition to, a Congressional appropriation. One is the electoral process, the retribution by the voters against a President who overreaches. However, if that process suffices as a restraint against the President, it ought also to suffice as a restraint against Congress' overly zealous use of the appropriations process to hamstring the President. Sidak's other limits specified conditions under which the President may spend without an appropriation. Those conditions would be useful if one were willing to concede that Clause 7 requires no more than responsible bookkeeping. Making that concession, however, would eviscerate this clause, a result that Sidak's arguments do not justify.

The central issue in the scholarly debate on the appropriations clause focused on whether that clause limited the President's powers, such as the power to conduct foreign relations. Although, as Part II indicates, some cases on pardons clarified that issue, the debate included far more political theorizing than legal analysis. Finally, a case made the state of the law on that issue clear (OPM v. Richmond, 1990). Because his salary exceeded the allowed amount, Richmond was denied disability benefits, even though an official had assured him that he would receive them. The only appropriation that might have authorized payment specified that the money was to be used to pay benefits under the law. The payments were denied because they were not authorized by the law, so there was no appropriation under which they could be paid, and they could not be drawn from the treasury without an appropriation. The Court greatly clarified the appropriation clause's effect when it generalized: "[a]ny exercise of a power granted by the Constitution to one of the other branches of Government is limited by a valid reservation of congressional control over funds in the Treasury." The Court used as an example a principle that earlier decisions ought to have made ineluctable: "[j]ust as the pardon power cannot override the command of the Appropriations Clause, so too judicial use of the equitable doctrine of estoppel cannot grant respondent a money remedy that Congress has not authorized." Thus, the appropriations clause has as much force as any other constitutional provision.

Although the most interesting and important issue about the appropriations clause is the amount of authority that it gives to Congress as against the executive branch, courts have also had to deal with the more technical question of the precision that is required for an appropriation to be valid and thus to allow spending without violating Clause 7. In *Cincinnati Soap*, the Court had been flexible but mainly because the spending was to benefit a dependency, to which this country owed an unusual duty of care. After that decision, it was still unclear whether courts would be flexible in less unusual circumstances. It turned out that they will be flexible. A Court (Republic Nat. Bank Miami v. United States, 1992) held that a statement that in certain circumstances "property shall be returned forthwith to the claimant or his agent" was an appropriation. Indeed, that Court wrote that "I have difficulty imagining how an 'appropriation' of funds determined on appeal not to belong to the United States could ever be more specific." The Court failed to imagine a conventional appropriation that set aside money for that purpose, which is the function that appropriations perform.

Although § 9 did not figure as prominently in the debates over framing and ratifying the Constitution as did a number of other provisions, it has generated some interesting and important case law. A fair amount of that case law arose out of such crises in the history of this country as the Civil War, the Cold War, and the Vietnam War. That case law, unfortunately, is far from consistent. Many of the issues remain to be settled, and in some of them courts need to choose between competing lines of cases. These generalizations will be substantiated and the current state of the law on § 9 clarified in Part II.

NOTES

1. An excellent account of Sir Thomas More's legal troubles appears in Peter Ackroyd, *The Life of Thomas More* (New York: Doubleday, 1998).

2. For a brief history of the writ of habeas corpus see Fay v. Noia, 372 U.S. 391 (1963).

3. William Blackstone, *Commentaries on the Laws of England* (Chicago and London: University of Chicago Press, 1979: facsimile of the first edition).

4. 1 Blackstone, *Commentaries*, 46.

5. 1 Blackstone, *Commentaries*, 373.

6. 1 Blackstone, *Commentaries*, 132.

7. 2 Max Farrand, *The Records of the Federal Convention of 1787* (New Haven and London: Yale University Press, 1966), 220.

8. 2 Farrand, *Records*, 222.

9. 2 Farrand, *Records*, 220.

10. 2 Farrand, *Records*, 369.

11. 2 Farrand, *Records*, 370.

12. 2 Farrand, *Records*, 416.

13. 2 Farrand, *Records*, 371.

14. 3 Farrand, *Records*, 210–11.

15. 3 Farrand, *Records*, 334–35.

16. 2 Farrand, *Records*, 334.

17. 3 Farrand, *Records*, 328.

18. 2 Farrand, *Records*, 376.

19. 2 Farrand, *Records*, 376.

20. 2 Farrand, *Records*, 448–49.

21. 2 Farrand, *Records*, 617.

22. 2 Farrand, *Records*, 95.

23. 2 Farrand, *Records*, 220.

24. Bernard Bailyn (ed.), *The Debate on the Constitution* (New York: Library of America, 1993), Part I, 89.

25. Bailyn, *Debate*, Part I, 210.

26. Bailyn, *Debate*, Part I, 814.

27. 3 Farrand, *Records*, 212.

28. Bailyn, *Debate*, Part III, 395.

29. 3 Farrand, *Records*, 161.

30. Bailyn, *Debate*, Part II, 706.

31. 3 Farrand, *Records*, 254.

32. Bailyn, *Debate*, Part II, 20.

33. Bailyn, *Debate*, Part II, 152.

34. 3 Farrand, *Records*, 157.

35. Bailyn, *Debate*, Part I, 647.

36. Bailyn, *Debate*, Part I, 557.
37. Bailyn, *Debate*, Part II, 41.
38. Bailyn, *Debate*, Part II, 711.
39. Bailyn, *Debate*, Part II, 711.
40. Bailyn, *Debate*, Part II, 237.
41. Bailyn, *Debate*, Part I, 349.
42. Bailyn, *Debate*, Part II, 626.
43. Bailyn, *Debate*, Part I, 396.
44. Bailyn, *Debate*, Part II, 728–29.
45. Bailyn, *Debate*, Part II, 237.
46. Bailyn, *Debate*, Part II, 711.
47. Bailyn, *Debate*, Part II, 539.
48. 3 Farrand, *Records*, 365.
49. 3 Farrand, *Records*, 213–14.
50. 3 Farrand, *Records*, 149–50.
51. The privilege of the writ was also suspended in part of South Carolina in 1871 because of activity by the Ku Klux Klan, in the Philippines in 1905 and in Hawaii during World War II.
52. John Hart Ely, "The American War in Indochina, Part I: The (Troubled) Constitutionality of the War They Told Us About," *Stanford Law Rev.*, 42 (1990) 899.
53. Armed Forces Appropriations Act, 1972, Pub. L. No. 92–156, § 601(a).
54. Second Supplemental Appropriations Act, 1973, Pub. L. No. 93–50.
55. Further Continuing Appropriations Act, Pub. L. No. 97–377, § 793.
56. Kate Stith, "Congress' Power of the Purse," *Yale Law J.* 97 (1988) 1343–96.
57. J. Gregory Sidak, "The President's Power of the Purse," *Duke Law J.* (1989) 1162–1253.

PART II

PROHIBITED GOVERNMENT ACTS AND COMMENTARY

The first eight sections of Article 1 of the U.S. Constitution explicitly confer powers on, and impose duties on, Congress. Article 1's tenth and final section specifies constraints that undoubtedly apply to the states. The entity to which § 9 is addressed sometimes is Congress, sometimes is another specified entity, and sometimes is not clear to one who reads only the section's text. The common element of the clauses in § 9 is their prohibitive nature. Because they are addressed to more than one entity, if it were to have a title, prohibited government acts would serve well.

Clause 1 decrees that Congress may not prohibit the migration or importation of "persons" until 1808. It is clear from the debates at the Constitutional Convention and during the discussion about whether the Constitution should be ratified and according to the only case in which Clause 1 played a part, that "persons" refers not to all persons but only to slaves brought from Africa. Therefore, this clause is not a limit on Congress' power over immigration (under US Const, Art 1, § 8, Clause 4). For that reason, and because 1808 has long since passed, Clause 1 has no contemporary relevance. However, the case in which it was relevant, the *Dred Scott* case (Dred Scott v. Sandford, 1856), is one of the more famous of American cases. The case and the role of Clause 1 in it are discussed in Part I.

Clause 4 prohibits capitation and direct taxes (terms that the case law defines) except those taxes "laid" (imposed) in proportion to the census. That is, those taxes must be imposed on the basis of population. Similarly, § 2 of Article 1 states that "direct taxes shall be apportioned among the several states which may be included within this union, according to their respective numbers" and then specifies the means by which those numbers are to be determined. These provisions have generated significant case law and have an interesting history and substantial importance. However, it makes more sense to consider them along with other constitutional provisions on the federal government's taxing power in order to allow a unified treatment of the parts of the Constitution that relate to the life blood of governments in this country: tax money. These other provisions include the general grant of the power of taxation in Article 1, § 8, Clause 1 and the Sixteenth Amendment. For that reason, Clause 4 is covered in the volume in this series on Congress' taxing and borrowing authority.

Therefore, two of the clauses in § 9 are not covered in this analysis. In addition, Clause 8, which prohibits granting titles of nobility and accepting presents and certain other benefits by certain governmental officials, has generated no case law, although there are clues to the ways in which it should be interpreted. These clues are worth examining, so that clause will be discussed here. The remaining five clauses have been litigated enough times and are important enough to justify substantial treatment in this analysis. In fact, several of these clauses, as shown in Part I, establish important bulwarks of our free society.

Clause 2: Suspending the Privilege of the Writ of Habeas Corpus

CLAUSE 2. THE PRIVILEGE OF THE WRIT OF HABEAS CORPUS SHALL NOT BE SUSPENDED, UNLESS WHEN IN CASES OF REBELLION OR INVASION THE PUBLIC SAFETY MAY REQUIRE IT.

Habeas corpus is one of a number of writs (orders) that courts have at their disposal to accomplish, require, or prevent particular actions. By translating that Latin clause—"you have the body"—one begins to understand its function. A Court aptly understood the writ's function: "[i]ts root principle is that in a civilized society, government must always be accountable to the judiciary for a man's imprisonment; if the imprisonment cannot be shown to conform with the fundamental requirements of law, the individual is entitled to his immediate release" (Fay v. Noia, 1963).

Courts use this writ most frequently in the criminal law to order an authority that is holding someone in custody to produce that person so that the court can assess the detention's validity. Most of the persons who avail themselves of the writ have been convicted of a crime and wish to have a federal court determine whether the conviction comports with federal constitutional law. Others have been held in custody on the basis of a quasi-judicial proceeding or, in rare cases, on the basis of no proceeding at all. This writ is used less frequently in civil cases to determine the validity of a child custody decision or of a deportation order.

Liberty is the prize for obtaining a writ and then using the opportunity that it presents to convince a court that a detention is unlawful. Thus, the writ is very important. In fact, the writ of habeas corpus is one of the wonders of the Anglo-American legal system. Legal scholars and judges have much revered it. Blackstone, for example, called it "the most celebrated writ in the English law."[1] A Court wrote that "[t]he importance of the main question [whether a writ of habeas corpus should have been issued] presented by this record cannot be overstated; for it involves the very framework of the government and the fundamental principles of American liberty" (Ex Parte Milligan, 1966). Moreover, its importance extends beyond individuals and the judicial system: "[i]t is no accident that habeas corpus has time and again played a central role in national crises, wherein the claims of order and of liberty clash most acutely, not only in England in the seventeenth century, but also in America from our very beginnings, and today" (Fay v. Noia, 1863).

Before beginning an analysis of the current state of the law on Clause 2, it is important to note matters to which it does not apply. A significant amount of the federal courts' workload is dealing with incarcerated persons' petitions for the writ. This has changed because, at first, the federal writ was held to be unavailable to state prisoners (Ex Parte Dorr, 1845). Congress gradually extended the writ's reach and, in the Judiciary Act of 1867, extended it further so that it was available to state prisoners. The bases for the federal habeas corpus activity in regard to state prisoners is not this clause, however. They are the 1867 Judiciary Act and its successors, the inherent power of federal courts under Article 3 (see *Judicial Power and Separation of Powers: A Reference Guide to the U.S. Constitution* and *Courts' Jurisdiction: A Reference Guide to the U.S. Constitution*), and the application of the Bill of Rights to state action under the Fourteenth Amendment. However, the reference to the writ in Clause 2 is the only one in the U.S. Constitution. In contrast, some state constitutions grant to the courts the right to issue all writs or a list of writs, which is likely to include habeas corpus. As we will see, there is a fairly cogent argument that the reference in Clause 2 does provide the authority to the courts to issue this writ, but some courts have disagreed on this.

A number of courts have made that argument. That argument and other arguments on this issue are all dicta (statements that are unnecessary to the decision in a case) because courts clearly have the authority to issue the writ of habeas corpus, if not because of this clause then because of other reasons. The argument arises, of course, because Clause 2 limits the writ but does not clearly grant the authority to issue it. A limit implies that there is another source for this authority, that the authority is virtually certain to be granted later, or that the limit itself implicitly authorizes it. During the Civil War, a Court chose the third possibility: "[t]he terms of this provision [this clause] necessarily imply judicial action" (Ex Parte Yerger, 1869). That infelicitous prose seems to mean that because of this clause courts have the authority to issue writs of habeas corpus. That Court went on to assert that if courts have this authority, the Supreme Court, having the most important judicial powers, certainly has it. A later Court was more clear: "[t]he writ of habeas corpus as an incident of the federal judicial power is implicitly recognized by Article I, 9 cl. 2" (McNally v. Hill, 1934). This Court did, however, point out that after the Constitution was ratified, the Judiciary Act in effect (one has been in effect since 1789) also bestowed the power to issue the writ.

Other courts have asserted that Clause 2 does not authorize issuance of the writ. Again, one court stated its position rather obscurely, by referring to "the time that the Suspension Clause was written into our Federal Constitution and the first Judiciary Act was passed [in 1789] conferring habeas corpus jurisdiction upon the federal judiciary" (Fay v. Noia, 1963). The phrase about conferring the jurisdiction appears to be intended to modify only the first Judiciary Act, and the reference to Clause 2 in the same sentence then seems to mean that the clause did not confer this jurisdiction. Another Court was a bit clearer: "[t]he habeas corpus jurisdictional statute implements the constitutional command that the writ of habeas corpus be made available" (Jones v. Cunningham, 1963). This statement accords with one made by a very early court:

> [a]cting under the immediate influence of this injunction [the clause's implication that the authority to issue the writ must be given] they [the first Congress] must have felt, with peculiar force, the obligation of providing efficient means by which this great constitutional privilege should receive life and activity, for if the means be not in existence, the privilege itself would be lost, although no law for its suspension should be enacted (Ex Parte Bollman, 1807).

The response to that influence, as the Court pointed out, was the grant of authority to issue the writ that was included in the first Judiciary Act. Congress, in addition to recognizing the need for the writ, must also have recognized that there was no authority for it; otherwise it probably would not have granted that authority by statute. This position, that the clause does not itself authorize the writ but that it signals to Congress to do so, makes more sense than does the position that the clause does in fact authorize the writ. One could argue that the Framers knew the way to grant power; for example, they provided that "[t]he Congress shall have power to lay and collect taxes, duties, imposts and excises" (US Const, Art I, § 8, Clause 1). However, they did not, by means of similar wording in Clause 2, grant power to issue the writ of habeas corpus. Their decision not to do so is puzzling because they surely knew that habeas corpus was important.

The clause thus probably does not grant the power to issue writs of habeas corpus, but it certainly constrains the suspension of the privilege of them. An obvious first task that needs to be performed if one is to understand that clause's effect is to determine the entity or entities that the clause constrains. This entity or those entities are also the same ones that have the power to suspend the writ during the conditions that the clause names. The clause is not addressed to any particular entities; its prohibition is generally phrased. Because the Constitution is addressed to the federal government, this clause surely constrains it. One could also argue that, due to the clause's generality, it also constrains the states. Courts have not agreed. One Court made a structural argument, asserting that all of this section restricts only national, not state, action (Gasquet v. Lapeyre, 1917). For that proposition it cited three cases, all of which are on Clause 6 (Munn v. Illinois, 1876; Morgan's L. & T.R. & S.S.C. v. Board of Health, 1886, and Johnson v. Chicago & P. Elevator Co., 1886). The second of these cases does include a statement that "the ninth section...is...devoted to restraints upon the power of Congress and of the national government." But this argument falls short of being utterly compelling. First, the argument is circular: it states that Clause 6 applies only to the federal government because courts in three cases held that the entire § 9, including of course this clause, applies in that way. Also, the application of some of the clauses only to the federal government is not entirely clear. Finally, all three cases are about Clause 6, so one could argue that in respect to the other clauses the relevant statements are dicta. Nevertheless, it appears to be settled that Clause 6 restricts only the federal government.

Oddly enough, although Clause 2 applies only to the federal government, it applies, under certain circumstances, outside the borders of the United States. Courts have been willing to inquire into the issue of suspension of the writ in this country's dependencies. One such case involved Hawaii before it became a state (Duncan v. Kahanamoku, 1946). Another involved the Philippine Islands when they were a dependency (Fisher v. Baker, 1906). In both instances, Congress, exercising its authority over dependencies and territories, had enacted statutes about the suspension of the writ. Therefore, the court was actually inquiring into federal legislation as well as into the actions of the officials who had been given authority by the federal government over a dependency or territory.

However, the clause's reach beyond this country's borders is limited. At a time when Cuba was occupied by this country (shortly after the Spanish-American War), a citizen of the United States attempted to induce a court in this country to afford him some constitutional protections. The Court's response was that habeas corpus protection and other rights "have no relation to crimes committed without the jurisdiction of the United States against the laws of a foreign country" (Neely v. Henkel, 1901). *Neely* did not deal with Clause 2, but one can assume that the same principle would apply to it. For one thing, no official of another country has the authority to suspend the privilege of the writ under this clause.

Another puzzle about Clause 2 is the meaning of "privilege," since suspension of "privilege" is the clause's subject. In an early case, Justice Taney, presiding in a federal circuit court on a temporary basis, as Supreme Court justices once did in addition to their primary duties, rather than in the Supreme Court, assumed that the thing suspended is the enforcement of the "civil process of the United States" (Ex Parte Merryman, 1861). A few years later a court made a clearer and more explicit explanation: "[t]he suspension of the privilege of the writ of habeas corpus does not suspend the writ itself" (Ex Parte Milligan, 1866). In other words, this clause is about instances in which officials who are holding persons in custody are given permission or orders not to respond to writs of habeas corpus. The clause does not refer to courts discontinuing the issuance of the writ, either on their own volition or in the highly unlikely event (due to the separation of powers doctrine) that they were ordered to do so.

Because Clause 2 is not addressed to any particular entity, the identity of the entity that has the power to suspend the privilege of the writ is an issue. The earliest court that discussed this issue did not decide it because that issue was not part of the case (Ex Parte Bollman, 1807). The Court's position was that

> [i]f at any time the public safety should require the suspension of the powers vested by this act [the first Judiciary Act] in the courts of the United States; it is for the legislature to say so. That question depends on political considerations, on which the legislature is to decide.

This reasoning is not adequate. First, the conclusion is a non sequitor, and, second, the premise is faulty. The question depends most fundamentally on an assessment of whether there is an emergency of sufficient magnitude to justify suspending the privilege of the writ. The executive branch, because it has easier access to the data that are pertinent to the decision, is in a better position to make this assessment than is the legislative branch. To be sure, the decision, particularly if it is to suspend the privilege, will have political ramifications, because it will take away a major protection of the liberties that citizens expect and will probably injure a faction and, in a crisis, perhaps one that has a national scope. Moreover, it does not follow from the existence of a political dimension that the legislative branch should decide whether to suspend the writ. Presidents, too, are political creatures and accountable to the voters.

A later Court made a more incisive argument: "it would be difficult to say, since this great writ of liberty is usually provided for by the ordinary functions of legislation...that it ought not to be deemed...within the scope of the legislative power of Congress" (Prigg v. Com. of Pennsylvania, 1842). After removing the double negative, one is left with the proposition that if Congress has provided for the writ and specified its dimensions—which it did in the first Judiciary Act—it ought also to have the power to suspend the privilege of the writ. This argument incorrectly assumes that the Judiciary Act, not Clause 2, created the writ. This argument from symmetry has some attraction. However, the argument from capacity, that the executive has more ability to assess the dimensions of an emergency, is perhaps more compelling.

Ex Parte Merryman, described earlier, was also important because in it the Court squarely faced for the first time the question of the locus of authority to suspend the privilege of the writ (Ex Parte Merryman, 1861). Justice Taney decided the case and wrote the opinion while sitting on a federal circuit court, so that his opinion has less precedential value than do Supreme Court opinions. Nevertheless, it is an important case and presents forceful arguments for the proposition that only Congress has authority to suspend the writ. In this case, President Lincoln had proclaimed the state of emergency that was necessary to activate the power to suspend the privilege and had delegated the decision about the suspension itself to a military officer. Taney used a number of arguments to support his contention that the President had acted beyond his constitutional powers.

One of his arguments was that all § 9 is devoted to Congress, so that Clause 2 applies only to that body. However, Clause 8 is addressed to "the United States" and prohibits executive branch employees, among others, from accepting gifts from other countries. Also, the major function of Clause 7 is to prohibit the executive branch from spending without the authority of an appropriation. Moreover, even if Taney had been correct in regard to his facts, it does not necessarily follow that all the clauses in a section of the Constitution need be directed to the same entity. In general, structural arguments—arguments that base an interpretation about a provision in the Constitution on its relation to other parts of the Constitution—ought to be treated with skepticism.

In Ex Parte Merryman, Taney also argued that the President has only limited powers, that in regard to protecting the life, liberty, and property of citizens his or her only power is to execute the laws. In fact, he claimed that the President has no power to execute the laws himself or herself but only the power to "take care" that others do so. This is an accurate statement of some of Article II, § 3. However, Taney again slightly misinterpreted the facts. He forgot, for example, that the Constitution gives the President the power to make treaties and installs him or her as the commander in chief of the armed forces. Both functions can be used to protect life, liberty, and property. Again, too, even if Taney had been right about the facts, there is a gap in the chain of logic: it does not follow that the virtual absence of power elsewhere in the Constitution means that there also is a void in a particular clause.

Taney's final major argument was based on legal precedent and, in particular, on Ex Parte Bollman, 1807. He quoted at length Justice Marshall's opinion, which did in fact agree with Taney's position. As mentioned, however, Marshall's remarks that only Congress has the power to suspend the privilege of the writ are dicta and thus have no value as precedents. Marshall's remark is a conclusory statement supported only by another conclusory statement: that the question is political. In short, Marshall and Taney agreed, but Marshall's opinion, not being a precedent, does not support, much less by itself justify, Taney's opinion.

Taney's opinion is a strongly worded statement that Lincoln's actions were unconstitutional, but one is likely to be surprised by its conclusion:

> I shall, therefore, order all the proceedings in this case, with my opinion, to be filed and recorded in the circuit court of the United States for the district of Maryland, and direct the clerk to transmit a copy, under seal, to the president of the United States. It will then remain for that high officer, in fulfillment of his constitutional obligation to "take care that the laws be faithfully executed," to determine what measures he will take to cause the civil process of the United States to be respected and enforced.

In one of the few law review articles written on Clause 2, Martin S. Sheffer attempted to rebut Taney's opinion in Ex Parte Merryman.[2] Taney seems impertinent at the conclusion of his opinion in *Merryman*. He is remembered today, almost invariably with disfavor, principally for his opinion in the *Dred Scott* case.

Nevertheless, Taney deserves his due. Accomplishing that requires examining Sheffer's article, which also makes it possible to look at the arguments for and against the proposition that the President has the authority to suspend the privilege of the writ.

Sheffer summarized the arguments of Attorney General Bates, who defended Lincoln's order to suspend the privilege of the writ. Bates began with the principle of separation of powers, which, he asserted, implies that none of the branches is subordinate to either of the others. The President, then, is not subordinate to the judicial branch if that compromises his or her ability to perform duties given by the Constitution. Bates argued that obeying, or allowing subordinates to obey, writs of habeas corpus during a civil war is thus not required of a President, who, under the Constitution, is the commander in chief. Bates also adumbrated his belief that the President ought to be active and energetic, a view like Alexander Hamilton's. Bates argued that it also followed from that view that a President must be able to act to suppress a rebellion unimpeded by writs of habeas corpus. Bates also argued that Taney himself had taken such a view of the presidency in an earlier case (Luther v. Borden, 1849). Sheffer was particularly impressed by the last of Bates's arguments, thinking that it negated the opinion in Ex Parte Merryman.

Bates' first argument is a bit too simple. Separation of powers is not absolute; there are areas of shared power, and courts have found ways to harmonize Constitutional provisions that are directed at two branches of government. His second argument is an example of political theory, not a legal argument. It is his third argument that has force, and Sheffer is right to be interested in it. However, to assess its validity accurately one needs to look more closely at Luther v. Borden. Taney did write in it that the "President's assessment of an emergency situation is conclusive and binding on other political branches." Bates and Sheffer concluded that Taney cannot have it both ways. Either in times of emergency, the President has the authority to act vigorously, including the authority to ignore writs of habeas corpus, or he does not.

However, Luther v. Borden is about a declaration of martial law, which is not the same thing as the suspension of the privilege of the writ of habeas corpus. In fact, either action may occur without the occurrence of the other, although it is likely that a declaration of martial law will be followed by a suspension of the privilege. Even more damaging to the argument that Bates and Sheffer advanced is the fact that in Luther v. Borden, the President was acting under the authority of a statute. That is, Congress had authorized the President to declare martial law. The facts of that case do not make it grounds for asserting that the President has independent authority that derives from this clause to suspend the privilege of the writ.

Listing occasions when the privilege has been suspended might cast some light on the question of whether the President has the authority to suspend it. President Lincoln suspended the privilege during the Civil War (litigated in Ex Parte

Merryman, 1861), but Congress later ratified this action. The Governor of the Philippines, acting under the authority of a federal statute, suspended it in 1905 (litigated in Fisher v. Baker, 1906). The Governor of Hawaii, acting under the authority of a U.S. statute, suspended it during World War II (litigated in Duncan v. Kahanamoku, 1946). Thus, in the instances appearing in the case law, Congress either authorized the suspension before it occurred or ratified it afterwards, but the actual suspension was the result of an action by the head of the executive branch of the jurisdiction.

At this point, the puzzle about whom or what may suspend the privilege of the writ remains unsolved. An important clue is the disposition of Ex Parte Merryman, because this case is the only one in which the authority of the President to suspend the privilege was litigated. The disposition is not congruent with the opinion. The disposition was literally sending the President a message. In the opinion, Justice Taney argued that Lincoln had acted unconstitutionally. At first solving the puzzle appears to be more difficult. However, the incongruity of the disposition and opinion might be the answer. If in the future a suspension by the President is litigated, it is difficult to imagine that a court would interfere. Taney was an implacable opponent of Lincoln and utterly convinced that Lincoln had acted unconstitutionally, but he would not order the President to reinstate the privilege, order an official to bring forth a prisoner, or otherwise take a substantive action to resist the President. Instead he made a mere gesture, based on a finding of unconstitutionality. Surely no other Supreme Court justice would order the President to reinstate the privilege. Thus, it might not matter whether the President has the power to suspend the privilege of the writ of habeas corpus. Any President assuming that he or she has this power and using it in conditions that obviously are an emergency will almost certainly be able to exercise the power unimpeded by a Court.

Another issue concerning Clause 2 is the nature of suspension. The reference to emergencies in the clause suggests that the clause is about refusing to respond to *all* writs of habeas corpus issued in the area in which the emergency is occurring and during a specified time period or until the order to suspend is revoked. Both the geographical scope and the temporal scope would likely be specified in the order to suspend. However, courts have confused matters by considering instances that do not represent all writs issued in a particular location or during a particular time period but only a class of writs. Courts have further complicated the issue by considering failures to grant a writ of habeas corpus rather than only failures to honor writs that have been granted. That is, they have considered actions that a literal reading of the clause does not cover. They could have disposed of those cases by declaring that Clause 2 does not apply to either situation. By proceeding beyond that point in the kind of case just described, courts have made it necessary to distinguish between suspending the writ (while pretending this "privilege" does not appear in the clause) and limiting the issuance of the writ.

In one case, the plaintiff assumed the clause has a broader scope than it actually has. The plaintiff argued that Clause 2 was violated by a statute that provided for free trial transcripts only if a judge certified that the claim was not frivolous and that the transcript was needed to decide the case (United States v. Maccollom, 1976). The plaintiff reasoned that the transcript was an indispensable part of the writ and, therefore, denying it free of charge in any instance was a suspension of the writ. The court held that the statute limited the writ rather than suspending it, but did not go far enough in its finding. Refusing to weigh the effect of the statutory requirements on the grounds that the "privilege" of the writ was not at issue would have prevented many later arguments that a different impediment was significant enough to be a suspension.

Another plaintiff argued that a statute violated this clause by specifying that the same claim may not be made in more than one habeas corpus action (Felker v. Turpin, 1996). Again, the court could have disposed of the case quickly by pointing out that the plaintiff was not arguing about a suspension of the privilege or about all writs in an area during a stated time period, so Clause 2 did not apply. Instead, the Court wrote that the rule was similar to the rule of res judicata (that an issue that has already been decided may not be reasserted). The term used in regard to more than one request in a case for a writ of habeas corpus is abuse of the writ. The result makes good sense, particularly in light of the flood of habeas corpus petitions that persons imprisoned by the states have let loose on the federal courts. Here again, the Court failed to foreclose future arguments that a statutory constraint on the use of the writ amounts to a suspension.

A more difficult case arose when a plaintiff asserted that requiring that a criminal conviction must be challenged by means other than a writ of habeas corpus was a suspension of the writ (Swain v. Pressley, 1977). This was more difficult because the restriction applied to a larger class. That is, it more nearly approached the size of the class affected when, say, President Lincoln suspended the privilege of the writ during the Civil War. Specifically, the plaintiff argued that, if another means of challenging a conviction was required, it must be exactly commensurate with the writ and that the statute in question required the judgment to be made by judges of the Superior Court of the District of Columbia rather than by federal judges. He argued then that the Superior Court judges did not have lifetime tenure and their salaries could be reduced while they were in office. The vulnerability to retribution against those judges that those two facts created made the other means of testing the conviction incommensurate with a habeas corpus petition directed to a federal court. The Court responded that the statute required an adequate and effective remedy, not one that was commensurate with an appearance in a federal Court made possible by a successful petition for a writ of habeas corpus. The court's dealing with the merits of the case rather than asserting the inapplicability of the clause to the facts seems to be another troubling mistake like the ones made in the two cases just mentioned.

Another issue that Clause 2's text presents is the nature of an emergency. Unfortunately, most of the cases shed little light on this issue. Some cases are about situations, such as the bombing of Pearl Harbor, that were obviously an emergency, so that issue does not arise. Others are about situations that obviously are not emergencies, such as recent cases in which courts have considered whether a limit placed on the right to petition for a writ of habeas corpus suspends the writ. The political price of suspending the privilege of habeas corpus in a situation that is not certainly an emergency will ensure that it is unlikely to happen. Thus, probably there will never be a borderline instance in regard to which a Court will have to decide whether an emergency did exist.

The final issue about Clause 2 is the relation between suspension of the privilege and martial law. Sheffer asserted that under the rules of martial law as they existed during the Civil War military courts supplanted the judicial system. A case from that era suggests otherwise (Ex Parte Milligan, 1866). The confederate soldier who wanted to use the writ was arrested in Indiana when the Confederate army was not in action in that state. The commander of a military district had ordered his arrest, and he was then tried by a military commission. The Court acknowledged that this clause allowed suspension of the privilege but cautioned that it "goes no further. It does not say after a writ of habeas corpus is denied a citizen, that he shall be tried otherwise than by the course of the common law." Therefore, the trial should have been held in a nonmilitary court. In fact, the Court wrote that "[m]artial rule can never exist where the courts are open." The Court's other reason for thinking that martial law should not have been instituted is that "martial law cannot arise from a threatened invasion [as opposed to an actual invasion]." In short, suspending the privilege of the writ under the authority of Clause 2 does not automatically institute martial law or deny persons their other trial rights. The propriety of instituting martial law and the propriety of suspending the privilege are separate questions. There can properly be martial law without suspension of the writ, and there can properly be suspension of that writ without martial law.

In summary, Clause 2 is unusual for several reasons. First, it has a strong political dimension. The questions of whether a situation justifies suspension of the privilege and of who has the authority to suspend it are likely to be answered according to political considerations, not according to judicial interpretations of the clause, because existing opinions do not illuminate these issues and future opinions are not likely to do so either. Second, the clause has the potential to generate litigation in which the prerogatives of the executive and legislative branches are possibly in conflict or at issue or both. This would occur if a President suspended the writ in a situation that was not an emergency. However, because of the political considerations already mentioned, that outcome, too, is unlikely. Third, until recently, Clause 2 became an issue only during emergencies, thus making litigation infrequent but highly charged. The recent willingness of courts to consider limits to the writ itself under this clause rather than foreclosing that option by stating that the clause does not apply to that issue is disturbing. This willingness distorts the clause's meaning and might lead to a considerable amount of litigation. That trend ought to be reversed. A reversal of this trend would put the case law back on the right track, and plaintiffs who had meritorious claims would probably be able to frame them in terms of another constitutional provision.

Clause 3: Bills of Attainder and Ex Post Facto Laws

CLAUSE 3. NO BILL OF ATTAINDER OR EX POST FACTO LAW SHALL BE PASSED.

This tersely worded clause prohibits two kinds of legislation. Because of the nature of these kinds of laws, a legislative body that has the right to enact them has the power to oppress its citizens. Both kinds of laws offend the notion of fundamental fairness held by many citizens of this country. Clause 3, therefore, at least potentially, affords important protection against these two types of legislative tyranny. One must qualify the statement in the previous sentence with "potentially" because the willingness of courts to use Clause 3 to restrict Congress has varied. During a few eras, courts have used Clause 3 boldly. However, many other times courts have been hesitant to employ the clause and thus quick to find arguments that it does not apply to the facts that are being litigated.

It is noteworthy that the statements of these two prohibitions appear not only in the same clause but also in the same sentence. Their common purpose of preventing congressional overreaching makes this linkage appropriate. Also, in many cases, plaintiffs have argued that a legislative act violates both prohibitions. Thus, I will analyze some cases under both topics. It is more likely that a bill of attainder is also an ex post facto law than that an ex post facto law is also a bill of attainder. One reason for that is that the general applicability of most ex post facto laws does not accord with the narrow applicability of the typical bill of attainder. Conversely, if Congress desires that a person or a small group of persons suffer punishment and there is an applicable criminal law in effect, an attractive option is to allow the judicial process to take its course. In this instance, no law would be enacted. However, if there is no applicable criminal law and if Congress wants punishment to occur immediately and to be directed at a particular person or persons, it must enact a law that might offend both parts of Clause 3.

Clause 3 relates to several other parts of the Constitution. The least important relation is with Article 3, § 3, Clause 2, which, among other things, provides that "no attainder of treason shall work corruption of blood, or forfeiture, except during the life of the person attainted." The common element is, of course, the reference to "attainder." Interpretation of the two clauses has proceeded quite independently. The relation with part of § 10, Clause 1 of Article 1 is much closer. Section 10, Clause 1 states in part that "[n]o state shall...pass any bill of attainder, ex post facto law, or law impairing the obligation of contracts." The logical response by a state to these prohibitions is to place them in their own constitutions. State courts' interpretation of these prohibitions might or might not strictly follow federal courts' interpretations of the same prohibitions as applied to Congress. For example, the Wisconsin constitution prohibits bills of attainder and ex post facto laws (US Const, Art I, § 12). Although Wisconsin courts have interpreted the prohibition against bills of attainder in much the same way that federal courts have interpreted them, Wisconsin courts have not automatically adopted federal courts' interpretations. After a 1974 case, the Wisconsin Supreme Court decided to begin accepting all federal court interpretations of the prohibition against ex post facto laws (State ex rel. Mueller v. Powers, 1974). Congress' power to impeach and then convict is an exception to the prohibition against bills of attainder. Under Art I, § 3, after an impeachment, the U.S. Senate has the power to impose the following punishments: "removal from office, and disqualification to hold and enjoy any office of honour, trust or profit under the United States."

Bills of Attainder

With three important exceptions, this analysis of Clause 3 as it relates to bills of attainder will not consider prohibitions against their passage by states. *Limits on States: A Reference Guide to the U.S. Constitution* analyzes all these cases. One exception is an early case on bills of attainder (Cummings v. Missouri, 1866). The U.S. Supreme Court issued that opinion and one in a case (Ex Parte Garland, 1866) that involved this clause on the same day. They are crucial cases and the Court intended that, together, they would form the contours of the law on that subject. To a large extent they have done so. Courts that have taken an expansive view of this clause have followed them; other courts that have taken a more restrictive view of Clause 3 have had to work their way around the decisions. Moreover, a vigorous dissent in Ex Parte Garland, which stated that it also applied to Cummings v. Missouri, is one of the better arguments for a restrictive view of the prohibition against bills of attainder. For these reasons, these two cases must be considered together.

Two other exceptions are Fletcher v. Peck (1810) and Ogden v. Saunders (1827). These cases are the source of the doctrine that "bill of attainder" as it is used in Clause 3 means more than bills that impose a sentence of death, that the term also includes bills that impose less severe penalties and were under common law called bills of pains and penalties.

First, the unusual word "attainder" needs to be explained. The dissent in Ex Parte Garland cited a legal dictionary that defined "attainder" as the corruption of blood that in common law accompanied a death sentence (Ex Parte Garland, 1866). "Corruption of blood" means incapacity, under the law, to receive or distribute property by means of inheritance. This secondary result of being convicted of a capital crime extended the punishment to the defendants' heirs. From these definitions, one can fashion a conception of the way that Clause 3 should be interpreted. In fact, Raoul Berger, a much more recent commentator, did so. The interpretation that logically follows from these definitions, so that argument goes, is that the clause prohibits only legislative enactments that decree both a death sentence and corruption of blood. Berger also used as a reason for his opinion the confusion that he alleged has resulted from judicial attempts to apply the term to other kinds of punishment as well. He argued that Clause 3 should be interpreted to apply only to the kinds of acts that were bills of attainder under English common law.[3] However, a significant number of acts of Parliament that are similar to bills that imposed death sentences imposed less severe punishments such as banishment and revocation of the right to vote. In addition, adopting Berger's position would in fact nullify the clause, because it is highly unlikely, for political reasons, that Congress would pass a law that condemned a person to a death sentence and effected corruption of blood. Each provision of the Constitution ought to have at least a minimal effect, which is another sound argument against Berger's position.

It makes little sense to adopt Berger's suggestion and retain, unexpanded and unmodified, the meaning that bill of attainder had in English common law. However, it is useful to know something about those bills, including the types, of English legislative acts that Clause 3 was added to the Constitution to forestall. Examining some members of that species chills the reader. One of the more important historically is quoted in a 1977 case on bills of attainder:

> WHEREAS, *James*, duke of *Monmouth* has in an hostile manner invaded this kingdom, and is now in open rebellion, levying war against the King, contrary to the Duty of his Allegiance, Be it enacted by the King's most excellent majesty, by and with the advice and consent of the lords spiritual and temporal, and commons in this Parliament assembled, and by the authority of the same, that the said James duke of Monmouth stand and be convicted and attainted of high treason, and that he suffer pains of death and incur all forfeitures as a traitor convicted and attainted of high treason. (Nixon v. Administrator of General Services, 1977)

In the above instance, a group of officials constituting a legislative body interrupted their other work to issue the command that a man—albeit one alleged to be a traitor—was to be put to death and his heirs forbidden from inheriting his property. This kind of legislative act was not only an English phenomenon. Colonial legislatures had enacted similar legislation, mainly to wreak revenge against supporters of England during the American Revolution.

In short, Clause 3 deals with matters of the utmost importance, not only to potential victims of bills of attainder but also to the polity as a whole. Bills of attainder impose penalties by legislative fiat rather than by the carefully honed methods of courts. Also legislatures are likely to pass bills of attainder in times of crisis, when pressure from constituents might overwhelm even the most cool-headed and circumspect of legislators. In *Nixon*, the Court described "a major concern that prompted the bill of attainder prohibition: the fear that the legislature, in seeking to pander to an inflamed popular constituency, will find it expedient openly to assume the mantle of judge—or, worse, still, lynch mob" (Nixon v. Administrator of General Services, 1977). As another court noted, "[w]hen our Constitution and Bill of Rights were written, our ancestors had ample reason to know that legislative trials and punishments were too dangerous to liberty to exist in the nation of free men they envisioned. And so they proscribed bills of attainder" (United States v. Lovett, 1946).

Alexander Hamilton, one of the more brilliant of these "ancestors," played a major part in shaping the Constitution and defending it during the debate on its ratification. Hamilton foreshadowed the position that some judges took many years later:

> Nothing is more common than for a free people, in times of heat and violence, to gratify momentary passions, by letting into the government principles and precedents which afterwards prove fatal to themselves. Of this kind is the doctrine of disqualification, disfranchisment, and banishment by acts of the legislature. The dangerous consequences of this power are manifest. If the legislature can disenfranchise any number of citizens at pleasure by general description, it may soon confine all the votes to a small number of citizens at pleasure by general descriptions, it may soon confine all the votes to a small number of partisans, and establish an aristocracy or an oligarchy; if it may banish at discretion all those whom particular circumstances render obnoxious, without hearing or trial, no man can be safe, nor know when he may be the innocent victim of a prevailing faction. The name of liberty applied to such a government, would be a mockery of common sense.[4]

One can best begin to understand the current state of the law on bills of attainder by defining that term, which, in turn, is most expeditiously done by determining the elements that constitute it. Courts have not been totally consistent on this issue, but eventually they propounded a definition that has become standard.

The companion cases of Ex Parte Garland and Cummings v. Missouri established the most widely accepted definition of bills of attainder. Before stating this definition, it is useful to note the dissent that applies to both cases, because it indicated that the definition that has persisted was a new departure when it was announced. This dissent purported to derive its definition from an empirical analysis of English bills of attainder and it stated a number of the identifying characteristics of bills of attainder: they effected corruption of blood; they were pronounced by the legislative branch, not the judicial branch, of government; the sentence and the punishment were not determined by any previous law; the accused was not likely to be present during deliberations on the bill; and the rules of evidence were inapplicable in legislative proceedings that might result in enacting a bill of attainder. The writer of the dissent explained that the process that Parliament used to enact a bill of attainder violated the principles of separation of powers and due process of law. The dissent also stated that strict adherence to the English common law meaning of bill of attainder would require that its victim or victims either be named in the bill or easily determined from it. However, some of the victims of English bills of attainder belonged to classes that were as nebulous as the ones that were identified in the legislation that was litigated in Cummings v. Missouri and Ex Parte Garland. The writer concluded the portion of his dissent on bills of attainder by implicitly proposing a slightly different set of criteria: "[a] statute, then, which designates no criminal, either by name or description—which declares no guilt, pronounces no sentence, and inflicts no punishment—can in no sense be called a bill of attainder." In short, the dissent's position closely resembled that of Raoul Berger.

The dissent's position in regard to corruption of blood has some merit. However, to accept this position, one needs to accept that the views of the Framers of the Constitution, if not dispositive, are at least highly pertinent in interpreting the Constitution. (See *A Reference Guide to the U.S. Constitution: Constitutional Interpretation.*) There is, of course, some support for limiting interpretation of the Constitution to the Framers' intent, for adopting the original intent school of interpretation. That view, however, is a distinctly minority position. Those who accept that mode of interpretation can cite Article 2, § 3, Clause 2 on the limit on the duration of corruption of blood in regard to every "attainder of treason." That is, some can argue from that provision that the Framers associated bills of attainder with corruption of blood. In other words, the Framers assumed that every bill of attainder would include a decree of corruption of blood and, in adding Clause 2, they intended to limit the temporal extent of the invariable corruption of blood. To accept this theory, one must make the illogical assumption that the absence of a provision that effects corruption of blood is sufficient to make a legislative act something other than a bill of attainder. That is a long leap, and taking it would make Clause 3 virtually null, because then this clause would apply only to bills imposing the death penalty.

There are several other problems with the dissent's view. First, this view assumes that "bill of attainder" has the same meaning in Clause 3 that it had in English common law as it existed when the U.S. Constitution was drafted. In general, this is far from an overpowering argument in regard to the Constitution in general; in regard to Clause 3, it is even less convincing because of the absence of debate on the clause during the Constitutional Convention. Second, another problem is the factual error already pointed out: the enactment by Parliament of bills that resembled bills imposing death sentences but that imposed a different penalty. A counter argument is that the other bills are bills of pains and penalties and should not necessarily be treated the same way as bills of attainder. The third problem with the dissent's viewpoint is that the absence of a previous law is a more appropriate identifying quality of an ex post facto law—in fact, it is the main identifying quality of that kind of law—than it is of bills of attainder. As mentioned, some bills of attainder are not also ex post facto laws. This point also runs counter to the historical argument, because laws against treason, for example, were no doubt applicable to persons who were victims of bills of attainder. In any event, the meaning of "punishment" in this clause seems to be by far the most difficult element in the jurisprudence on the clause.

The dissent was reacting to a definition that was less elaborate and more general (and thus more widely applicable) than was the definition that one could derive from English common law and that the dissenter would have preferred. The Court in *Cummings* defined a bill of attainder as a "legislative act that inflicts punishment without a judicial trial." It also remarked that bills of attainder may be directed either against an individual or against a class and that bills of attainder may punish absolutely or conditionally. The Court, thus, did not include some of the characteristic features of common law bills of attainder, such as a proclamation of guilt, in the definition of that kind of legislative act. Its main contribution, however, was substituting "punishment" for "sentencing to death" or other very severe penalties as one of the identifying criteria. The Court did not explain the reasoning that supported some of its decision about the definition, but it did produce its reasoning about the use of "punishment." This reasoning fits more logically later in this discussion.

Later courts have generally accepted the definition of bill of attainder that the Court formulated in those two cases, although some courts that have done so have proposed minor adjustments to it. Thus, Ex Parte Garland and Cummings v. Missouri determined the course of the law on bills of attainder. This is not to say that the expansive view of this concept has prevailed. The courts in two much more recent cases have specified that the definition should include one more element so that the bill of attainder must impose punishment on a designated person or a designated class of persons (United States v. Lovett, 1946; United States v. Brown, 1965). The Court in *Cummings* had mentioned this criteria but had not included it in the definition that it propounded. Adding this element also brings the definition closer to the understanding of the concept in common law and to the definition proposed by the dissent in Ex Parte Garland and Cummings v. Missouri. In proposing this clarification, the Courts in *Lovett* and *Brown* were not looking for a way to rule that a legislative act was not a bill of attainder. In fact, both Courts held that the act in question was a bill of attainder. The definition included in the two early opinions, as modified by the two later opinions, is the law on the subject. For example, an even later court adopted a definition that is a paraphrase of the one that would be derived from the four earlier cases: "a law that legislatively determines guilt and inflicts punishment upon an identifiable individual without provision of the protections of a judicial trial" (Nixon v. Administrator of General Services, 1977). The failure to include bills that impose punishment on a class of persons is either a slip or a reflection of the fact that the bill in question referred to only one person.

However, later courts have not followed the bold lead of the courts in the cases discussed above. As Michael Lehmann[5] has demonstrated, federal district courts have been particularly zealous at manipulating the terms of the core definition and at proposing other considerations, employing both strategies with the intent to make the doctrine only narrowly applicable. As we proceed, we will see some of the methods that the U.S. Supreme Court has used and that have had the same result. The Supreme Court's decisions have varied considerably on bills of attainder. Some evince a broad conception of bills of attainder while others evince a very narrow conception of them.

The first element in the definition of bill of attainder—that it must be a legislative act—has created few problems of interpretation. Any action by Congress short of passing a bill or a concurrent resolution that is to be presented to the President under Article 1, § 7 would not be legislation. For instance, a joint resolution would not be such. Moreover, unless the President vetoes a bill and the veto is overridden, Presidential approval is required for a bill to become a law. This fact in turn means that the prohibition in Clause 3, like the other prohibitions in § 9 that have to do with legislation, also is directed at the President. The use of "bill" and "passed" in the clause also makes it clear that the clause restricts legislation, not unilateral action by the executive or judicial branches of government. These matters are self-evident and have not been the subject of litigation. The only difficulty about this element is that one of the cases on the prohibition in Article 1, § 10 against states passing bills of attainder deals with a provision in a state constitution (Cummings v. Missouri, 1866).

The part of the definition of bill of attainder that has caused by far the most trouble for courts is the requirement that the bill must inflict punishment. If the Court in Cummings v. Missouri and Ex Parte Garland had taken the course that Raoul Berger recommended many decades later, and had specified that a bill must impose a death sentence in order to be a bill of attainder, courts would have avoided this problem. In fact, there would have been so few cases on this prohibition that they probably would have avoided all problems on it. By conflating bills of attainder and bills of pains and penalties, as defined by English common law, this Court both breathed life into this prohibition and made it much more difficult for courts to deal with the question whether particular legislative acts are bills of attainder.

The main support that the Court in *Cummings* presents for its assertion that bills of attainder can inflict punishment other than death is one of Chief Justice John

Marshall's opinions (Fletcher v. Peck, 1810). The Court in *Cummings* later quoted part of that opinion:

> [w]hatever respect might have been felt for the State sovereignties, it is not to be disguised that the framers of the Constitution viewed with some apprehension the violent acts which might grow out of the feelings of the moment, and that the people of the United States, in adopting that instrument, have manifested a determination to shield themselves and their property from the effects of those sudden and strong passions to which men are exposed. The restrictions on the legislative power of the States are obviously founded in this sentiment; and the Constitution of the United States contains what may be deemed a bill of rights for the people of each State: "No State shall pass any bill of attainder, ex post facto law, or law impairing the obligation of contracts."

The Court's definition of bill of attainder followed that quotation.

Fletcher v. Peck was a contract case, and the last phrase in the part of Article 2, § 10 that the Court quoted was the portion that was relevant to this case. Marshall cryptically presented his argument, so some explication is necessary. He appeared to mean that the three prohibitions in this clause of the Constitution, including the one that is relevant to the case, serve the same purposes because they appear in the same clause. They must protect property as well as persons because virtually all contracts are agreements about the former, not about the latter. The Court in Cummings accepted the conclusion that bills of attainder can threaten property as well as life, even though Marshall's statement about that kind of bill was a dictum. Later in his opinion in Fletcher v. Peck, Marshall more clearly connected the three constitutional prohibitions:

> [t]his rescinding act would have the effect of an ex post facto law. It forfeits the estate of Fletcher for a crime not committed by himself, but by those from whom he purchased. This cannot be effected in the form of an ex post facto law, or bill of attainder; why, then, is it allowable in the form of a law annulling the original grant?

Marshall was referring to the attainting function—the denial of the right to transfer property by will—that was included in English bills of attainder. His points were that the prohibition against bills of attainder prevents attainting and that because the three prohibitions serve the same function of protecting property and life, state legislatures may not in effect take away property by passing laws that impair contracts.

In another case (Nixon v. Administrator of General Services, 1977), Chief Justice Burger noted that the Court in *Cummings* had another precedent available to make the same point (Ogden v. Saunders, 1827). In Ogden, too, the Court asserted its belief that the three prohibitions appear together because their common effect "is a general provision against arbitrary and tyrannical legislation over existing rights, whether of person or property." The important part of the quotation for interpreting the prohibition against bills of attainder is the last phrase. Because this statement about bills of attainder was not necessary to the decision in the case, it has no precedential value, but it makes a cogent point.

Thus, the Court in *Cummings* stretched a point by using a dictum to support its position that bills of attainder do not necessarily impose the death penalty. Regardless of the correctness of its logic, that Court established a conception of Clause 3 that has persisted. As a result, courts need to make the much more difficult determination of whether a bill inflicts punishment instead of the obvious determination of whether it imposes the death penalty. As a matter of public policy, the Court's broader conception makes good sense, because it gives the prohibition some force and thus protects citizens against a legislative branch of government that may be too inflamed by a crisis to abstain from meting out punishment.

Not only may a bill that does not impose the death penalty be a bill of attainder but also so may a bill that has none of the earmarks of a criminal law. Although the parties in *Cummings* were litigating a fine and incarceration, the basic purpose of the law under which the plaintiff was convicted was to forbid persons who would not, or could not, take an oath that they had remained loyal to the United States during the Civil War and continued to remain loyal to it from holding public office or offices in corporations, from teaching, from holding property in trust for the use of a religious organization (Cummings was a priest), and from engaging in certain other specified acts. That is, the real issue was the oath, and failing to take it resulted in civil penalties. Cummings' criminal conviction resulted from his preaching and teaching although he had not taken the oath. The issue in Ex Parte Garland was an oath that lawyers were required to take.

Again, the basic purpose of the act was to deny to persons who refused to take the oath the opportunity to do certain things; in this case the act denied the plaintiff the ability to practice law (a civil penalty). Similarly, in *Lovett*, the penalty was loss of a job (United States v. Lovett, 1946). In fact, both Ex Parte Garland and United States v. Lovett were civil cases; in neither was a criminal penalty an issue. If the main purpose of the acts that were litigated in these three cases was to impose a criminal penalty or a penalty that closely resembled a criminal penalty, it would have been easier for the courts to distinguish bills of attainder from other bills. The test would have been definite and easy to administer. However, courts have confronted the much more difficult task of deciding whether bills imposed punishments.

Michael Lehmann[6] attempted to rebut a Minnesota court that had held that a bill imposing only civil penalties could not be a bill of attainder. Lehmann pointed out the civil nature of Ex Parte Garland and United States v. Lovett, although he considered Cummings v. Missouri to be a criminal case. However, he also argued that bills of attainder imposed punishment and when a legislature imposes punishment, "it has adjudged its victim to be...guilty of a crime." He did admit that the "crime" might not be on the statute books. Lehmann assumed that which he was attempting to prove: that a bill imposing punishment was a criminal law and thus in the tradition of common law bills of attainder. Lehmann is more convincing in his final point on this issue, that the proper question for a court to consider in a bill of attainder case is not whether the bill is criminal but whether it is, on the one hand, punitive or, on the other hand, regulatory.

In addition to the imposition of criminal penalties, another feature of a bill that would indicate a punitive purpose is a declaration of guilt. As the dissent in Ex Parte Garland asserted, most bills of attainder at English common law explicitly declared guilt. The writer of this dissent argued that the absence of this declaration in the legislative act litigated in this case was one indication that the legislative act was not a bill of attainder. The majority opinion in this case did not include a declaration of guilt in its definition of bill of attainder. In *Lovett*, the court explicitly rejected the inclusion in the bill of a declaration of guilt as an identifying characteristic of bills of attainder (United States v. Lovett, 1946). The Court wrote:

> [t]he fact that the punishment is inflicted through the instrumentality of an Act specifically cutting off the pay of certain named individuals found guilty of disloyalty, makes it no less galling or effective than if it had been done by an Act which designated the conduct criminal. No one would think that Congress could have passed a valid law, stating that after investigation it had found Lovett, Dodd, and Watson "guilty" of the crime of engaging in "subversive activities," defined the term for the first time, and sentenced them to perpetual exclusion from any government employment.

Therefore, this argument is not a potential aid to courts that are trying to define punishment in bill of attainder cases.

Having rejected a few clear-cut tests for determining whether a bill imposed punishment, courts were forced to devise tests to accomplish this. Their usual strategy has been to divide bills into categories. The most useful kind of categorization for this purpose has been constructing dichotomies. If a Court could divide all bills into those of "type x" and those of "type y," and if "x" indicated that a punishment was inflicted and "y" indicated that no punishment was inflicted, then categorizing the bill being litigated into an "x" or "y" would determine whether it inflicted punishment and would go a long way toward determining whether the bill was a bill of attainder. In some cases, a Court held that a bill of attainder may be either an "x" or "y," while in other cases, it constructed a scheme that had more than two categories, making the test less efficient. Even more unfortunate was the fact that as cases proliferated so did schemes of categorization. One could respond to this state of affairs by saying that the cases on bills of attainder depend heavily on their facts or by saying that the case law is confused because the courts continue to propose new schemes of categorization.

One dichotomy that courts have used is "activity–person or group." The Court in Flemming v. Nestor (1960) used this dichotomy. That case was about a person who had been deported because he had been a Communist and also was, under a statute, denied social security benefits for that same reason (Flemming v. Nestor, 1960). The Court's main analytical tool was this dichotomy:

> [w]here the source of legislative concern can be thought to be the activity or status from which the individual is barred, the disqualification is not punishment even though it may bear harshly upon one affected. The contrary is the case where the statute in question is evidently aimed at the person or class of persons disqualified.

The source of this dichotomy, according to the Court, is a statement in Cummings v. Missouri: "[the oath] was required in order to reach the person, not the callings. It was exacted, not from any notion that the several acts designated indicated unfitness for the calling, but because it was thought that the several acts deserved punishment." However, the Court misread the earlier opinion. It is generally accepted that the quotation from Cummings means that the constitutional provision was not designed to ensure that clergymen were qualified (that is what "reach the callings" means, as indicated by the reference in the next sentence to "unfitness for the callings") but to punish persons like Cummings.

The dissent in Flemming v. Nestor implied, quite convincingly, that the logic of the dichotomy is false, by stating that the enactment was aimed at "an easily ascertainable group." The activity identified the persons subject to the act; there is no definite difference between attacking a proscribed activity and attacking a person who performed that activity. Nestor felt no differently about losing his social security benefits than he would have if the bill had been phrased so as to threaten him more directly and more explicitly. More to the point, the same result would have ensued as to him and to everyone who engaged in the proscribed activity if they had been named in the act.

A Court that declared an act to be a bill of attainder also used this dichotomy as one of the means of arriving at this conclusion (United States v. Brown, 1965). Using that dichotomy thus appears to be a permissible approach. According to the Court in *Brown*, the legislation did not identify certain actions or characteristics that would bar persons from holding an office in a labor union, but it specified that members of the Communist Party had performed these actions and had those characteristics and were thus barred from office. The Court pointed out that in another case the legislation had been held not to be a bill of attainder because the legislation referred to activities, not to persons or groups (Communist Party v. Subversive Activities Control Board, 1961). The Court further argued that the earlier Court had clearly implied that, if the legislation's designated targets had been named the legislation would have been a bill of attainder. Next the Court argued against the government's assertion that the act in *Brown* was not different in this respect from a particular conflict of interest statute. The conflict of interest statute was based on an assessment of temptations that would apply to everyone, not only to a class of persons, and thus focused on general characteristics, not on a particular group.

The decision in *Brown* is impressive because it takes the bill of attainder clause seriously and because the Court in that case stood up against anti-"subversive" mania. However, the decision perpetuated the "activities–person or group" dichotomy. The Court could have arrived at the same result by a different route. For example, it could have disputed the government's assertion that the conflict of interest statute was indistinguishable from the statute that was at issue in the case by arguing that the other statute specified criteria relevant to holding the position; whereas, membership in the Communist Party was not relevant to holding an office in a labor union. Later we shall see that a Court, in passing, mentioned a distinction that would have made more sense than either the "activities–group or person" dichotomy and the analysis of relevance.

Courts have also used a "right–privilege" dichotomy. They have held that denying a right is punishment but that denying a privilege is not punishment. The origin of this dichotomy is the dissent in Ex Parte Garland: "[t]he right to practice law in the courts as a profession, is a privilege granted by the law, under such limitations or conditions in each state for government as the law-making power may prescribe. It is a privilege, and not an absolute right" (Ex Parte Garland, 1866). Although the writer of this dissent did not connect that statement to a later statement that the bill being litigated did not impose a punishment, he seems to intend that link. However, the majority opinion in this case and its companion, Cummings v. Missouri, held that making it impossible for someone to engage in an occupation can be punishment and that a bill that has this effect can, therefore, be a bill of attainder. Moreover, a bill that drove three persons out of their jobs was a bill of attainder (United States v. Lovett, 1946).

In contrast, two courts have used this dichotomy in order to aid their argument that certain bills were not bills of attainder. One of these courts called the denial of social security benefits "the mere denial of a noncontractual governmental benefit. No affirmative disability or restraint is imposed" (Flemming v. Nestor, 1960). The dissent thought otherwise. It pointed out that the benefits "may well be this exile's daily bread." It also responded caustically to the majority opinion's dismissal of the argument that the plaintiff had paid into the social security fund with the understanding that he would receive benefits in return:

> [t]he Court consoles those whose insurance is taken away today, and others who may suffer the same fate in the future, by saying that a decision requiring the Social Security system to keep faith 'would deprive it of the flexibility and boldness in adjustment to ever-changing conditions which it demands.' People who pay premiums for insurance usually think they are paying for insurance, not for "flexibility and boldness."

A later Court quoted the characterization of the denial of social security benefits in the majority opinion in Flemming v. Nestor to bolster its argument that the denial of student aid to persons who had not registered for the draft was not punishment (Selective Service v. Minn. Public Int. Res. Gp., 1984). The dissent argued that the bill violated the Fifth Amendment's prohibition against requiring self-incrimination. But a more successful dissent would have referred directly to earlier holdings on bills of attainder by arguing that denial of student aid was punishment. This case seems analogous to Flemming v. Nestor, and just as the dissent in that case could have pointed out that Nestor's social security benefits might have been his daily bread, a dissent in this case could have pointed out that the student aid might have been the difference between the litigants remaining in college and their leaving. A dissent could have added that being forced to leave college would prevent the students from entering a number of occupations. This argument would have made this case analogous to Ex Parte Garland, Cummings v. Missouri, and United States v. Lovett.

In short, there are two lines of cases on the "right–privilege" dichotomy. One line, which begins with the landmark cases Ex Parte Garland and Cummings v. Missouri, holds that preventing someone from engaging in an occupation is punishment. This act clearly being a privilege, not a right, these cases cast doubt on the dichotomy's validity. Another line of cases, however, asserted that dichotomy's validity. One logical conclusion that can be drawn from the difference in opinion is that the line between a right and a privilege is not distinct as some courts have thought, certainly not distinct enough to be the prime underpinning of a decision.

Courts' frequent recourse to another dichotomy, "punishment–regulation," indicates a major conceptual problem that has developed in the case law. The problem has arisen from competing interests. In order to ensure the health, safety, and welfare of their citizens—to exercise their police powers—governments must regulate occupations. However, individuals who wish to engage in occupations have an interest in being able to do this. Denying them access to an occupation is a detriment, perhaps even a punishment, which would potentially make any law a bill of attainder if it regulates entry into an occupation. There may be a way to avoid this unwelcome result. In an ideal system of justice, bills that regulate ought to be upheld against the assertion that they are bills of attainder, and bills that punish under the guise of regulation ought to be declared unconstitutional bills of attainder. The difficulty, of course, is distinguishing between the two functions.

Both of the cases, Ex Parte Garland and Cummings v. Missouri, that have determined the case law's direction involved the regulation of entry into an occupation, in the former case the practice of law and in the latter case the ministry. The majority opinion in *Cummings* conceded that states have the right to regulate occupations but asserted that the dispositive question is "whether that power has been made in the present case an instrument for the infliction of punishment against the inhibition of the Constitution." The court answered the question by determining that the qualifications that the state constitution specified were not relevant to the occupation to which they apply. For example, having left a state to avoid being drafted into the Union army in the Civil War has no bearing on one's qualifications to be a priest. The Court in Garland made the same concession and proposed the same question as did the court in *Cummings*. The Court in *Garland* also found that, because *Garland* had been denied permission to practice law, punishment had been inflicted. It stated that it made that finding for the same reasons as had the Court in *Cummings*, which would mean that it had applied the relevancy test. The Court also noted that that denial had abrogated a Presidential pardon.

The dissenting opinion that applies both to *Garland* and *Cummings* took a different view of the issue. It argued that the qualifications that the federal statute and the state constitution placed on entry into these occupations were relevant: "[t]hat fidelity to the government under which he lives, a true and loyal attachment to it, and a sincere desire for its preservation, are among the essential qualifications which should be required of a lawyer, seems to me to be too clear for argument." The dissent did not discuss the relevance of the qualifications at issue in *Cummings* to the priesthood. It would have been difficult to make a convincing argument on that point, and the dissent's argument about the qualifications for attorneys, particularly in light of the fact that the Civil War was concluded by the time the oath was to be taken, was tenuous, which might be indicated by the falsely bold claim that it is too clear for argument.

The regulation–punishment dichotomy appeared in an unusual form in another case (Communist Party v. Subversive Activities Control Board, 1961). An act of Congress denied certain kinds of employment to members of "Communist-action organizations" and imposed restrictions and penalties on those organizations. The court responded:

> [l]egislatures may act to curb behavior which they regard as harmful to the public welfare....So long as the incidence of legislation is such that the persons who engage in the regulated conduct...can escape regulation merely by altering the course of their own present activities, there can be no complaint of an attainder.

That is, the Court did not determine whether the qualifications were relevant to the occupations but used a test of escapability. It implied that regulation becomes punishment only when it is inescapable. The difficulty with the test is that one can argue cogently that forcing some persons, but not all persons, to choose between maintaining their sincerely held beliefs and entry into, or continuation in, a particular occupation is itself a kind of punishment. The escape will be punishment to some who accomplish it. In short, responding "it is their choice" is much too facile.

In *Brown*, although the Court did not explicitly invoke the "regulation–punishment" dichotomy, it implicitly based its analysis on that dichotomy, and the Court asserted that a statute is regulatory only if it identifies the persons whom the statute affects by means of qualities that are relevant to the conduct that the statute regulates (United States v. Brown, 1965). That is, the relevancy test used in Ex Parte Garland and Cummings v. Missouri appeared in this case also. In *Brown*, the purpose of the statute was to regulate political strikes, and it was directed at members of the Communist Party. The Court responded to a challenge of this statute: "[i]n a number of decisions, this Court has pointed out the fallacy of the suggestions that membership in the Communist Party, or any other political organization, can be regarded as an alternative, but equivalent, expression for a list of undesirable characteristics." In other words, there was not a close enough fit between the means used to identify the persons to whom the statute applied and the statute's purpose. The statute, therefore, imposed punishment rather than regulated conduct.

The writer of a strongly worded, at times vituperative, dissent was not impressed. It is difficult to follow that dissent because it is not totally accurate about the majority opinion and because its organization is somewhat random. However, one of the objections it raised is that the majority based its decision in part on the fact that the category (membership in the Communist Party) in regard to the regulation that the statute instituted was both underinclusive and overinclusive. This statement seems to mean that, according to the majority, others besides members of the Communist Party favored political strikes and that not all members of the Communist Party favored political strikes. The dissent's argument seems to be that, in this respect, the majority opinion is self-contradictory. However, the dissent actually supported the majority's view because it demonstrated that the quality was not relevant enough to the regulation to make the act an exercise of the police power rather than a bill of attainder. To phrase it differently, the dissent inadvertently helped the majority demonstrate that the criterion in the act and the act's regulatory purpose were not rationally related to each other.

The line of cases that uses the "punishment–regulation" dichotomy makes good sense. Determining whether legislatively established requirements are relevant to their purpose has helped courts to protect victims of statutes that purport to regulate but actually punish. This determination has allowed the government to proceed with legitimate regulation. This test is also well established in the case law, having appeared in a number of cases over a long time span. The difficulty, of course, is determining relevancy. However, courts are in the business of matching legal doctrines to sets of facts, and they have a much easier time doing this if the doctrine is rational.

Determining whether the alleged punishment is one traditionally imposed by bills of attainder or nontraditional is another method that employs a dichotomy and that is used to determine whether a statute is a bill of attainder. Statutes that impose one of the traditional punishments have been thought to be more likely to be bills of attainder. A court noted that the traditional punishments included imprisonment, banishment, and confiscation of property (Nixon v. Administrator of General Services, 1977). However, the court did not list a death sentence, which was probably the most common punishment imposed by English bills of attainder. *Nixon* was about the restrictions that had been applied to the papers of former

President Richard Nixon. Several features of the statute at issue convinced the court that these restrictions were not tantamount to confiscation. The dissent cogently retorted that the number of deprivations that are punishment for purposes of this clause has been steadily growing. This point demonstrates the conceptual problem inherent in this dichotomy because there is no reason why the list of deprivations that are punishments must be frozen because of the decisions in many cases in which courts held that nontraditional deprivations may be punishments cast considerable doubt on the precedential value of this case.

Nevertheless, a later court began its analysis of a statute by claiming that "[i]n deciding whether a statute inflicts punishment, we have recognized three necessary inquiries" (Selective Service v. Minn. Public Int. Res. Gp., 1984). The first inquiry listed was "whether the challenged statute falls within the historical meaning of legislative punishment." The answer was that denying student aid to persons who did not register with the Selective Service System was not a punishment that bills of attainder traditionally imposed. As it had in *Nixon*, in this case the court short-circuited analysis rather than using rational means to analyze the relation between the law and the facts.

Another basis of the decision in United States v. Brown is the distinction that the court drew between rulemaking and specification (United States v. Brown, 1965). It stated,

> [t]he statute does not set forth a generally applicable rule decreeing that any person who commits certain acts or possesses certain characteristics (acts and characteristics which, in Congress' view, make them likely to initiate political strikes) shall not hold union office, and leave to courts and juries the job of deciding what persons have committed the specified acts or possess the specified characteristics.

Rulemaking, the Court implied, is a characteristic of a valid regulatory act; whereas, specification is a characteristic of a bill of attainder. Later in the opinion, the Court blurred the lines between the two functions by stating that identifying a group that has precisely the characteristics thought to be relevant is really a shorthand way of stating the characteristics and thus indicated that Congress had made rules rather than specified the group to which the statute applied.

This "traditionally–nontraditionally imposed punishment" dichotomy has several advantages. It reflects the concern for separation of powers that frequently is manifested in the case law on bills of attainder. It also reflects two criteria that have generally been accepted in distinguishing bills of attainder from other kinds of legislation. One of these criteria is that in bills of attainder punishment is meted out without the safeguards that would apply in a court. The other criteria is that the statute names or characterize victims in such a way that they can easily be identified. The first two of these advantages derive from the Court's attempt to distinguish the proper work of the legislative branch from the proper work of the judicial branch. It accords with a characteristic of common law bills of attainder—that they name the victim—although this characteristic no longer appears often in acts that are litigated under Clause 3. This dichotomy also makes it more likely that Congress will reflect about causes and effects—that is, about public policy issues—rather than about persons and groups it wishes to punish.

This dichotomy, according to the dissent in *Brown*, also has several disadvantages. The dissent attacked it because it does not follow the precedent of *Douds* (Communications Ass'n. v. Douds, 1950). The statute at issue in this earlier case, although it specified the Communist Party, was held not to be a bill of attainder. The dissent was correct that *Brown* overruled *Douds*. The dissent claimed less convincingly that this case also invalidated all conflict of interest statutes that apply to identified or identifiable groups. That is not quite accurate because the majority opinion makes an exception for statutes that name groups if the name is an exact equivalent of pertinent characteristics. The dissent also accepted the Solicitor General's argument that the statute involved in this case is indistinguishable from a particular conflict of interest statute relating to bankers. The dissent in *Brown* claimed that both statutes are overinclusive and underinclusive. The dissent also did not accept the majority's argument that the statute in *Douds* is based on a general understanding of human nature; whereas, the statute in *Brown* simply names a group and applies only to that group, not to anyone who happens to be in the general position described in the banking statute. The dissent also made much of the fact that "[t]he Communist Party's illegal purpose and its domination by a foreign power have already been adjudicated." This may have been true, although it is unlikely that every member of the Communist party is likely to call a political strike, which is the real issue, and the result that the statute was designed to prevent if the statute was actually regulatory rather than punitive.

The dissent's point about the majority's attempt to distinguish the banking statute from the statute at issue in *Brown* is plausible at first glance. However, William Lehmann demonstrated that the majority opinion actually made good sense.[7] Lehmann conceded that it is difficult to distinguish between statutes that use a shorthand label to stand for a collection of qualities and those that punish a particular group. He also conceded that the majority opinion in *Brown* failed to clarify this distinction by defining punishment but instead wrote about the various purposes that punishment might serve. However, Lehmann argued that in *Brown* the majority opinion's section on rulemaking and specifying and in particular the section in which it attempted to distinguish the banking statute from the statute that was at issue in the case were based ultimately on its view that the label used by the statute in *Brown* did not fit the purposes of that statute and thus was not relevant. If so, that opinion is one of a line of cases that stretches back to Ex Parte Garland and Cummings v. Missouri. It may or may not be so. The majority opinion is tangled, and it probably would have been more convincing had it avoided some detours and simply argued that the identification of the group affected was not related closely enough to the statute's purpose—was not relevant enough—for the statute to be regulatory rather than punitive. Therefore, the act was a bill of attainder.

One of the dichotomies that is used most commonly to determine whether a statute imposes punishment is "retrospective–prospective." The former label refers to statutes that impose a burden because of a past action or condition. The latter label refers to statutes that impose a burden because of an action that occurs or a condition that arises after the bill becomes a law. That is, a retrospective law imposes a burden because of something that has already happened and thus because of something beyond the current control of anyone who fulfills the law's requirements. According to the decisions in cases that employ this dichotomy, retrospective application indicates that the burden imposed is punishment and that Congress has decided that the action or condition—or, more likely, a person or group—deserves to be punished. In contrast, prospective laws allow persons who might be affected by them to determine whether they will escape the burden. This feature indicates that the law is regulatory. Regulation certainly intends to determine in the future whether an action has been performed or a condition achieved and thus whether someone ought to suffer for it. It is literally impossible to regulate actions and conduct that have already occurred.

This dichotomy appeared in both the landmark bill of attainder cases. In the case of Ex Parte Garland the oath required attorneys to make five affirmations. One affirmation was to uphold the Constitution, and the court considered it irrelevant to the case because it was "promissory," that is, it was a promise about future conduct. The other four affirmations were about participation in the Confederacy and thus were retrospective. The Court labeled the requirement that attorneys take the oath "a legislative decree of perpetual exclusion" and concluded that exclusion "for past conduct can be regarded in no other light than as punishment for such conduct," which in turn meant that the statute was a bill of attainder. The oath at issue in Cummings v. Missouri required thirty affirmations. The Court noted that "it is retrospective; it embraces all the past from this day." This was one of the factors that led the Court to conclude that the provision in Missouri's constitution that was at issue was punitive.

It is important to recognize that the Court in these two cases did not hold that only bills that imposed burdens because of prior, completed behavior can be bills of attainder. This would have run counter to the meaning of the term as evidenced by English common law bills of attainder, some of which imposed burdens if certain kinds of behavior occurred after the bill was enacted. It also would have narrowed the definition of punishment without any basis in precedent or logic. Instead, the Court held that imposing burdens for past, irrevocable behavior is strong evidence that a legislative act is a bill of attainder.

The dissent that applied to both cases acknowledged that some of the actions that were subjects of the oaths had already occurred, but it argued that all of them were evidence of a disposition and thus that their relevance extended into both the present and the future. Both the past conduct and the future conduct, the dissent continued, "have reference to [a prospective attorney's] disposition to support or to overturn the government, in whose functions he proposes to take part." Many past actions do demonstrate the presence of propensities. However, the dissent ignores the unique qualities of the Civil War. The states of both litigants had seceded from the union; that war was unique in this country's history; and one like it will almost certainly never occur again; and it had concluded. To claim that everyone who had participated in the Confederacy had a disposition to overthrow the government strains credulity.

This dichotomy lay in abeyance until much later, when Justice Frankfurter, in writing a concurring opinion, adverted to it (United States v. Lovett, 1946). He presented his view of the nature of common law bills of attainder and then drew several conclusions from that view: "[t]here was always a declaration of guilt either of the individual or the class to which he belonged. The offense might be a pre-existing crime or an act made punishable *ex post facto*." Frankfurter's prose is gnarled, but he appears to mean that in every bill of attainder, the offense was either an action that was a crime when it was committed at some time in the past or an action that was committed in the past and was made a crime afterwards by the statute in question. In either case, Congress would have made a declaration of guilt and in either case it would have imposed a burden retrospectively. In the former kind of bill of attainder the offense that existed when the act that violated it was committed would be specified. However, Frankfurter's understanding of common law bills of attainder is badly flawed and he leaves out some of the more important identifying characteristics. More important, he does not seem to know that many of these bills imposed punishment that would apply if a specified act were committed in the future.[8] He thus not only went well beyond Ex Parte Garland and Cummings v. Missouri, in which the courts held that retrospective application was evidence that a bill was a bill of attainder, but also did so on tenuous grounds. Luckily, he did so in a concurring opinion, and, therefore, his position has no value as a precedent.

However, a few years later, the Court in *Douds* clearly took the position that Justice Frankfurter appeared to take (Communications Ass'n v. Douds, 1950). It distinguished *Garland* and *Cummings* on the grounds that the conduct in these cases was irrevocable; whereas, the plaintiff in *Douds* could in effect revoke the conduct, membership in the Communist Party, that Congress believed to be symptomatic of future unacceptable behavior. There are several problems with this holding. The Court itself recognized one: "[o]f course, the history of the past conduct is the foundation for the judgment as to what the future conduct is likely to be." This concession reminds one that past actions and present actions are not so easily distinguishable as one might think. Furthermore, this concession indicated that the act was in fact retrospective. Another problem is the twisting of the holding in the earlier cases. Under these cases, retrospective laws are likely to be bills of attainder, but under *Douds*, prospective laws, even ones that have a tinge of retrospectivity, are not bills of attainder. The Court in this case simply asserted its position without regard for precedent or even, as Justice Frankfurter had done, albeit not quite accurately, without deriving its position from an examination of common law bills of attainder. The Court also assumed that the only punishment that the statute imposed was denial of the ability to hold an office in a labor union, and it minimized this punishment by claiming that anyone could avoid it by taking the oath. The Court ignored the other punishment of the requirement of an oath, which applied only to a few persons and required them to choose among three unpleasant alternatives: renouncing their political position, subscribing falsely to an oath and agreeing not to hold an office in a labor union.

A case similar to *Douds* (which also involved registration of the Communist Party) that had a similar result and similar reasoning (Communist Party v. Subversive Activities Control Board, 1961). In this case, the Court conceded more forthrightly than had the court in *Douds* that the act, although in a sense prospective, also had a tinge of retrospectivity:

> [t]he fact that activity engaged in prior to the enactment of the legislation may be regarded administratively and judicially as relevant to a determination that an organization is presently foreign-controlled and presently works to advance the objectives of the world Communist movement, does not alter the operative structure of the Act. The incidents which it reaches are nonetheless present incidents. The past is probative of these.

The meaning of "operative structure" is far from clear, but one would think that something that is probative of the incidents that an act "reaches" is probably part of the act's "operative structure." In addition, the problems that were noted in regard to *Douds* apply to this case.

Within a few more years, the "retrospective–prospective" dichotomy was well established, despite its foundation in quicksand. As mentioned earlier, a case that involved a statute denying student aid to persons who had not registered for the draft arose (Selective Service v. Minn. Public Int. Res. Gp., 1984). In this case, the Court assumed that, if it could demonstrate that the act in question was purely prospective, it would also demonstrate that the act is not a bill of attainder. It attempted this gambit by asserting that any person who had received notice of failing to comply with the registration act could regain eligibility for student aid by registering within thirty days. The court cited the legislative history, by merely mentioning it, rather than quoting some of it, and the act's phrasing to try to make its point. However, if the legislative act that is pertinent to the litigation is unambiguous, its legislative history is irrelevant. The act in fact is clear, and its meaning is not that which the court ascribes to it. According to the statute, the action that must be performed within thirty days after receipt of notice is to "establis[h] that he has complied with the registration requirement" in the Selective Service Act. It does not say that the required action is, in fact, to register. The "registration requirement" to which reference is made is to register within thirty days after the person becomes eighteen years of age. Those thirty days were over long ago for the plaintiffs. The grace period is designed, if one reads it literally, to allow persons to *establish* that they did register in a timely fashion and thus to demonstrate that their student aid had unlawfully been denied. The literal meaning makes perfect sense, and there is no justification for going beyond it. If a drafting error was made, Congress must live with it. All that having been said, the conclusion that remains is that the act is totally retrospective. This fact, according to *Garland* and *Cummings*, does not prove that the act is a bill of attainder, although it is strong evidence that it is, and it certainly negates the argument that the act is totally prospective and thus not a bill of attainder.

Despite certain conceptual problems in them, there thus appears to be a fairly long line of cases that use the "retrospective–prospective" dichotomy in order to uphold legislative acts against attacks that are based on Clause 3. However, Chief Justice Warren devastated *Douds* (United States v. Brown, 1965). First, he got the history right:

> [h]istorical considerations by no means compel restriction of the bill of attainder ban to instances of retribution. A number of English bills of attainder were enacted for preventive purposes—that is, the legislature made a judgment, undoubtedly based largely on past acts and associations, that a given person or group was likely to cause trouble...and therefore inflicted deprivations upon that person or group in order to keep it from bringing about the feared event. It is also clear that many of the early American bills attainting the Tories were passed in order to impede their effectively resisting the Revolution.

Next, Chief Justice Warren strongly challenged the decision in *Douds*: "[w]e think that the Court in *Douds* misread *Lovett* when it suggested that that case could be distinguished on the ground that the sanction there imposed was levied for purely retributive reasons." He asserted that the purpose of the statutes that was at issue in these cases were identical: to purge certain groups of certain kinds of persons based on the "tendencies" of these persons. In other words, Chief Justice Warren recognized that bills of attainder can be prospective, something that should have been clear many years before. The dissent in Brown correctly asserted that *Brown* overruled *Douds*, although it stated that the Court in *Brown* accomplished that by holding that inferences that were based on past behavior could not be made in order to predict future behavior and then to form the basis for the imposition of sanctions. A more accurate description of the situation is that *Brown* overruled *Douds* by dealing more rationally with the "retrospective–prospective" dichotomy. That is, the Court in *Brown* rejected the notion that declining to base punishment on past acts or conditions would prevent a bill from being a bill of attainder. If

Douds was overruled, then Communist Party v. Subversive Activities Control Board, which is virtually identical to *Douds* (and in which the court appeared not to notice the devastation that *Brown* had done to *Douds*), was wrongly decided and thus ought to be overruled. Moreover, the decision in Selective Service v. Minn. Public Int. Res. Gp., because it rests on the foundation of the "retrospective–prospective" dichotomy and ignores *Brown*, probably is no longer good law either.

United States v. Brown, thus, is the other side of the coin, one side of which appeared in the two landmark bill of attainder cases. These early cases held that retrospective laws ought to be suspected of being bills of attainder. *Brown* demonstrated that it does not follow from this proposition that prospective laws were not bills of attainder. There were enough conceptual muddles in earlier cases, most notably the failure to realize that past and future actions could be inextricably intertwined and misreadings of history before *Brown* in order to foreshadow that case and in order to induce a court in an earlier case to set this dichotomy right, but it did not happen until *Brown* was decided.

One of the more sophisticated attempts to define punishment for purposes of Clause 3 is the construction of a four-part examination (Nixon v. Administrator of General Services, 1977). The first test is whether the disadvantage that was imposed has traditionally been imposed by bills of attainder. At first glance, that is a sensible test, but there are several flaws in it. As the Court admitted, the list of traditional disadvantages has grown. For example, denying access to particular occupations is a fairly late development in this country, not an advantage that has a long history of protection in common law. However, under the holdings of Ex Parte Garland and Cummings v. Missouri, this amounts to punishment. More fundamentally, it is more rational to examine not the kind of disadvantage that was imposed but the reason why it was imposed. For example, as we have seen, denial of access to a particular occupation can be either a punishment or a means of regulating this occupation. This test also did not have strong roots in the case law.

The second part of the examination is to determine the function of imposing the disadvantage. Determining its purpose would have been a clearer way of describing this test. This test does have strong roots in the case law, for instance in the cases that are based at least in part on the "regulation–punishment" dichotomy. The court in *Nixon* advised determining an act's function by looking at its phrasing and examining its legislative history. However, these methods might reveal either nothing illuminating or something misleading.

The third test is determining Congress' motivation. English bills of attainder proclaimed guilt, which would have made this test irrelevant to them. The Court advised examining the act's legislative history. As the Court in *Nixon* claimed, the Court in *Lovett* had used this test; in fact, it had done so meticulously. However, this test is difficult to use and even more difficult to use convincingly. The dissent in United States v. Brown makes a fairly strong argument that the majority opinion, because it relies on the degree of generality of the statute in question and does not recognize that legislative bodies frequently try to solve problems piecemeal rather than all at once, misread Congress' motives.

The final test is "to inquire into the existence of less burdensome alternatives by which that legislature (here Congress) could have achieved its legitimate non-punitive objectives." The last phrase is based on the belief that the results of the test are available. Other difficulties with this test are that it has no basis in the case law, that it depends on imagining other possible bills rather than analyzing the one at issue and that it might lead to absurd results. Regarding the last of these problems, it is not clear whether the Court meant, for example, that a bill ordering the confiscation of a person's property might not be a bill of attainder because Congress could have imposed a death sentence. Despite these problems, the Court ought to be given credit for attempting to find a rational test and, specifically, for proposing an examination consisting of a number of tests so that the issue can be looked at from several angles, which in turn makes a credible decision more likely.

Courts have frequently used one of the tests in *Nixon* to determine Congress' motives. One opinion stated that to determine whether a bill is a bill of attainder requires "an interpretation of the meaning and purpose of the section, which in turn requires an understanding of the circumstances leading to its passage" (United States v. Lovett, 1946). The Court in *Lovett* meant that it would examine the legislative history to determine Congress' motives. It proceeded to describe at substantial length the actions over a long period of time of the House Committee on Un-American Activities, which consisted of dogged attempts to discover "subversives" and to remove them from governmental positions or otherwise to forestall their purposes. The committee's chairperson told the House of Representatives that the three persons who eventually litigated this case were unfit for government service, and he insisted on adding to an appropriations bill a rider that would preclude paying their salaries. The record thus appears at first glance to make it clear that the motive for the rider was to punish the three employees.

The matter is not quite so clear, however. Justice Frankfurter, in his concurrence, mentioned that the Senate had resisted adding the rider and that President Franklin Roosevelt had objected to it because he did not think that the three employees were "subversives." To enact the rider, the House of Representatives needed the concurrence of the Senate and, barring a veto and subsequent override, needed the President's signature. One could argue that the Senate and the President did not have the same motives as the House, so that it makes no sense to conclude that the motives of the entities that enacted the bill demonstrate that the rider was intended to punish and was thus a bill of attainder. However, the actions of the Senate and the President are good evidence that, although they did not intend punishment (indeed, the Senate doggedly tried to prevent it), they believed that the rider was intended to punish.

The situation in *Lovett* is symptomatic of the search for the elusive element of motivation, which is roughly as difficult as the search for legislative intent. That search has two inherent difficulties. One difficulty is establishing a logical link between motivation (or intent) and effect (or meaning). In regard to literary works, W.K. Wimsatt and Monroe Beardsley wrote that either the work accurately reflected the author's intent or it did not.[9] In the former instance, the intent was superfluous because it revealed nothing that one cannot determine from the text. In the latter instance, the intent was misleading. The same analysis applies to the texts of legal opinions. The other difficulty is that, even if one can demonstrate the logical link between either motivation and effect or between intent and meaning, it is ludicrous to assert that a body as diverse as Congress ever has a unitary motive or intent.

More recently another court attempted to determine Congress' motive (Selective Service v. Minn. Public Int. Res. Gp., 1984). It wrote that

> [t]he District Court also ignored the relevant legislative history. Congress' purpose in enacting 12(f) was to encourage registration by those who must register, but have not yet done so. Proponents of the legislation emphasized that those failing to register timely can qualify for aid by registering late. The District Court failed to take account of this legislative purpose.

This attempt to determine motivation is considerably less rigorous than the one in *Lovett*, but, like the court in that case, the court in this case assumed that the attempt would yield meaningful results. As we have seen, if a court accurately determines Congress' motivation, this motivation does not match the effect that one discerns by reading the statute literally.

Courts in other cases have been much more skeptical about the value of determining Congress' motivation. In Flemming v. Nestor (1960), the Court, responding to the litigant's claim that the bill's legislative history demonstrated that Congress' motive was to punish, wrote "[w]e observe initially that only the clearest proof could suffice to establish the unconstitutionality of a statute on such a ground. Judicial inquiries into Congressional motives are at best a hazardous matter, and when that inquiry seeks to go behind objective manifestations it becomes a dubious affair indeed." Undeterred, the Court in a case (Communist Party v. Subversive Activities Control Board, 1961) that was litigated in the next year quoted the passage in *Flemming* about the clearest proof being required and then proceeded to argue that Congress' motivation was clearly not to punish. This later Court began its search for motivation by examining the act's text. It took at face value the act's statement of its purpose, although this kind of statement can easily be manipulated, specifically to induce a Court to declare constitutional the act in which it appears. This Court then perfunctorily interpreted the act's legislative history:

> [n]or does the legislative history contain any such suggestion [that the act was clandestinely intended to impose punishment]. Rather, the Committee reports on the bills from which the

Act derived express an object "to require the Communist movement in the United States to operate in the open rather than underground," and "to expose the Communist movement and protect the public against innocent and unwitting collaboration with it."

One would have thought that examination of motivation was more arduous work than that.

To decide whether a statute inflicts punishment, courts that were searching for precedents even resorted to cases that did not involve the prohibition against bills of attainder. For example, in the case involving former President Nixon (Nixon v. Administrator of General Services, 1977), the court referred to an Eighth Amendment (prohibiting cruel and unusual punishment) case (Trop v. Dulles, 1958) and to a Fifth Amendment (requiring due process of law) and Sixth Amendment (requiring various safeguards in criminal trials) case (Kennedy v. Mendoza-Martinez, 1963). The Court in an earlier case (Flemming v. Nestor, 1960) also adverted to Trop v. Dulles, as well as to two deportation cases. These other constitutional provisions, particularly the Eighth Amendment, involve the concept of punishment and, therefore, in some cases on them the term is defined. However, consulting these cases rests on the premise that a word necessarily has the same meaning in different parts of the Constitution. That premise is less than overwhelmingly compelling, but there are precedents that future courts can use in bill of attainder cases to justify consulting cases on other parts of the Constitution.

As one can readily see, tracing attempts by courts to discover a valid way to determine whether an act inflicts punishment, and thus might be a bill of attainder, takes a considerable amount of time. The reason for this is, of course, that courts have tried many tests. That in turn suggests that none of the tests is obviously correct. It also suggests that at this point a Court that has to decide a bill of attainder case would have at its disposal a large panoply of tests and, if it likes, could choose whichever one or ones would lead to the result that it prefers. In short, the case law on punishment, which unfortunately has become the most important subject in the law on bills of attainder, is in disarray. To sort out the law on punishment and, indeed, on bills of attainder, courts need to agree on a test or minimize the emphasis on punishment, so that chaos on that subject will not lead to chaos on the constitutional prohibition against bills of attainder.

The third element of bills of attainder is that they designate a person or group. This requirement entered the case law at a late date. It does not appear in either of the decisions that set the course of the law on this prohibition (Ex Parte Garland, 1866; Cummings v. Missouri, 1866). In *Cummings*, the definition of bill of attainder is "a legislative act which inflicts punishment without a judicial trial." In fact, the group on which the act operated not only was not named but also, because of the way it was described, its membership was difficult to determine. The Court in the other of these cases (Ex Parte Garland) did not explicitly define bill of attainder, perhaps because it considered that doing this in the companion case sufficed. The writer of the dissent that applied to both cases remarked at one point that English bills of attainder "declared certain persons attainted," which is close to declaring that these bills designated a person or group. However, when the dissenter listed the elements of bills of attainder, he did not include designation of their victims.

The majority opinion in *Lovett* stated that it did not depart from earlier case law; of *Garland* and *Cummings*, it remarked "[t]hey stand for the proposition that legislative acts...that apply either to named individuals or to easily ascertainable members of a group in such a way as to inflict punishment on them without a judicial trial are bills of attainder." The bill in this case clearly met the requirement of specification because it named the three individuals to whom it applied. It is not so easy to answer the question whether the two early cases stand for the proposition that to be a bill of attainder a bill must either name its victims or describe them in such a way that they are easily ascertainable. As we have seen, in neither case did the bill fulfill this requirement. Also, in neither case did the bill name its victims. Michael Lehmann claimed that some of the elements that persons had to swear to in the oaths in these cases were nebulous.[10] His implication is that the persons to whom the provision in the Missouri Constitution and the federal statute applied were not easily ascertainable and that therefore *Lovett* mischaracterized these cases and imposed a requirement without precedent. However, in both cases, the punishment was imposed directly not for the acts but for failing to take an oath. Although the persons who could not take the oath would have been difficult to determine at the time, the persons who had in fact not taken it probably could easily have been ascertained. If the persons who took the oath did not have copies of the oaths they had signed, a governmental agency probably had copies, or at least had a record of the persons who had taken the oath. In any event, a list of persons who had taken the oath could be constructed and then compared to a list of persons who were engaged in the occupations for which taking the oath was required. The court in *Lovett* probably was thinking that the earlier cases were about taking oaths, not about aiding the Confederacy, and thus thought that it was following *Garland* and *Cummings* rather than striking out on its own. In either event, writing that portion of its opinion more clearly would have helped others to understand the court's position.

The best way to understand the reactions of later courts to this development in *Lovett*—whether it was a clarification of earlier cases or a new departure—is by describing them in chronological order.

The court in the next relevant case (Communist Party v. Subversive Activities Control Board, 1961) implicitly accepted that failure to specify a target person or group would prevent a bill from being a bill of attainder. It claimed that the statute in question identified actions and qualities rather than specifying a group and for that reason and others was not a bill of attainder. However, the bill was replete with definitions that were precise enough to make it ineluctable that its target was the

Communist Party. In short, the opinion adhered to a conception of bills of attainder that now seemed magically to have precedential value, but it distorted the facts very badly as well.

The next Court (United States v. Brown, 1965) that considered the problem of specification drew an inference from the previous case. First, the Court in *Brown* held that the bill in *Communist Party* was not a bill of attainder partly because it identified characteristics rather than naming a victim. Then, the Court in *Brown* inferred that if the bill had specified a victim, it would have been a bill of attainder. The bill in *Brown* explicitly named the Communist Party as its target. This point led into an explication of the dichotomy of "rulemaking–specification." The Court later dismissed the government's argument that because no individuals had been named, there was no specification. According to the Court in Brown, the description of the targets was clear enough for the individuals who were subject to the statute to be readily identifiable. The dissent's response focused on its charge that the majority's point about the category being both underinclusive and overinclusive did not make sense. However, as we have seen, this response distorted the majority opinion. The majority did write that the victims were specified, and although it was not done explicitly (by naming persons), it was done clearly (by naming the group to which they belonged). The Court held that this form of specification fulfills the requirement, which was set forth in *Lovett*, that the victim or victims must be designated if a bill is a bill of attainder. This opinion negated possible arguments that *Communist Party* had established the principle that declining literally to name victims would prevent a bill from being a bill of attainder.

In the next case (Nixon v. Administrator of General Services, 1977), the Court faced the same situation in regard to specificity as had the Court in *Lovett*: the victim (this time there was only one) was explicitly named. The Court held that the naming by itself did not make the bill a bill of attainder. One reason for that conclusion was that the case was about former President Nixon's papers and that the papers of all of the other former Presidents were already stored in their presidential libraries. Thus, the issue of ownership of, and the proper location of, presidential papers applied only to one former President. The Court held that the bill was not a bill of attainder. Thus, it believed that specific designation of the person or persons to whom a bill applied was a necessary but not a sufficient cause that would result in a bill being a bill of attainder. In fact, the Court in *Nixon* defined bill of attainder as "a law that legislatively determines guilt and inflicts punishment upon an identifiable individual without provision of the protections of a judicial trial."

Unfortunately, the Court continued to develop the theme of specificity by writing that Nixon was "a legitimate class of one." Determining whether a class is "legitimate" is an exercise that one would expect in a case on the Fourteenth Amendment's requirement of equal protection of the laws, not in a case on Clause 3. The writer of the majority opinion also remarked that the prohibition against bills of attainder "was not intended to serve as a variant of the equal protection doctrine." As Michael Lehmann noted, this remark negated the argument of the dissent in *Brown* that the case had introduced the concepts of overinclusiveness and underinclusiveness, two other concepts usually seen in equal protection cases, into the case law on bills of attainder.[11] To be a "legitimate class of one," Nixon would have had to be unique. The dissent asserted that Nixon's "uniqueness does not justify serious deprivations of existing rights." The dissent correctly was disturbed that uniqueness, a new element, was introduced into the law on bills of attainder. However, the dissent, too, took the concept of uniqueness seriously enough to consider the justified and unjustified consequences instead of bluntly stating that uniqueness is irrelevant, because only specification, not specification that has the correct scope, is required.

In 1984, the Court dealt with a number of arguments that a statute denying student aid for persons who failed to register for the draft was unconstitutional (Selective Service v. Minn. Public Int. Res. Gp., 1984). The Court devoted almost all the section of its opinion on the allegation that the statute was a bill of attainder to the issue of whether the bill imposed punishment. However, at the end of that section it laconically remarked, "[b]ecause 12(f) does not single out an identifiable group that would be ineligible for Title IV aid or inflict punishment within the meaning of the Bill of Attainder Clause, we hold that the District Court erred in striking down 12(f) as an impermissible attainder." The Court appeared to mean that singling out an identifiable group is one of the identifying characteristics of bills of attainder, which is in line with the case law. However, its statement that no identifiable group was singled out does not square with the facts. Persons who were required to register for the draft within thirty days after they became eighteen years of age yet failed to register certainly constitute an easily identifiable group. In fact, partly because of the statute in question, almost certainly there was a list of these persons.

Although courts have not always convincingly applied the facts in cases to the requirement that the victim or victims of a bill must be specified, it is clear that specification, either explicit or implicit, is necessary if a bill is to be a bill of attainder. In easy cases on this issue, such as *Lovett* and *Nixon*, the bill at issue named the person or persons to whom it applied. Failing that, a bill can fulfill the specification requirement by stating characteristics that will allow the victim or victims to be easily identified.

The final identifying characteristic of bills of attainder is that they do not provide the safeguards that are required in a judicial trial. The most egregious example of this element is the procedures that led to three federal employees losing their jobs until they prevailed in court (United States v. Lovett, 1946). As discussed earlier, after some members of Congress objected to summarily adding to an appropriations bill a rider that would accomplish that purpose by denying funding for the employees' positions, the House of Representatives reached a compromise that would require the Appropriations Committee to determine whether the charges against the employees were well founded. The chair of that committee extolled the process: "we will expedite adjudication and disposition of these cases and thereby serve both the accused and the Government." Expedite they did, but the court painted a lurid portrait of the proceedings by means of which they did so:

> [t]hose charged with "subversive" beliefs and "subversive" associations were permitted to testify, but lawyers including those representing the agencies by which the accused were employed were not permitted to be present. At the hearings, committee members, the committee staff, and whatever witness was under examination were the only ones present. The evidence, aside from that given by the accused employees, appears to have been largely that of reports made by the Dies Committee, its investigators, and Federal Bureau of Investigation reports, the latter being treated as too confidential to be made public.

These procedures certainly did fall short of the ones that would have been used in a judicial trial. In fact, they were exactly the kind of procedures that led to the enactment of common law bills of attainder and that this prohibition was designed to prevent. They also well deserved the court's comment on the general problem that they illustrated: "[w]hen our Constitution and Bill of Rights were written, our ancestors had ample reason to know that legislative trials and punishments were too dangerous to liberty to exist in the nation of free men they envisioned. And so they proscribed bills of attainder."

The presence or absence in a statute of the protections that are afforded in judicial trials is almost always very easy to determine. One possible exception is the statute at issue in one of the cases involving the Communist Party (Communist Party v. Subversive Activities Control Board, 1961). This statute provided that before an organization was required to register as a supporter of the Communist Party, which could result in a number of negative consequences, there must be an administrative hearing, which was subject to review by the courts. The Court concentrated on the other elements and did not deal with this one at any length. Thus, it is still not settled whether the possibility of a trial in the future is enough to satisfy this requirement. It certainly would be enough if Congress, by statute, merely created a generally applicable crime and then let the judicial process run its course. However, even in this instance Congress had interposed an intermediate step and had put persons in jeopardy not because of the kind of actions that are characteristic of crimes but because of such things as joining a political party.

This element indicates that the prohibition against bills of attainder is related to two other constitutional doctrines. One is the separation of powers. That is, the element is intended to ensure that adjudication will be the responsibility of courts instead of Congress. Separation of powers was an issue in one of the two landmark cases (Ex Parte Garland, 1866) because that case was about an oath that was required of lawyers. The court noted that "[a]ttorneys and counselors are not officers of the United States; they are not appointed in the manner prescribed by the Constitution for the election and appointment of such officers. They are officers of the court, admitted as such by its order." Both the majority opinion and the dissent stated that Congress may impose qualifications on prospective lawyers. The majority held that it may not do this in order to punish anyone. The dissent considered the qualifications to be similar to those already in effect and thus neither extraordinary nor punitive.

In other cases, the court adverted to the separation of powers doctrine not because a legislative body was regulating admission to the bar but because it was accused of adjudicating. In the other landmark case (Cummings v. Missouri, 1866), the court included this element in its definition of bill of attainder and remarked that in passing a bill of attainder "the legislative body, in addition to its legitimate functions, exercises the powers and office of judge; it assumes, in the language of the text-books, judicial magistracy."

After explaining the political theory that supported the doctrine of separation of powers, a court wrote:

> the Bill of Attainder Clause not only was intended as one implementation of the general principle of fractionalized power, but also reflected the Framers' belief that the Legislative Branch is not so well suited as politically independent judges and juries to the task of ruling upon the blameworthiness of, and levying appropriate punishment upon, specific persons (United States v. Brown, 1965).

When it considered the facts of the case, that court decided that:

> [t]he statute does not set forth a generally applicable rule decreeing that any person who commits certain acts or possesses certain characteristics...shall not hold union office, and leave to courts and juries the job of deciding what persons have committed the specified acts or possess the specified characteristics.

The other constitutional doctrine that Clause 3 buttresses is the guarantee of due process of law under the Fifth and the Fourteenth Amendments. Immediately after making its statement about separation of powers, the court in *Cummings* made a statement about due process:

> [in enacting a bill of attainder, the legislative branch] pronounces upon the guilt of the party, without any of the forms or safeguards of trial; it determines the sufficiency of the proofs produced, whether conformable to the rules of evidence or otherwise; and it fixes the degree of punishment in accordance with its own notions of the enormity of the offense.

The dissent in this case lists some of the attributes of due process in its definition of bills of attainder: "[t]he investigation into the guilt of the accused, if any such were made, was not necessarily or generally conducted in his presence, or that of his counsel, and no recognized rule of evidence governed the inquiry."

The next issue that has appeared in cases about this clause is the limit on the entities who may assert that doctrine. In two of the cases, the result seemed obvious. South Carolina litigated the controls placed on it by the Voting Rights Act of 1965 because of its previous voting discrimination (South Carolina v. Katzenbach, 1966). It alleged, among other things, that the act was a bill of attainder. The court responded that "courts have consistently regarded the Bill of Atttainder Clause...only as protections for individual persons and private groups." Dicta in earlier cases do state that, but this case is the first in which that was held. The same Court also remarked, in dicta, that states do not have standing to assert this doctrine on behalf of their citizens. Moreover, in some circumstances citizens are barred from asserting the doctrine. In a case in which an individual who had been accused of violating Cuba's law against embezzlement and was resisting extradition to face that charge, the court held that the clause did not apply to citizens of the United States who were charged with violating the law of another country (Neeley v. Henkel, 1901).

However, in two other cases in which the kind of entities that might assert a violation of this constitutional provision was an issue, the result was far from obvious and the majority decisions induced powerful dissents. In one case, a person had been convicted of violating a law that prohibited members of the Communist Party from holding office and having any other important position in a labor union (Dennis v. United States, 1966). The plaintiff claimed that the conviction must be reversed because, under *Brown*, which was decided in the previous year, the law under which he had been convicted was an unconstitutional bill of attainder and thus no law at all. The plaintiff had lied about his affiliation, and the Court held that "a claim of unconstitutionality will not be heard to excuse a voluntary, deliberate and calculated course of fraud and deceit." One could argue that an action is either constitutional or unconstitutional, regardless of a plaintiff's behavior. In a similar case (Bryson v. United States, 1969), the plaintiff had been indicted for falsely denying that he was a Communist. The Court held that the invalidity of the statute under which the question was asked did not negate the jurisdiction of the National Labor Relations Board (NLRB) to proceed against the plaintiff. However, it could be argued that the statute's invalidity had nullified the plaintiff's wrongdoing and that, therefore, the NLRB should not have proceeded against him.

The dissent in *Dennis*, by Justice Douglas, asserted that the Court denied the plaintiff due process of law by failing to rule on the constitutionality of the statute under which he was convicted. It noted that the indictment charged, as it was required by previous decisions to do, that the defendant had interfered with "lawful" functions of government. The dissent then pointed out that if the statute in question was a bill of attainder none of its requirements was a lawful function of government. The dissent then challenged the majority opinion's assertion that there were precedents for denying the plaintiff the chance to attack the statute that formed the basis of his conviction, and it dealt with each of the alleged precedents.

The dissent concluded that the majority made up the law that is the basis for its decision. Justice Douglas also dissented in *Bryson* and made a similar argument: that the plaintiff had not interfered with a lawful function of the National Labor Relations Board because the statute under which he was convicted was a bill of attainder and thus not a law.

The majority decisions in *Dennis* and *Bryson*, although law, have a number of other problems. One is that they might be used as precedents in other kinds of cases. For example, if their logic makes sense, no Court should allow someone who has been convicted of violating a state criminal statute to use a writ of habeas corpus in order to litigate in federal court the constitutionality of that statute. That result seems unjust and would overturn a considerable amount of case law. These two decisions also place the Court in the position of upholding a bill of attainder despite the constitutional prohibition against passing them. In short, the decisions that this kind of legislation may not be passed but under certain circumstances it may be enforced cannot be appropriate.

Looking back over all the bill of attainder cases, one sees some inconsistency and failure to follow precedent, some assertions of legal doctrines that have no basis in the law, and some decisions that are very difficult to defend. This state of affairs probably pertains to most branches of the law that have been the subject of a substantial number of cases. The disturbing features of the law on bills of attainder are that the bills' intent to punish has become the most important and contentious element that courts use to determine whether a bill is a bill of attainder and the Court, rather than arriving at one method of deciding whether particular disadvantages are punishments, has used very many methods.

The proliferation of methods to determine a bill's intent suggests that courts, at least in some cases, are asking the wrong question. A different question is worth considering. Let us try to imagine the results if the first question that courts asked when presented with a bill of attainder case is whether the act or condition that triggered the disadvantage was political. If it was not political, then the Court would be left with its current jurisprudence on bills of attainder. One would hope that the Court would then improve this jurisprudence. If the relevant act or condition was political, the court Could determine whether there was any disadvantage created and, if there was, could then decide that the statute was a bill of attainder. In the political cases, the problem of assessing disadvantages to determine whether they are punishments would instantly vanish. This is an improvement over the present state of the law, but a Courts' inquiry must not end there.

The proposed new approach should also accord with traditional views on the nature of bills of attainder. Determining whether a bill is aimed at a political group does accord with the nature of most of the bills of attainder that were enacted by Parliament and colonial legislatures. Of the statute at issue in one case, a Court wrote that it "inflicts its deprivation upon members of a political group thought to present a threat to the national security...[S]uch groups were the targets of the overwhelming majority of English and early American bills of attainder" (United States v. Brown, 1965). There were exceptions, of course. The exceptions will be accommodated because applying the current state of the law to statutes that are not directed at political beliefs, actions, or groups will allow future nonpolitical bills to be ruled bills of attainder.

If courts declare that all bills that impose any measure of punishment for political reasons are bills of attainder, this clause will become an effective means of protection against political tyranny. At least one of the Framers of the Constitution was thinking along those lines. In the *Federalist Papers* number 84, Alexander Hamilton answered the charge that the Constitution was seriously flawed because it had no bill of rights. He answered that the Constitution contained "a number of such provisions," and he cited several that are included in this section, among them Clause 3, the prohibition against bills of attainder. The case law has not made this prohibition resemble a bill of rights. Rather, in many of the cases courts have found a way to validate the infliction of hardship on people because of their political actions or beliefs.

Separating bill of attainder cases into two categories and making it easier for plaintiffs who have been punished for political reasons to prevail would also reflect the fact that a major function of the prohibition against bills of attainder is to reinforce the separation of powers. That is, Congress, being a political body, is most likely to impose punishment wrongly for political reasons than for other reasons. Therefore, redress ought to be more easily obtained by those who are wronged by Congress for this reason than by those who are wronged by it for other reasons. This in turn would shift some of the burden of deciding guilt to the courts, where political concerns, and, more to the point, transient political concerns, are much less substantial.

One counterargument to this proposed change is that it would leave Congress powerless to deal with truly dangerous acts that are politically motivated. However, the federal statutes are replete with crimes against the state and with other laws that could be used to punish overt acts. If none applies when danger from this source appears to Congress to be likely, Congress can enact other criminal laws that will apply to the situation. The point is that the decision on punishment should be left to the courts, particularly when political vengeance is the most likely motive for inflicting the punishment.

The most convincing test of this proposed change in the way courts deal with bill of attainder cases is to determine the results that would have occurred under the proposal in the cases that have been decided already. Anyone who determines this is likely to notice that it is almost always obvious whether politics are at work in a case. Only two cases require some thought on this issue. One is the case in which persons were denied student aid because of their failure to register for the draft (Selective Service v. Minn. Public Int. Res. Gp., 1984). Anyone who is familiar with the Vietnam War era would recognize that failing to register for the draft at that time was a political act. The most difficult case to characterize is the one brought by former President Richard Nixon (Nixon v. Administrator of General Services, 1977). Although Nixon was, of course, a political figure, perhaps the consummate political individual of our era, the actions that brought about his downfall were for the most part ordinary crimes. Also, the majority opinion argued cogently that the purpose of the act was preservation of the papers of someone who had shown a willingness to destroy evidence, not punishment for political behavior. The result is not absolutely clear-cut, but *Nixon*, ironically, appears to be a nonpolitical case. The cases that are easy to characterize are all political. Two involve affiliation with the Confederacy (Cummings v. Missouri, 1866; Ex Parte Garland, 1866). Seven involve affiliation with the Communist Party (United States v. Lovett, 1946; Communications Ass'n v. Douds, 1950; Flemming v. Nestor, 1960; Communist Party v. Subversive Activities Control Board, 1961; United States v. Brown, 1965; Dennis v. United States, 1966; Bryson v. United States, 1969).

Thus, there have been ten political cases brought to court under this clause. If the proposed method of deciding political bill of attainder cases had been used, six of these cases would have been decided differently (Communications Assn v. Douds, 1950; Flemming v. Nestor, 1960; Communist Party v. Subversive Activities Control Board, 1961; Dennis v. United States, 1966; Bryson v. United States, 1969; Selective Service v. Minn. Public Int. Res. Gp., 1984). In each of those cases, the bill would have been declared an unconstitutional bill of attainder, and the victims of the bill would have prevailed. Persons will differ about whether those results would have been better, but strong arguments can be made that they would have been better.

In summary, the case law on bills of attainder is less impressive than one would wish. Occasionally courts took forthright stands and framed convincing arguments for doing so. However, other opinions are highly dubious. The cases as a group lack consistency, as indicated by the many methods used to determine whether punishment has been imposed. A new direction is needed if Clause 3 is to become an important bulwark of freedom, as it appeared to be in the early cases of *Cummings* and *Garland*. The change proposed above is at least worth consideration.

Ex Post Facto Laws

With only a few exceptions, analysis of the prohibition against ex post facto laws will be confined to the constitutional prohibition that applies to the federal government. The prohibition against passage by state legislatures of this kind of law, which appears in Article 1, § 10, is covered in *Limits on the States: A Reference Guide to the U.S. Constitution*. The exceptions are an early case on the prohibition applicable to the states that marks the beginning of a line of cases that takes one of the two possible positions on the important issue of whether a civil law can be ex post facto (Cummings v. Missouri, 1866). The second state case included a statement, in dictum, that was used as a precedent by the court in Cummings v. Missouri (Fletcher v. Peck, 1810). The third state case is an even earlier case that appears to contain the first definition of "ex post facto law" in the case law. This case takes the other possible position on the issue of whether only criminal laws can be ex post facto (Calder v. Bull, 1798).

In interpreting this prohibition, the courts have not frequently considered its purpose. But examining possible purposes will cast some light on the prohibition against ex post facto laws and help explain some of the reasons why the Framers included this prohibition in the Constitution. One statement of a purpose and of that purpose's significance is "the principle on which the Clause is based—the notion that persons have a right to fair warning of that conduct which will give rise to criminal penalties—is fundamental to our concept of constitutional liberty" (Marks v. United States, 1977). In other words, this provision induces the government and the judiciary to provide notice, which is also a reason for the requirement of due process of law that the Fifth and Fourteenth Amendments establish. In turn, requiring notice promotes fundamental fairness, which is one of the glues that holds together just societies.

The Court in an early case (Calder v. Bull, 1798) traced the prohibition against states passing ex post facto laws to the social compact. This was a notion that was prominent in the political thought of the era in which the Constitution was written and in which that case was decided: "[t]he people of the United States erected their Constitution, or forms of government, to establish justice, to promote the general welfare, to secure the blessings of liberty; and to protect their persons and property from violence" (Calder v. Bull, 1798). In particular, the Court went on to write:

> [t]here are certain vital principles in our free Republican government, which will determine and over-rule an apparent and flagrant abuse of legislative power; as to authorize manifest injustice by positive law; or to take away that security for personal liberty, or private property, for the protection whereof the government was established. An ACT of the Legislature (for I cannot call it a law) contrary to the great first principles of social compact, cannot be considered a rightful exercise of legislative authority.

In short, a government that punishes a citizen after the fact for an action that was lawful when it was committed has broken the social compact by acting arbitrarily. If it can do so with impunity, no citizen can rest easy.

Ex post facto laws, then, are a class of laws that have a retrospective effect. For a long time, courts have been aware of the potential for injustice of this kind of law. In an ex post facto case, the Court alluded to "the settled rule that courts uniformly refuse to give to statutes a retrospective operation, where rights previously vested are injuriously affected, unless compelled to do so by language so clear and positive as to leave no room to doubt that such was the intention of the legislature"

(Cook v. United States, 1891). The courts' wariness of retrospective laws does not mean that they are all unconstitutional ex post facto laws or even that all of them violate some provision of the Constitution. The judge who linked the prohibition against ex post fact laws to the social compact wrote that "the true distinction is between ex post facto laws, and retrospective laws. Every ex post facto law must necessarily be retrospective; but every retrospective law is not an ex post facto law; The former, only, are prohibited" (Calder v. Bull, 1798). The problem, of course, is to determine into which of these two categories to place a law that is challenged on the basis of this prohibition.

The most serious impediment to making this determination is deciding whether laws that impose either a civil or criminal penalty can be ex post facto laws or whether only the latter can be that kind of law. Obviously, if both kinds of laws potentially are ex post facto, this prohibition has a much broader scope. Another result of this determination is that the decision about whether a particular law is ex post facto can be more difficult. This occurs because courts have developed generally agreed upon, effective tests for determining whether laws that impose criminal punishments are ex post facto; whereas, they have not done this for laws that impose civil punishments. The determination has not been made definitively so there are two lines of cases. This, then, is the central issue in the case law on the prohibition against the federal government's enactment of ex post facto laws.

One can quickly discover many of the subsidiary issues that are related to this central question by closely examining the first important case on ex post facto laws (Calder v. Bull, 1798). This case resolved a dispute about property that had been transferred in probate proceedings, so the case was certainly civil, not criminal. The plaintiff argued that the legislature, by reversing a court order after the right to the property had vested, had passed an ex post facto law. After delivering a strong statement that ex post facto laws that imposed a criminal penalty and other kinds of retroactive laws were repugnant to the social compact, the Court propounded a definition that many later courts adopted:

> I will state what laws I consider ex post facto laws, within the words and the intent of the prohibition: 1st. Every law that makes an action, done before the passing of the law, and which was innocent when done, criminal; and punishes such action. 2nd. Every law that aggravates a crime, or makes it greater than it was, when committed. 3rd. Every law that changes the punishment, and inflicts a greater punishment, than the law annexed to the crime, when committed. 4th. Every law that alters the legal rules of evidence, and receives less, or different testimony, than the law required at the time of the commission of the offence, in order to convict the offender.

All four varieties of ex post facto laws, according to that definition, relate to crimes. The case being civil, the argument that the law was ex post facto did not prevail. If all courts had subscribed to the definition in Calder v. Bull, the ex post facto prohibition would apply only to criminal cases.

Some courts have diverged from this definition, but it has been influential enough to make examination of its basis useful. One of its problems is that the court demonstrated an incomplete understanding of English ex post facto laws:

> [t]he prohibition against [state legislatures] making any ex post facto laws was introduced for greater caution, and very probably arose from the knowledge, that the Parliament of Great Britain claimed and exercised a power to pass such laws, under the denomination of bills of attainder, or bills of pains and penalties; the first inflicting capital, and the other less, punishment.

Thus, the court conflated bills of attainder and ex post facto laws. A bill of attainder is not necessarily an ex post facto law and vice versa, so the conflation is inappropriate. The court also appeared to assume that all English bills of attainder inflicted criminal punishment. Making this assumption is the only logical way to use the statement about English law to buttress the court's conclusion that all ex post facto laws are criminal. However, this assumption is not valid in respect to either English or American bills of attainder. In fact, a few lines later, the court lists as an example of an ex post facto law the banishment of Lord Clarendon, which was not a typical criminal punishment. Therefore, his banishment does not seem to fit into any of the court's four categories of ex post facto law. This passage is not totally clear, but it seems to formulate a syllogism: all ex post facto laws are also bills of attainder; all bills of attainder are criminal; therefore, all ex post facto laws are criminal. Both the major premise and the minor premise are invalid, so the syllogism is invalid.

The Court's other argument for its definition is bizarre. The Court begins this argument by remarking that there are several kinds of retrospective laws and then creates a dichotomy consisting of protections of citizens' "personal security" and protections of their "private rights." The next point is that the prohibition against ex post facto laws was not included in the Constitution to protect private rights, because the prohibitions against making anything but gold and silver coins a tender in payment of debts (US Const, Art I, § 10, Clause 1) and the prohibition against passing laws that impair contracts (US Const, Art I, § 10, Clause 1) protect private rights. Again, the court seems to be formulating a syllogism: the Constitution must protect both personal security and private rights; it protects private rights elsewhere; therefore, the prohibition against ex post facto laws protects personal security and, therefore, is a criminal provision. The major premise is dubious; the minor premise is weak because it specifies only two protections, one of which is trivial; and the conclusion certainly does not follow from the premises. This syllogism, too, is faulty.

The Court's final argument was that its conception of ex post facto laws accorded with the best contemporary opinion on the subject. It cited William Blackstone's commentaries and "the author of the Federalist." The court did not cite the passage in the commentaries, but it probably had in mind Blackstone's statement that a law is ex post facto "when after an action (indifferent in itself) is committed, the legislator then for the first time declares it to have been a crime, and inflicts punishment upon the person who has committed it."[12] The later reference is to the *Federalist Papers* number 84, by Alexander Hamilton. In a passage about three of the provisions in this section, including the one on ex post facto laws, Hamilton wrote "[t]he creation of crimes after the commission of the fact, or, in other words, the subjecting of men to punishment for things which, when they were done, were breaches of no law" is an instrument of tyranny. Hamilton may have only been giving an example of a kind of ex post facto law; he did not mention the other three kinds of criminal ex post facto laws that the court in Calder v. Bull mentioned. It is certainly not clear that he meant that all ex post facto laws are criminal. The court also quoted the definition of "ex post facto law" in the constitutions of Massachusetts, Maryland, North Carolina and Delaware, which were in effect when the U.S. Constitution was framed. These constitutions are good evidence of the conception of the term ex post facto that was held at least by the delegates to the Constitutional Convention from these states.

This last argument is by far the strongest of the four that the Court constructed. However, it, too, is flawed. Another court (Cummings v. Missouri, 1866) quoted Blackstone's definition of "punishment":

> [s]ome punishments consist in exile or banishment, by abjuration of the realm or transportation; others in loss of liberty by perpetual or temporary imprisonment. Some extend to confiscation by forfeiture of lands or movables, or both, or of the profits of lands for life; others induce a disability of holding offices or employments, being heirs, executors, and the like.

If one applies that definition to the first and third categories of ex post facto laws in Calder v. Bull, one concludes that some ex post facto laws inflict non-criminal punishments. Moreover, Joseph Story, an early analyst of the Constitution, believed that ex post facto laws "embrace all retrospective laws, or laws governing or controlling past transactions, whether...of a civil or criminal nature."[13]

In sum, the first three of the court's arguments for its proposition that all ex post facto laws are criminal in nature are easily refuted. The fourth argument is somewhat, but not totally, convincing. Limiting the prohibition in the way that the Court in that case limited it might be the wisest choice. Moreover, as we shall see, although there are other arguments that could have been made for imposing this limit, the arguments that the Court makes for its position are tenuous. Nevertheless, in regard to the issue of whether all ex post facto laws are criminal laws, Calder v. Bull stands at the beginning of a line of cases.

The opinion in one of this line of cases (Johannessen v. U.S., 1912) includes the statement that the "prohibition [against ex post facto laws] is confined to laws respecting criminal prosecution, and has no relation to retrospective legislation of any other description." For this proposition, it cited Calder v. Bull, a treatise, and a note. *Johannessen* involved deportation, which was a civil proceeding, so that general statement should have sufficed to dispose of the argument that the law in question was ex post facto. However, the Court then began to retreat from its position. It acknowledged that in two earlier cases the Court had held that laws depriving persons of the right to vote for non-criminal actions when they were committed were ex post facto laws, but it did not question that result. The difficulty is that laws denying the right to vote are not "laws respecting criminal prosecution." The Court then embarked on a series of arguments: no punishment was inflicted; nothing was made unlawful that was lawful when it was done, and it imposed no new penalty. In sum, the Court seemed to begin to assume that some ex post facto laws are civil. If the Court had not made that assumption, it would not have had to attempt to distinguish the case it was deciding from the two others that involved voting. One possible conclusion is that after the two cases about voting rights Calder v. Bull was no longer a convincing precedent.

Despite the weaknesses in the logic in Calder v. Bull and the questionable (because it cited a dictum as a precedent) use of that case as a precedent in Johannessen v. United States, a line of cases has formed. A later Court (Mahler v. Irby, 1924) remarked that "[t]he inhibition against the passage of an ex post facto law by Congress in section 9 of article 1 of the Constitution applied only to criminal laws," and it cited the other two cases as its authority for that statement. However, the court in this case, like the Court in *Johannessen*, then began to state arguments that were apparently based on the assumption that civil laws can be ex post facto. However, the Court also stated that the law did not increase punishment, which is a consideration that is relevant to criminal laws, and that the law was an exercise of the police power (the power of a government to protect the health, safety, and welfare of its citizens), which is a consideration that is relevant to civil laws.

The beginning of the line of cases holding that civil laws may be ex post facto is a state case about the loss of title to land (Fletcher v. Peck, 1810). An act of the legislature had rescinded a land grant because of a crime that was committed by the person from whom the plaintiff bought the land. Justice Marshall defined "ex post facto law" more broadly than had the Court in Calder v. Bull, stating that it is one "which renders an act punishable in a manner in which it was not punishable when committed" and that "such a law may inflict penalties on the person, or may inflict pecuniary penalties which swell the public treasury." He did not assert that the law challenged in that case was ex post facto but that it had "the effect of an ex post facto law." That is, he claimed that the punishment, although not criminal, was of a type that an ex post facto law could inflict. The status of that remark is open to question. In a sense this remark has value as a precedent in cases on the prohibition against ex post facto laws because it allowed Marshall to form the analogy leading to his conclusion that the law was equivalent to an ex post facto law and thus unconstitutional. It would then follow that Marshall in effect expanded the meaning of ex post facto law to include civil laws. Conversely, Marshall did not write that the law was an ex post facto law. Moreover, it seems logical to conclude that an ex post facto law must impose additional punishment on the person who committed the act that later was to be determined to be criminal or criminal-like. This case is not the most solid of foundations for a line of cases.

The Court that explained Fletcher v. Peck at length asserted that its facts were analogous to the state case that it was deciding (Cummings v. Missouri, 1866). The provision in the Missouri constitution that was being litigated did not define a crime or directly inflict a punishment in the usual sense of the word but, like the law in Fletcher v. Peck, it had the same effect. The provision wreaked on certain persons a deprivation that amounted to a punishment. The provision, which required persons who wished to engage in certain activities to take an oath, the main purport of which was that they had not aided the Confederacy, therefore violated the prohibition against ex post facto laws. As a result of that holding, the proposition that civil laws may be ex post facto was more firmly established.

A dissent that applied to both Cummings v. Missouri and another case (Ex Parte Garland, 1866) vigorously disputed the results and reasoning of these cases. Its writer quoted the definition of ex post facto laws in Calder v. Bull and, failing to mention Fletcher v. Peck, asserted that this definition had never been denied or modified. One of the dissent's points was that taking an oath was not a criminal proceeding, so the law requiring it cannot be ex post facto. It continued that the earmarks of criminal proceedings were not in evidence, because there was no charge, no prosecution, and no implication of guilt. The dissent maintained that "the fatal vice in the reasoning of the majority is in the meaning which they attach to the word punishment." This was a crucial point because if there was no punishment the law could not have been a member of either of the two classes of ex post facto laws into which it could most plausibly have been placed: a law that punished an act that was innocent when it was performed and a law that increased the punishment for an act that has occurred. In regard to Ex Parte Garland, the dissent wrote that denying admission to the bar for failing to take the oath does not punish, in fact has no real effect, because the actions that were the subject of the oath were, by themselves, grounds for that denial. This statement conveniently ignored the fact that the requirement of the oath would make public the persons who performed these actions and that a law does not escape classification as an ex post facto law because another law or an administrative practice has the same effect. The dissent's final point was that a government has the right to regulate entry into the legal profession. That is true, but the issue here is whether in so doing it enacted an ex post facto law. The dissent was correct that the reasoning and the result of Calder v. Bull did not foreshadow the reasoning and the results of Cummings v. Missouri and Ex Parte Garland. However, its counterarguments lack force.

The next case in the line that begins with Fletcher v. Peck was about liability for a tax on tobacco and a penalty that resulted from that liability (Burgess v. Salmon,

1878). A tax had been paid and the tobacco on which the tax was imposed had been stamped to indicate that payment only a few hours before a law that increased the tax rate was enacted. As the Court acknowledged, litigation about those kinds of liability was civil. The Court noted that the federal government could have proceeded against the taxpayer either in a criminal action or in the civil action that it had chosen. If it had done the former, the act would have been ex post facto. Therefore, the law that the government used was the equivalent of a criminal law and was ex post facto. The court added a generalization: "the ex post facto effect of a law cannot be evaded by giving a civil form to that which is essentially criminal." Imposition of a tax and penalty do not seem "essentially criminal." That holding is too broad. It would have made more sense to hold either that a civil law is ex post facto if it is used in a situation in which the effect is exactly the same as that which would be obtained by using a criminal law or that a civil law is ex post facto if civil trappings were added to an essentially criminal prosecution in order to obscure its real nature. Although the reasoning in this case is not very convincing and the case could be a precedent in, and lead to irrational results in, many cases, the court's point about giving a civil form to an essentially criminal law, as we shall see, indicated a way to reconcile the two lines of cases about the issue of whether a civil law can be ex post facto.

For a while the view that civil laws can be ex post facto was stated mainly in dissents. For example, Justice Douglas traced the development of both positions on that issue (Marcello v. Bonds, 1955). He believed that a law compelling deportation for a drug offense that had been committed earlier ought to have been ruled unconstitutional, even though deportation proceedings were civil cases. He argued that deportation was a severe punishment, which is true, and that there was no rational connection between the imposition of the penalty of deportation and "the *present* [emphasis added] desirability of the alien as a resident in this country." As to the latter statement, he was arguing that the punishment must have been for a past act. Thus, Douglas believed that the case fell into one of the long-recognized categories of ex post facto laws: it added a punishment for an act that had already been the cause of punishment.

Justices Douglas, Black, and Brennan wrote vigorous dissents in a case in which the Court held constitutional an act that denied payments of social security benefits to persons who had been deported because they once belonged to the Communist Party (Flemming v. Nestor, 1960). Again, the case was civil. Justice Douglas confined his arguments to the issue of whether the act was a bill of attainder, but the other two justices also dealt with the ex post facto issue. Justice Black asserted that the act causing the deprivation inflicted punishment for a past act and thus was ex post facto. Justice Brennan agreed that the denial of social security benefits was punishment and wrote that "[t]he framers ordained that even the worst of men should not be punished for their past acts....Today's decision is to me a regretful retreat from Lovett, Cummings and Garland." Those justices convincingly argued that for many persons loss of social security benefits caused severe financial hardship and that in the 1950s Congress was highly motivated to punish present and former members of the Communist Party.

In a recent case (Landgraf v. USI Film Products, 1994), the Court assumed, without argument, that a civil law can be ex post facto and probably would have ruled that a particular law was ex post facto if it had been clearly retroactive. Part of the law, the Civil Rights Act of 1991, authorized punitive damages if the defendant engaged in a discriminatory practice with malice or reckless indifference to federally protected rights. The court wrote that "[t]he very labels 'punitive' or 'exemplary' damages, as well as the rationales that support them, demonstrate that they share key characteristics of criminal sanctions." This is reminiscent of the court's analysis in Burgess v. Salmon. Although an award of damages would have gone to the plaintiff, not to the government, as would a fine, an award of this kind of damages is at least similar to, if it is not in fact, a punishment. The Court almost wrote that allowing punitive damages for past acts would be ex post facto. It wrote instead that allowing punitive damages would "raise a serious constitutional question." However, the application of the law was prospective only.

As should by now be clear, the issue of whether a civil law can be ex post facto intertwines with the issue of the meaning of punishment. For example, judges who argue the affirmative on the first issue sometimes base their position in part on the assertion that the disadvantage that the law caused resembled criminal punishments. Conversely, judges who argue the negative on the first issue sometimes base their position partly on the assertion that the civil law in question imposed a disadvantage but that that disadvantage was not really a punishment. One can most readily understand the latter issue by examining two cases in which strong dissents were written.

The Court wrote that the oath at issue in the case about fitness to practice law was "a legislative decree of perpetual exclusion. And exclusion from any of the professions or any of the ordinary avocations of life for past conduct can be regarded in no other light than as punishment for such conduct" (Ex Parte Garland, 1866). The Court did state that the legislature's regulation of the legal profession, which is primarily responsible to the judicial branch of government, was particularly egregious. It recognized the right of legislatures to propound qualifications that lawyers must fulfill, but it asserted that the legislature may not do this to punish prospective lawyers. Despite the Court's remarks on the uniqueness of the legal profession, its statement about denying access to avocations was phrased very generally, and the Court recognized the great seriousness of that denial.

In contrast, the dissent argued that practicing law was a privilege, not a right, that attaching qualifications to that privilege was well within the powers of the legislative branch of government, and that loyalty to the country was an obvious qualification for persons who seek to practice law in its courts. In other words, the dissent's position was that denying a privilege was not punishment and that the reason for the denial was rational. One could argue that the "privilege–right" dichotomy is false. It would certainly be no comfort to someone who has been denied his or her chosen means of earning a living to be told that only a privilege, not a right, has been revoked. That is, the dichotomy seems to be irrelevant to the issue of whether a punishment or something that can be given a less disturbing label has been inflicted. The dissent took much less seriously than did the majority the denial of entry into a line of work. Moreover, the right of a legislature to impose qualifications for entry into vocations, although indisputable, was also not relevant to the issues in this case. The issue was whether punishment had been inflicted. A legislature can impose qualifications either to regulate or to punish. Similarly, the reasonableness of the qualifications did not negate their punitive nature if they were punitive. However, the dissent implicitly made a valuable point. A government must be able to regulate activity, including participation in an occupation. If all the laws that do this are ex post facto, they are voidable, and regulation, therefore, will eventually cease. Courts need to balance a government's need to regulate with the interests of individuals requiring protection from ex post facto laws. This balance cannot be struck if courts imply that the right to regulate is absolute or nearly absolute and decline to examine the effects on those who were regulated and the purpose of the regulation.

In the case on the denial of social security benefits (Flemming v. Nestor, 1960), the court found that there was no punishment and hence no violation of the prohibition against ex post facto laws. Thus, the sides are reversed: the majority argued that there was no punishment, and the dissent argued that there was punishment. The majority employed a number of arguments.

One of the majority's arguments was to distinguish laws that were aimed at an activity or status, which do not inflict punishment, from those that were aimed at a person or persons, which might inflict punishment. The difficulty with this argument is that a definite line cannot be drawn between the two. A law that might be ex post facto is highly unlikely to name an individual. Thus, it will affect a number of persons because they have engaged in a particular activity or have had a particular status. These same persons will be affected and for the same reasons regardless of whether the ostensible target was the person or the activity. The distinction appears to be both virtually meaningless and impossible to draw.

The majority opinion also constructed a second dichotomy: "present–past." It quoted the opinion in another case that was not about ex post facto laws (De Veau v. Braisted, 1960):

> [t]he question in each case where unpleasant consequences are brought to bear upon an individual for prior conduct is whether the legislative aim was to punish that individual for past activity, or whether the restriction of the individual comes about as a relevant incident to a regulation of a present situation, such as the proper qualifications for a profession.

This dichotomy, too, is false. In the typical ex post facto case an individual suffers a deprivation in the present, in order to effect a present regulation, but the actions that led to the deprivation were done in the past. Thus, the dichotomy collapses because the present and past are not totally distinct. The past actions are indications or causes of the present status. Even if it were intact, separating the two kinds of instances appears to be impossible.

The Court also attempted to analyze the motives of Congress. It noted that the court in Cummings v. Missouri was well aware of the heated atmosphere that existed soon after the Civil War and that the atmosphere motivated the constitutional provision that was litigated in this case. It would be logical to note, as one of the dissenters did, that the anti-Communist hysteria of the 1950s was very similar to, and was just as good evidence of a punitive motive as, the situation that pertained shortly after the Civil War. The majority opinion also noted the difficulty of discerning the motives of Congress, which was a valid response to the problem, but then proceeded to try. In addition to that difficulty, searching for the motive of Congress is focusing on the wrong actor. It would make more sense to focus on the victim in order to determine whether he or she has been punished and, if so, to determine the things that the victim had done to allegedly deserve that punishment.

The majority also downplayed the significance of the denial of social security benefits, which it denominated "a non-contractual government benefit," and of which it wrote "[n]o affirmative disability or restraint is imposed." The first point was both factually inaccurate and irrelevant. Payment of social security taxes created an implied contract that the government will in turn pay social security benefits. Also, there was no logical connection between the absence of a contract—even if this were the case—and the absence of punishment. A denial of a sum of money would have exactly the same monetary effect whether it was due under a contract or for another reason. The difference between an "affirmative disability" and a mere disability is far from clear, but it is clear that the plaintiff was denied social security benefits, which was certainly a disability, particularly because he was also deported and appears to have been impecunious.

In his dissent, Justice Black took a more clear-headed view of the results of the government's action. He pointed out that the plaintiff had paid into the social security system with the expectation of getting benefits in return. He also pointed to the distinct possibility that the money that was not paid to the plaintiff "may well be this exile's daily bread." Justice Brennan's position was that the law:

> is a congressional enactment aimed at an easily ascertainable group; it is certainly punishment in any normal sense of the word to take away from any person the benefits of an insurance system into which he and his employer have paid their moneys for almost two decades.

These justices examined the effect on the targets of the law, not the nature of the deprivation or the motives of Congress. Justice Douglas, also examining the effect on the law's targets, noted that denying social security benefits was analogous to denying compensation, which the court in United States v. Lovett had found to be accomplished by means of an unconstitutional ex post facto law. He also argued that the "'penalty exacted has one of the classic purposes of punishment—to reprimand the wrongdoer, to deter others'" (quoting Trop v. Dulles, 1958).

Thus, there are two lines of cases on the nature of punishment. One line was built on the assumption that a penalty must be severe and clearly like criminal penalties to be punishment. This view makes it difficult for a target of a legislatively imposed penalty to prevail in an ex post facto case, while making it easy for the government to regulate conduct—and to inflict penalties—and yet avoid having the laws that do so ruled unconstitutional. The other line of cases focuses on the victim and is willing to label many kinds of penalties as punishments. This view, of course, makes it easier for plaintiffs to win ex post facto cases. In addition to this fundamental disagreement, even by examining only two cases, one can see that there are many ways to analyze the issue of the nature of punishment. The result is considerable confusion on this issue. One would have hoped that agreement on the nature of punishment would have clarified the larger issue of whether the exaction of civil penalties can make a law ex post facto, but that has not happened.

We have noted in passing that both the majority and one of the dissenters in Flemming v. Nestor considered the motives of Congress to be relevant in determining whether a law was ex post facto. The majority conceded that "[j]udicial inquiries into Congressional motives are at best a hazardous matter, and when that inquiry seeks to go behind objective manifestations it becomes a dubious affair indeed." Nevertheless, it risked that hazard. However, the Court shifted the burden of the hazard to the plaintiff. The plaintiff was thus put in an impossible position because the court declared a type of evidence to be pertinent, even though it declared inquiry into it "hazardous," and then shifted the burden of proof in regard to that evidence to the plaintiff. However, the Court itself also looked at the legislation and, cursorily, at its legislative history and concluded that there was not enough evidence to justify a finding that Congress had been most concerned with the action in question, joining the Communist Party. This finding appears to be inconsistent, because joining the party was the reason for the denial of the social security payments. The majority opinion also fell short of being convincing on this issue when it responded to the argument that persons who voluntarily resided abroad were not denied benefits. This seems to be convincing evidence that the law was intended to penalize only persons who had been deported. However, the majority responded that Congress might have failed to consider them or thought there were so few of them that it was not worth considering them. These arguments are at best disingenuous. The common-sense view of the omission is that Congress did not want to punish them; it wanted to punish deportees, particularly those who had been deported because they had once belonged to the Communist Party.

In his dissent, Justice Black asserted that the "general fashion of the day—that is, to punish in every way possible anyone who ever made the mistake of being a Communist in this country"—reveals Congress' motive. Justice Douglas stated that Congress' motive was to punish, that is, to reprimand and deter. He cited a revealing comment by a member of Congress, who admitted that the law's purpose was to terminate benefits "because of illegal entry, conviction of a crime, or subversive activity." Justice Brennan examined the law, in particular in regard to its treatment of the classes of persons who lived abroad yet retained their social security benefits and concluded from that examination that Congress' motive must have been to punish persons who had committed certain actions.

In two cases, the Court assumed that Congress' motives were relevant, but instead of inquiring into them and stating reasons to believe that certain motives were operating, it merely stated its view of these motives. One of these statements appeared in a case on deportation:

> Congress by the act of 1920 was not increasing the punishment for the crimes of which petitioners had been convicted, by requiring their deportation if found undesirable residents. It was, in the exercise of its unquestioned right, only seeking to rid the country of persons who had shown by their career that their continued presence here would not make for the safety or welfare of society. (Mahler v. Erby, 1924)

An even more self-assured statement of Congress' motives that was similarly lacking in support appeared in a recent case:

> [n]or could anyone seriously contend that the compensatory damages provisions smack of a 'retributive' or other suspect legislative purpose. Section 102 reflects congress' desire to afford victims of discrimination more complete redress for violations of rules established more than a generation ago in the Civil Rights Act of 1964. (Landgraf v. USI Film Products, 1994)

Those cases provide ample precedents for courts that wish to inquire into motives. However, collectively they provide a good reason to agree with the Court in Flemming v. Nestor that inquiry into the motives of Congress is at best hazardous. These cases offer no consistency on the proper way to determine intent. Rather, they illustrate that the search for a legislative body's motives or intent will almost certainly conclude with a result that will leave most readers unconvinced. The reason for the futility of the process is not that no obviously efficacious method has been found to determine legislative motive or intent but that there is no such thing as a motive or an intent of a legislative body.

Unfortunately, courts, in determining whether a law is punitive and might therefore be ex post facto, have eschewed a method that has considerable promise and also could be used with far more possibility of success than a chase after the will-of-the-wisp of legislative motive or intent. The dissent in the case about denying entry into the legal profession for persons who aided the Confederacy (Ex Parte Garland, 1867) argued that persons were unfit to practice law. This conclusion is arguable, but the important point is that the dissenter was aware that it made sense to determine whether a penalty was rationally related to the reason why it was imposed. This makes sense because if the penalty rationally relates to the reason for its imposition then the law that imposed the penalty is far more likely to be regulatory than if there is no rational relation between the two, in which case the law is likely to be punitive.

Later courts did not follow this course. In fact, one Court that had an excellent situation in which to use that test implicitly rejected it (Murphy v. Ramsey, 1885). That case was a suit for damages by persons who were prevented from voting because they had practiced bigamy. The Court stated that inquiring into whether a person who wished to vote was a bigamist was

> precisely similar to an inquiry into the fact of nativity, of age, or of any other status made necessary by law as a condition of the elective franchise. It would be quite competent for the sovereign power to declare that no one but a married person shall be entitled to vote.

The point was that a government could deny the right to vote on any grounds. Even setting aside problems with the First Amendment and the equal protection doctrine, the statement is untenable in regard to Clause 3. It is difficult to find a rational relation between being a bigamist and competence to vote (that is, on this basis, the case was wrongly decided) and between not being married and competence to vote. In contrast, it is not difficult to find a rational relation between age and competence to vote. Although persons can argue cogently about the age at which the franchise should be bestowed—and it has changed over the years—no one can cogently argue that everyone, regardless of age, should be allowed to vote.

If the relevance of the penalty to the action or status for which it was imposed had been a decisive test in all ex post facto cases, many of them would have been decided differently. For example, it would have been difficult to establish that there was a rational relation between a penalty and the reason why it was imposed in regard to denying social security benefits because of deportation for membership in the Communist Party (Flemming v. Nestor, 1960), deportation for violation of the Selective Service Act (Mahler v. Erby, 1924), deportation for past membership in the Communist Party (Harisiades v. Shaughnessy, 1952; Galvan v. Press, 1954), deportation for violation of a narcotic law (Marcello v. Bonds, 1955), deportation for being a prostitute (Bugajewitz v. Adams, 1913), and deportation for having committed blackmail (Lehmann v. Carson, 1957).

Because the essence of ex post facto laws is their imposition of penalties for past actions, fixing the action in the time continuum is sometimes a problem, although that task is often easily performed. The greatest difficulties arise when the action is continuing. The cases in which that problem arose indicate that even if a person has committed an action in the past that both has an effect continuing into the present and was made illegal after it was committed, then the person is not the victim of an ex post facto law if he or she also has violated another part of the same law that proscribed a current condition.

A case that involved the Anti-Trust Act of 1890 illustrates this problem of classifying continuing actions (United States v. Trans-Missouri Freight Ass'n, 1897). The plaintiff argued that it had executed a contract before a law that potentially applied to it took effect and that application of the law to the contract would give the law an ex post facto effect. The Court had an easy time with this argument. It stated that the "statute prohibits the continuing or entering into such an agreement for the future." That is a rough paraphrase of the statute. The statute actually specified that "[e]very person who shall make any such contract or engage in any such combination or conspiracy, shall be deemed guilty of a misdemeanor." It would have been clearer if the Court had stated that the failure to abrogate the contract was evidence that the unlawful combination or conspiracy had remained in existence until the present. That is, the second prohibition in the statute, not the first, had been violated. The present violation, notwithstanding the fact that the contract had been executed before the law was passed, was enough to ensure that the law was not ex post facto.

The law in Murphy v. Ramsey (1885) similarly sanctioned both a past event and an effect of it that continued into the present. As noted earlier, a federal law that applied to United States territories stated that bigamists may not vote. The past event was the wedding of a person who was already married, and the continuing effect was the simultaneous marriage to another person. The Court's analysis was inconsistent. At one point it stated that bigamy was entering into a bigamous marriage and "is complete when the relation begins." This seems to mean that the act was over at this point rather than continuing. However, later in its decision, the Court stated that someone who is in the "state and condition of a bigamist or a polygamist" may not, under the law, vote. This seems to mean that bigamy was a continuing condition. However, the law under consideration also specified that anyone who cohabits with more than one person may not vote. The Court should have confined its analysis to cohabitation rather than also making contradictory statements about bigamy. Its confusion illustrates the difficulty of dealing in an ex post facto case with events that have continuing effects. The case would have been much more difficult if the law had stated only that bigamists, not also persons who are cohabiting with more than one person, may not vote. Then the Court would have had to decide whether bigamy was a wedding of someone who was already married, and thus completed, or simultaneous marriage to more than one person, and thus continuing.

A different kind of timing problem arose in a case involving controls on petroleum (United States v. Powers, 1939). Congress had passed a law specifying that actions that the defendant appears to have taken were illegal and that the act expired on June 16, 1937. Two days before the act was scheduled to expire it was amended to delay its expiration until June 30, 1939. The defendants argued that prosecutions begun against them after the original expiration date were ex post facto. The Court might have logically pointed out that the actions that were prosecuted were taken during the time when the act was in effect under its original sunset date, that the date when prosecution began was irrelevant to the question of whether the act was ex post facto and that the act thus was not ex post facto. Instead, the Court held that the act as amended was the same as the original act, which was true except for the change in the expiration date, but that was the main fact in the case. Therefore, the Court held, there was no new act that had an ex post facto effect. The Court apparently assumed that this finding was necessary to negate the plaintiff's argument that the act of June 14, 1939, had made it possible to prosecute an action that could not have been prosecuted before the act became law and that the new act thus subjected the plaintiffs to ex post facto punishment. However, the category of ex post facto laws that the Court seems to have had in mind is laws that make illegal an act that was legal when taken; it has nothing to do, and all of the other categories of ex post facto have nothing to do, with the ability to prosecute. The question of the holding in this case remains. It might be a narrow one: that an act that delays an expiration date and thus makes prosecution possible but makes no other changes to the original act is not ex post facto. This holding would be unusual because the change in the expiration date was not needed to make prosecution possible, but it would cause the least trouble. A broader reading is that an act that merely extends an expiration date is not a new act and thus cannot be ex post facto. This is both unusual and very troublesome, because some of these acts can make actions that were legal when taken (because they occurred after the original expiration date) illegal. This kind of act certainly ought to be ex post facto. However, the situation that pertained in the case is not common, so the case's meaning as a precedent is not very important.

The category of civil ex post facto cases on deportation bears careful attention, because it consists of many cases and because their results are totally consistent. In all of them courts have held that deportation is not punishment, so that any law that decrees deportation for an action that occurred in the past is not an ex post facto law. Another consistent feature of these cases is not nearly so obvious that the courts have declined either to examine or to take seriously the effects of deportation. These cases ought to be put in perspective by trying to communicate these effects. As anthropologists have discovered, in pre-industrial societies banishment is a common and greatly feared sanction for the most serious transgressions against the community. The seriousness of deportation perhaps will be dramatized by quoting the reaction of one exile, the writer Dante Alighieri. Dante was banished from his home city of Florence because he belonged to an unpopular political faction, an affiliation that, in the tumultuous times of late-medieval Florentine politics, was not prudent. To help prevent our descent into tumult, it would be wise to pay attention to his words:

> Thou shalt leave everything loved most dearly, and this is the shaft which the bow of exile shoots first. Thou shalt prove how salt is the taste of another man's bread and how hard is the way up and down another man's stairs. And that which shall weigh heaviest on thy shoulders is the wicked and senseless company with which thou shalt fall into that valley, which shall become wholly ungrateful, quite mad and furious against thee.[14]

The best way to understand the development of the application of the ex post facto doctrine to deportation cases is chronologically. In the first case, the issue was a law that required the deportation of persons who had become citizens by means of fraud (Johannessen v. United States, 1912). The plaintiff, having perpetrated a fraud, was not a sympathetic figure, a fact that in part determined the future course of the law on this subject. The Court held that there had been no punishment; the plaintiff had merely been stripped of something that, because of the fraud, never was rightfully his. It would have been best to conclude only that. However, the Court, citing Calder v. Bull and other sources, also stated that the prohibition against ex post facto laws applied only to laws that imposed criminal punishments. Then the court contradicted itself by approving the results of Ex Parte Garland and Cummings v. Missouri, even though the punishment in both of those cases was not criminal but denied the right to vote. This confusion is another reason why the law on ex post facto laws and deportation got off to a bad start.

The law that was at issue in the next case (Bugajewitz v. Adams, 1913) required deportation of alien women who were prostitutes. The Court held that "[i]t is thoroughly established that Congress has the power to order the deportation of aliens whose presence in the country it deems hurtful." To support this proposition, the Court cited a number of cases that were not about the prohibition against ex post facto laws. When it arrived at the specific question in the case, the Court tersely stated that the prohibition against ex post facto laws "has no application" and cited *Johannessen*. It could have interpreted *Johannessen* to mean that the prohibition does not apply in cases of fraud, in which citizenship had been improperly been granted and was revoked in order to return the deportee to the position that he or she was in before the fraud. It could also have recognized that the earlier Court conceded that some laws imposing non-criminal penalties are ex post facto. Instead, the Court simplified and hardened the precedent. After *Bugajewitz*, the law on the subject was that the ex post facto prohibition did not apply to any deportation cases.

The next case was a reprise of *Johannessen* (Luria v. United States, 1913). The plaintiff had fraudulently obtained citizenship by falsely claiming that he intended to remain in this country. Like the Court in *Johannessen*, the Court in *Luria* held that the plaintiff was not punished but merely divested of citizenship, to which he not been lawfully entitled. The court did not state that laws requiring deportation could not be ex post facto. This narrow reading of *Johannessen* made it possible for later courts to apply the doctrine to some deportation cases if they wanted to do so.

However, the next Court to rule in a case in which a law about deportation was challenged on the grounds that it was ex post facto reverted to a hard-line interpretation (Mahler v. Erby, 1924). The plaintiff had violated the Selective Service Act, rather than obtaining citizenship fraudulently. The Court, therefore, had the option of distinguishing *Johannessen* and *Luria*. Instead, even more decisively than had the court in *Bugajewitz*, the court in *Mahler* cut off the argument that deportation laws could be ex post facto. It cited *Bugajewitz* and another case to support its assertion that deportation was not punishment, which is very peculiar. It also stated that "[t]he right to expel aliens is a sovereign power, necessary to the safety of the country, and only limited by treaty obligations." Moreover, the Court added that the ex post facto doctrine applied only to criminal laws.

The next Court that considered the issue could have changed the course of the law (Harisiades v. Shaughnessy, 1952). The Court began its decision by stating that the cases decided up to this point indicated that the ex post facto prohibition applied only to criminal punishments and that deportation cases were civil. It did not state that deportation laws could not be ex post facto. Thus, rather than completely closing the door on the argument that the prohibition could apply to deportation laws, the court's decision left room for interpretation. The plaintiff had pointed out that "the ex post facto prohibition had been applied to what appeared to be civil disabilities" and cited Fletcher v. Peck, Cummings v. Missouri, Ex Parte Garland, and a case that was about the prohibition as it applies to state action. Moreover, the plaintiff reminded the Court that the Court in Burgess v. Salmon had held that the prohibition applied if criminal penalties were given a civil form. A logical inference from these precedents is that deportation—banishment—has been a criminal punishment for centuries and that although deportation cases were civil they ought to be subject to the ex post facto provision. Making this inference would have required reversing a number of cases. The Court had stated rational reasons to reverse those cases, and, one could argue, taking this action would have put on a much better course the law on the interaction between the ex post facto prohibition and deportation. The Court noted that the cases cited were known to other courts that had consistently declined to apply the prohibition to deportation cases and that the present Court also declined to do this.

Next even more serious doubt about following this course of denying plaintiffs in deportation cases the protection of the prohibition against ex post facto laws appeared. The majority in a deportation case (Galvan v. Press, 1954) that was decided the year after Harisiades stated that it was not writing on a clean slate. However, the Court in *Galvan* also stated that "since the intrinsic consequences of deportation are so close to punishment for crime, it might fairly be said also that the ex post facto clause, even though applicable only to punitive legislation, should be applied to deportation" (Galvan v. Press, 1954). The Court resisted the temptation to make that application: "whatever might have been said at an earlier date for applying the ex post facto Clause, it has been the unbroken rule of this Court that it has no application to deportation."

In the next case (Marcello v. Bonds, 1955), the majority quickly disposed of the ex post facto issue, stating that the prohibition does not apply to deportation and citing *Galvan* and *Harisiades*. However, the dissent argued in support of the contrary position. Justice Douglas noted that there were two lines of cases on the issue of whether the prohibition could apply to civil laws. He then stated that "[d]eportation may be as severe a punishment as loss of livelihood," which alludes to the deprivation inflicted in Ex Parte Garland and Cummings v. Missouri. He also distinguished *Mahler* and *Bugajewitz* on the grounds that the deportation in each case depended on a finding of a present reason, so that the laws were not applied retroactively. Furthermore, Justice Douglas distinguished *Johannessen* on the grounds that the deportation rectified a grant of citizenship that was fraudulently obtained. He made some powerful, but unavailing, arguments.

In the most recent case on deportation and the ex post facto prohibition, the majority did not even mention the pertinent provision in the Constitution but wrote that "Congress was legislating retrospectively, as it may do, to cover offenses of the kind here involved" and in a footnote cited several of the previous cases in this line (Lehman v. Carson, 1957). The dissenters cited the point that was made in the dissent in Marcello v. Bonds: that in a number of cases civil laws were held to be ex post facto. It then made a strong plea for reversing that line of cases:

> [w]hat is being done to these respondents seems to me to be the precise evil the ex post facto clause was designed to prevent. Both respondents are ordered deported for offenses they committed long ago—one in 1925 and the other in 1936. Long before the 1952 Act reached back to add deportation as one of the legal consequences of their offenses both paid the price society then exacted for their misconduct. They have lived in the United States for almost 40 years. To banish them from home, family, and adopted country is punishment of the most drastic kind whether done at the time when they were convicted or later. I think that this Court should reconsider the application of the ex post facto clause with a view to applying it in a way that more effectively protects individuals from new or additional burdens, penalties, or punishments retrospectively imposed by Congress.

The case law on the issue of whether a law that imposes civil penalties can be ex post facto and on the issue of the nature of punishment in ex post facto cases thus is inconsistent. There are two lines of cases on the first issue and considerable disagreement on the second. On the narrower issue of whether deportation cases are subject to the prohibition against ex post facto laws, the case law is consistent but many are dissatisfied with the results of these cases. The decisions in civil cases could be made more rational by holding that any kind of penalty that is inflicted for past political activity or affiliation is ex post facto. Like making that change for cases about possible bills of attainder, making that change for cases about possible ex post facto laws would make Clause 3 more similar to a clause in a bill of rights. It also would reflect that Congress is more likely to intend punishment if politics is an issue and would make the outcome of cases easier to predict.

The law is considerably more orderly in regard to the application of the ex post facto prohibition in criminal cases. One issue that has been resolved in criminal cases on this prohibition is a change in parole guidelines (Portley v. Grossman, 1980). In this case, the Parole Commission had revoked a person's parole because of two convictions, using the statutory parole guidelines then in effect, not the guidelines in effect at the time when the person was sentenced. Thus, they applied the newer parole guidelines retroactively. The Court assumed, but did not hold, that the ex post facto prohibition applied to the terms of parole. It then held that parole guidelines are only a framework for the Parole Commission's decision, that the "terms of the sentence originally imposed have in no way been altered" and that, therefore, the change in guidelines was procedural. ("Procedural" is an odd label to apply to a set of parole guidelines, which are part of the punishment for a crime.) That being so, the application of the new guidelines was not ex post facto. Because this is the only case on parole guidelines and the ex post facto prohibition, its holding is the law on the subject. However, that holding is somewhat troubling. Another view of this case is that the original sentence included the conditions of parole and thus included the parole guidelines that were in effect when it was imposed, so that changing those guidelines retroactively altered the sentence. Also, the change must at least have potentially increased the prison term, otherwise there would have been no need to litigate.

Another criminal case had unusual and complicated facts (Cook v. United States, 1891). This case was about a murder that was committed in the area that is now the Oklahoma panhandle, but at the time of the murder the area was part of a territory because Oklahoma was not yet a state. The defendant had been convicted in the Court for the northern district of Texas, which had jurisdiction over his case under a law that Congress enacted after the murder, instead of in the Court that had jurisdiction under the law in effect at the time of the murder. The law was certainly applied retroactively; the question was whether the person who was convicted was disadvantaged in such a way as to make the law ex post facto. The Court decided that the plaintiff had not been sufficiently disadvantaged:

> [t]he act of 1889 does not touch the offense nor change the punishment therefor. It only includes the place of the commission of the alleged offense within a particular judicial district, and subjects the accused to trial in that district rather than in the court of some

other judicial district established by the government against whose laws the offense was committed.

The Court might have considered whether the differences in the case law and rules of the two courts were substantial enough to make it likely that the outcome of a trial on the charge would have been different in one court than in the other. Nevertheless, under this case, a law changing the jurisdiction over a criminal trial after the offense was allegedly committed is not an ex post facto law.

Although the cases that have been examined so far are disparate and on some issues inconsistent, they all involve legislative acts that are alleged to have a retroactive effect. One conclusion that can be drawn from that common thread is that this ex post facto prohibition applies only to Congress, just as the prohibition in the next section of the Constitution applies only to state legislative bodies. A case in which a plaintiff attempted to convince a Court to extend the prohibition to the judicial branch of government confirmed this generalization (Marks v. United States, 1977). Citing Calder v. Bull and a case on the prohibition in the next section, the Court held that the prohibition applies to legislatures, not to the judiciary. This is an obvious conclusion from the wording of the prohibition: "[n]o...ex post facto Law shall be passed" because only a legislative body can pass a law. As an aside, the Court remarked that the principle on which the prohibition is based is that persons "have a right to fair warning of that conduct which will give rise to criminal penalties" and that the due process clauses of the Fifth and Fourteenth Amendments protect this right against action by the courts.

Thus, obviously criminal laws have rarely been challenged on the grounds that they violate the ex post facto prohibition; the factual circumstances in each of these cases have been unusual, and each law has withstood the challenge. A federal criminal law has never been held unconstitutional because it was one of the four types of ex post facto laws that were specified more than 200 years ago:

> I will state what laws I consider ex post facto laws, within the words and the intent of the prohibition: 1st. Every law that makes an action, done before the passing of the law, and which was innocent when done, criminal; and punishes such action. 2nd. Every law that aggravates a crime, or makes it greater than it was, when committed. 3rd. Every law that changes the punishment, and inflicts a greater punishment, than the law annexed to the crime, when committed. 4th. Every law that alters the legal rules of evidence, and receives less, or different testimony, than the law required at the time of the commission of the offence, in order to convict the offender. (Calder v. Bull, 1798)

Several minor themes in the case law on the prohibition against ex post facto laws remain to be clarified. They deal less with the substance of the law than the themes that have already been analyzed. Rather they deal with a function of laws other than their role in deciding cases, with methods of statutory interpretation that are especially pertinent to statutes that might be ex post facto.

One naturally thinks of constitutional provisions as means by which courts can invalidate laws. Indeed, this has been the main application of the ex post facto prohibition, although courts have struggled with the issues of whether the prohibition applies to civil laws; and, if they have concluded that the prohibition does apply to civil laws, then they have struggled to determine the conditions under which the prohibition ought to invalidate a law rather than merely invalidating one application of it.

The deterrent purpose of constitutional provisions is less obvious. However, in regard to criminal laws, that has been the dominant effect of the prohibition against ex post facto laws. Congress has recognized its obligation to avoid passing ex post facto criminal laws. In addition, the guidelines that appear in Calder v. Bull are clear enough for members of Congress to recognize easily the kinds of criminal laws that will violate the prohibition. Therefore, constitutional provisions serve as deterrants more often than tools to invalidate laws, but as John Milton wrote in a very different context, "they also serve who only stand and wait."[15]

The prohibition against ex post facto laws has performed another rather mundane but important purpose. It has influenced statutory interpretation. Two canons (rules) of statutory interpretation are applicable in these cases. One canon is that, if it is possible to do so in a reasonable way, statutes ought to be interpreted so as to avoid ruling them unconstitutional. This canon applies to all statutes. The second canon is that statutes ought not to be interpreted so as to give them a retroactive effect unless they clearly state that they are to have that kind of effect. Applying the latter rule can eliminate the retroactive effect of a statute, thereby preventing it from violating the ex post facto prohibition. Therefore, this canon has had a unique, and also an important, relation to this constitutional provision.

One Court went to great lengths to avoid interpreting a law so as to give it a retroactive effect, and it described its efforts in a very confusing way (Murphy v. Ramsey, 1885). This case, described earlier, dealt with denying the vote to polygamists and others who cohabit with more than one woman. Cohabitation refers to a present act, so prohibiting it does not make a law ex post facto. The Court had a more difficult time with the other offense. The law stated this offense thus:

> [e]very person who has a husband or wife living, who, in a territory or other place over which the United States have exclusive jurisdiction, hereafter marries another, whether married or single, and any man who hereafter simultaneously, or on the same day, marries more than one woman, in a territory or other place over which the United States have exclusive jurisdiction, is guilty of polygamy.

This seems clear: the offense is a marriage by someone who already has a spouse. The court, however, interpreted the offense as continuing to be married to more than one person, which would make the offense contemporaneous with the denial of the vote and thus not ex post facto. The court revealed the gyrations that it was going through by lapsing into a literal reading: "[t]he crime of bigamy or polygamy consists in entering into a bigamous or polygamous marriage, and is complete when the relation begins." Nevertheless, the court's position was that bigamy and polygamy meant remaining married (not being married) to more than one person and that the law was not ex post facto.

As described previously, in an even more convoluted opinion, another Court strove mightily to validate a conviction (Cook v. United States, 1891). A law that was enacted after a murder was committed gave the Court for the northern district of Texas jurisdiction over cases that involved capital crimes that were alleged to have been committed in an area that was a territory and became part of Oklahoma when it became a state later. Under an earlier law, the Court for the eastern district of Texas had jurisdiction over these cases. The court acknowledged the canon of statutory interpretation about attempting not to give a retroactive effect. However, it stated that Congress had clearly stated its intent to change the jurisdiction over the case retroactively by creating an exception to the law's rules of jurisdiction only for cases as to which prosecution had begun when the act became effective. That hardly seems to be a clear statement of an intent to make a law retroactive. In fact, the exception much more likely reflects the drafter's expectation that the law would be interpreted to have only a prospective effect and his or her identification of the event by which to measure the initial application of the law. That is, the best interpretation is that the law took effect when it was enacted, had only a prospective effect, and applied first to *offenses* committed on the law's effective date, not to *prosecutions* begun on its effective date. The Court's interpretation brought it into possible conflict with the prohibition against ex post facto laws. The Court avoided this problem by holding that changes in jurisdiction do not fit any of the categories of ex post facto laws.

Another unusual interpretation of a statute allowed a Court to decide that a statute did not apply retroactively and was thus not ex post facto (United States v. Trans-Missouri Freight Ass'n, 1897). The case involved the 1890 Anti-Trust Act. The court held that the act's prohibition of certain kinds of contract was not retroactive because the agreements in question had continued into the present. Unfortunately, the statute specified that "[e]very person who shall make any such contract...shall be deemed guilty of a misdemeanor." In other words, under the statute, *making*, not continuing to be bound by, a contract was the offense. The interpretation placed the criminal act in the past and, unless there were more contracts, would have made the act ex post facto. The Court should have looked at the rest of the statute, which made criminal the action of engaging in certain combinations or conspiracies. This part of the law referred to current violations and was thus not ex post facto. The defendant had violated these provisions as well, so conviction on these grounds would have been easy and would have given the case much more value as a precedent.

Another tortured, unnecessary interpretation of a statute was made more recently (Harisiades v. Shaughnessy, 1952). The court maintained that since 1920 federal laws have made it clear that anyone who became a member of the Communist Party would be deported. The Court meant that this outcome would have ensued during all that time period. However, it then admitted that another Court had held that anyone who ceased belonging to the Communist Party would not be deported (Kessler v. Strecker, 1939). Congress reacted by reversing the result of *Kessler*: "it supplied unmistakable language that past violators of its prohibitions continued to be deportable in spite of resignation or expulsion from the party." Therefore, according to the Court in *Harisiades*, the new law was not retroactive because it continued the law as it had been since 1920. However, the new law did not provide that former party members *continued* to be subject to deportation. The decision in *Kessler* was that the law at that time did not make these persons subject to deportation, and that law had the meaning that that court ascribed to it. The new law thus had a retroactive effect, notwithstanding the Court's statement to the contrary. The Court in *Harisiades* did not need to misread the statute. It also wrote that courts have consistently held that the prohibition against ex post facto laws does not apply to deportations. This fact alone would have resolved the case.

The law at issue in the other ex post facto case in which statutory construction was important stated that it was to "take effect upon enactment" (Landgraf v. USI Film Products, 1994). This law, like the statute in Cook v. United States, must have lacked an initial applicability provision. Effective dates, like the one quoted above, state the time when an act becomes law; initial applicability provisions state the event in the chain of events to which the law first applies. The Court used judicially constructed rules to determine the law's applicability. For example, it stated that a procedural change would first apply to trials that begin after the effective date. To avoid making the law ex post facto, the Court decided that the portion of the act that allowed punitive damages did not apply retroactively. That is, the Court tried both to follow accepted rules of interpretation that dealt with the effective dates of criminal laws and the rule that, if possible, statutes are to be read so as to be constitutional.

The prohibition against ex post facto laws, like the prohibition against bills of attainder, thus has resulted in some complex litigation and has raised difficult problems for courts. The courts have responded with some rational decisions and opinions but also with a substantial amount of inconsistency. They also have interpreted these prohibitions in such a way that they provide less protection than the prohibitions might have provided. If this section is a statement of rights that citizens have against encroachment by Congress, the courts have perhaps favored Congress too much in the cases on Clause 3.

Clause 5: Taxes on Exports

CLAUSE 5. NO TAX OR DUTY SHALL BE LAID ON ARTICLES EXPORTED FROM ANY STATE.

Article 1, § 10, Clause 2, sometimes called the import-export clause because it refers to both kinds of transactions, is similar to Clause 5 of § 9. The other clause reads:

> [n]o state shall, without the consent of the Congress, lay any imposts or duties on imports or exports, except what may be absolutely necessary for executing its inspection laws; and the net produce of all duties and imposts, laid by any state on imports or exports, shall be for the use of the treasury of the United States; and all such laws shall be subject to the revision and control of the Congress.

The book in this series on Article 1, § 10, *Limits on States: A Reference Guide to the U.S. Constitution*, covers that clause. However, looking briefly at it here will shed some light on Article 1, § 9, Clause 5.

In one case, the Court arrived by a round-about route at the meaning of "export" in this clause (Dooley v. United States, 1901). It consulted the definition of "import" that a Court formulated in a case on the other clause (Woodruff v. Parham, 1868). Because Clause 5 and the other one in § 10 have similar subject matter, courts often cited cases on both clauses to support interpretations of Clause 5. In the decisions, courts did not mention that they have conflated the two clauses, much less provide reasons for doing so. For example, in one case the Court cited cases on both clauses to support its position on the relevance of the fact that a general law (one that applied both to goods that were to be exported and to identical goods that were not to be exported) was at issue and to support its position on the constitutionality of taxing goods when they are in the process of being manufactured (A.G. Spalding & Bros. v. Edwards, 1923).

In addition, the existence of the other clause (US Const, Art I, § 10, Clause 2) makes it clear that Clause 5 applies only to the federal government, even though

Clause 5 does not identify the entity to which it is addressed. That is, it would have been illogical for the Framers to draft one provision and specify that it applies to the states and to draft another provision, which is worded similarly, and mean it to apply to both the states and the federal government. Probably because this reasoning is obvious, courts have simply asserted that Clause 5 applies only to the federal government without stating the reason for that assertion (Williams v. Fears, 1900; Fairbank v. United States,1901).

However, the conflation of the judicial interpretations of the two clauses does not mean that any development in the interpretation of one will be reflected in the interpretation of the other. Similarly, changes in the interpretation of the commerce clause (US Const, Article I, § 8, Clause 3) will not necessarily result in changes in interpretations of Article 1, § 9, Clause 5. In a recent case, for example, a corporation challenged the imposition of a tax on premiums that it had paid to foreign insurers in regard to exports of goods to its foreign subsidiaries (United States v. International Business Machines Corp., 1996). As we will see, the court in an earlier case had held that a stamp tax on insurance policies for goods that were to be exported violated Clause 5 (Thames and Mercy Marine Ins. Co. v. United States, 1915). The government conceded that the earlier case was a valid precedent but urged the Court to overrule it because of subsequent cases on the import-export clause and the dormant commerce clause, which is analyzed in *The Dormant Commerce Clause: A Reference Guide to the U.S. Constitution*. The court declined that gambit.

The court acknowledged that in 1976 it had declared constitutional certain nondiscriminatory taxes that had been challenged under the import-export clause (Michelin Tire Corp. v. Wages, 1976; Department of Revenue of Wash. v. Association of Wash. Stevedoring Cos., 1976). However, the court in United States v. International Business Machines Corp. (1996) noted that "our more recent Import-export clauses cases...caution that meaningful textual differences exist." Specifically, "tax," which appears in Article 1, § 9, Clause 5, is a broader term than is "impost," which appears in the import-export clause. Thus, a charge might not be forbidden by Article 1, § 10, Clause 2 because it was not an impost but it would be a species of tax and thus be forbidden under Clause 5. Second, the goals of the two clauses are not only different but also virtually the opposite. The import-export clause "was intended to protect federal supremacy in international commerce, to preserve federal revenue from import duties and imposts, and to prevent coastal States with ports from taking unfair advantage of inland States." In contrast, Clause 5 (the export clause) "specifically prohibits Congress from regulating international commerce through export taxes, disallows any attempt to raise federal revenue from exports, and has no direct effect on the way the States treat imports and exports." This contrast is too strongly worded. If the two sets of policies are not quite opposites, and if the only valid inference is that the Framers inserted two clauses because they intended them to have opposite effects, that is a rather irrational way to write a constitution. Regardless of that problem, the Court inferred that policy-based arguments for conforming the export clause's jurisprudence to that of the import-export clause were invalid. Finally, the Court pointed out that the facts of the present case differed significantly from the facts in the two import-export clause cases on which the government based its arguments.

The argument in the case that relied on a changing view of the dormant commerce clause was also unsuccessful. That clause, in general, forbids the states from enacting statutes that in certain ways inhibit the free flow of interstate commerce, an activity the regulation of which is predominately, under the wording of Article 1, § 8, Clause 3, reserved for the federal government. That is, the clause does not literally exist; it is based on the proposition that if regulation of interstate commerce is reserved for the federal government, then the states may not regulate it. First, the government argued that early cases on Article 1, § 9, Clause 5 rested on the view that the dormant commerce clause forbade the states from taxing interstate commerce. Second, in later cases, most notably Complete Auto Transit v. Brady (1977), the court allowed this kind of taxation if it fulfilled certain specified criteria. Therefore, the court should allow nondiscriminatory taxes on exports. This argument's ingenuity substantially exceeds its intellectual force. The Court in *International Business Machines* rejected it. It might simply have illustrated the many ways in which commerce clause jurisprudence and export clause jurisprudence had diverged since these analogies had been drawn. However, it pointed out that the export clause *explicitly* forbids imposing taxes on exports; whereas, the dormant commerce clause is a negative entity: its meaning rests on a statement that the commerce clause does not make but one that can be inferred from a statement in the clause. This difference, one would assume, justifies a considerably higher degree of flexibility for the dormant commerce clause than for the export clause.

The court in *International Business Machines* correctly asserted that the purposes of the export clause differ from those of the import-export clause. A logical way to begin explicating Clause 5 is to formulate its main purpose as meticulously as possible. The Court in an early case stated this purpose in absolute terms: "[t]he requirement of the Constitution is that exports should be free from any governmental burden" (Fairbank v. United States, 1901). It cited a familiar canard: "the power to tax is the power to destroy" and added that not only taxes in a literal sense but also charges that have the fiscal effect of taxes are destructive. The Court apparently assumed that this chain of logic justified its use of "any" in its statement of the clause's purpose.

A few years later, a Court took a more moderate position on the destructive force that the clause was designed to ward off: "the Constitution provides for a burden only by way of taxation or duty" (Armour Packing Co. v. United States, 1908). This Court thus adverted to the clause's wording instead of viewing taxation with alarm, and as a result expanded the clause's meaning. "Taxation" and "duty" as well as "exports" needed to be defined by case law, and this process resulted in the interpretation that the clause protects exports from considerably less than "any burden."

The first step in defining "tax" is to distinguish exactions under the taxing power—which is granted in Article 1, § 8, Clause 1 and the Sixteenth Amendment—and the commerce power, which is granted in Article 1, § 8, Clause 3 of the Constitution. Expressed in the simplest possible terms, the former power serves to raise revenue, and the latter power serves to regulate commerce. One way to decide whether an exaction is a tax is simply to accept as dispositive its label. A more rational way is to determine the exaction's purpose. An unusual concatenation of facts in an early case facilitates one's understanding of the difference (Pace v. Burgess, 1875). At one time tobacco was taxed and affixing stamps to it provided evidence that the tax was paid. However, tobacco that was to be exported was exempted from tax, as Clause 5 required. The exemption was a potential temptation to claim that one's tobacco was to be exported even if this was not the intent. The government's countermove was to require a different kind of stamp to be purchased and affixed to tobacco destined for export. The Court held that the latter kind of stamp was required merely "to separate and identify the tobacco which the manufacturer desired to export and thereby, instead of taxing it, to relieve it from taxation to which other tobacco was subjected." In other words, the stamps that tobacco to be exported bore helped to prevent fraud. The commerce clause provided the authority for requiring them. In contrast, the general tax was levied under the taxing power in order to raise revenue. A few years later another Court, following *Pace*, upheld an exaction for special stamps that were used to identify tobacco that was to be exported (Turpin v. Burgess, 1886).

A later Court correctly characterized Pace v. Burgess, pointing out that the charge for the stamps that were to be affixed to tobacco destined for export was designed to recover the costs of providing and affixing the stamps (Fairbank v. United States, 1901). That is, it was for the administrative expenses of regulation. The charge for stamps in *Fairbank* was designed to raise revenue, because a regulatory purpose was absent and there was a huge discrepancy between the costs incurred by exporters compared to the costs incurred by non-exporters indicated. Thus, this charge was a tax under Clause 5.

In deciding whether an exaction is designed for regulation or for revenue, courts will look beyond its label and even beyond the use of the money generated by it. In a recent case, the pertinent exaction was called a harbor maintenance tax (United States v. United States Shoe Corporation, 1998). Most likely, its proceeds were used for the purpose identified by its label. One can plausibly argue that maintaining harbors is a regulatory purpose, particularly because the taxpayers used the harbor. Moreover, all users of the harbor were subject to the exaction. For these reasons, the Court might have ignored the presence of "tax" in the exaction's label, and instead concentrated on the phrase "harbor maintenance" to decide that the exaction was a user fee, not a tax. However, the court noted that the tax was imposed on an ad valorem (according to value) basis. Thus, the amount paid bore no relation to the degree to which the harbor was used; whereas, a standard fee would have born a reasonable relation to this use. The Court held that the exaction therefore was not a user fee but a tax.

One can conveniently come to understand the meaning of "tax" in Clause 5 by first examining some exactions that were held not to be taxes and then examining some exactions that were held to be taxes. We have seen one exaction that was held not to be a tax: the charge for the stamps that identified tobacco that was intended for export and thus would be exempt from a general tax on that product (Pace v. Burgess, 1875). Another "cost," using the term in a very broad sense, was also held not to be a tax (Armour Packing Co. v. United States, 1908). To export goods lawfully, the shipper had to comply with the relevant established rate on file with the Interstate Commerce Commission. The shipper argued that the restriction coerced it into accepting lower rates than it could charge otherwise, which burdened its export business. The Court, reading the clause literally, responded that "the Constitution provides for a burden only by way of taxation or duty."

The income tax is, in common parlance, certainly a tax, but it is not a tax for purposes of Clause 5 (William E. Peck & Co. v. Lowe, 1918). The company had argued that the portion of its income taxes attributable to its export business were exempt under this clause. The Court held that the income tax is imposed on *net* income. That is, all the company's taxable income was aggregated, certain deductions were allowed, and net income was thereby calculated and then multiplied by a rate to arrive at the tax due. The court asserted that the tax was therefore remote from exportation. The court considered the remoteness in temporal terms, stating that if articles before exportation were not exempt under this clause neither was net income as calculated well after the exportation. Perhaps a better analysis would have been that, in regard to an income tax, the amount of tax that was attributable to exports was incalculable. This was because the intermingling of expenses in the calculation leads to the impossibility of rationally allocating deductions to the export business so as to set them off against income. That is, the company's entire business, not each separate function of it, was taxable, a fact that reflected the company's unitary existence. It follows that user fees, required rates, and the portion of income taxes that, were it possible, could be attributed to export are not taxes under Clause 5. In summary, the early view that this clause prohibits every burden on exportation has been considerably eroded (Fairbank v. United States, 1901).

At this point, one can divide the universe of exactions that are relevant to this clause into two parts: exactions on property and those that are not on property (required rates and portions of income taxes). Then, one can subdivide taxes on property into user fees (which are not invalidated by Clause 5) and taxes (which might be invalidated by Clause 5). The next step is to examine the kinds of property for which taxation has been an issue under this clause. One naturally thinks first of the property that is to be exported. Courts have considered the constitutionality of a number of taxes that were imposed directly on goods that were, or were intended to be, exported. Among them are filled cheese (Cornell v. Coyne, 1904), baseball equipment (A.G. Spalding & Bros. v. Edwards, 1923), and shoes (United States v. United States Shoe Corporation, 1998). The filled cheese was taxable, and the baseball equipment and shoes were exempt. These results did not depend on the fact that the property itself was taxed but on other factors.

More difficult cases involved the question of whether Clause 5's prohibition against taxing exports extends to taxes on property other than the goods that are to be exported. An example is a tax that is evidenced by a stamp and is imposed on bills of lading (a document that includes an acknowledgment of the receipt of goods and the terms under which they are to be transported and delivered). In *Fairbank*, another law that required carriers to issue bills of lading or similar documents to shippers and consignors was relevant because it required that goods could not legally be exported unless a bill of lading applied to them (Fairbank v. United States, 1901). The Court held that "[a] stamp tax on a bill of lading is in substance and effect equivalent to a tax on the articles included in that bill of lading and therefore a tax or duty on exports."

Another case involved a similar document: a charter party, a document that applies to an entire cargo in ways similar to those in which a bill of lading applies to part of a cargo (United States v. Hvoslef, 1915). As one would expect from the similarities of the two documents, the decision in the two cases was the same. The Court in the later case held that the tax was imposed on exportation. That is, although it was not imposed on goods that were to be exported, it was imposed on the process of exportation. The Court continued that "a tax on exportation is a tax on exports." To phrase it differently, "this constitutional freedom...plainly involves more than mere exemption from taxes or duties which are laid specifically upon the goods themselves."

In the same year the Court held that a stamp tax imposed on an underwriter of marine insurance that was written to cover a shipment for export was covered by Clause 5's prohibition (Thames & Mersey Marine Ins. Co. v. United States, 1915). The Court framed the case's dispositive question thus: "[i]s the tax upon such policies so directly and closely related to the 'process of exporting' that the tax is in substance a tax upon the exportation and hence within the constitutional prohibition?" By this time, the Court had begun to assume that Clause 5 applied not only to exports (goods) but also to exportation (the process of transporting goods out of this country). The issue in this case therefore became the propinquity to this process of the issuance of the document on which the tax was imposed. The next link in the chain of reasoning was finding that exporting requires "appropriate provision for indemnity against marine risks during the voyage." The fact that the case was heard during World War I, when goods that were shipped by sea were often at risk, probably made it more likely that the Court would come to this conclusion.

Moreover, the Court found that insurance policies are regarded in the trade, like bills of lading, as one of the ordinary "shipping documents": documents that were necessary in order to ship goods. Payment for the documents, which is the consideration for their transportation, includes payment for insurance. The final link in the chain of reasoning is that the "taxation does not deal with preliminaries, or with distinct or separable subjects; the tax falls upon the exporting process." The link between this process and "exports," the term in the clause, had already been made, so the tax was held to be unconstitutional. In a recent case, the federal government indicated its resignation to the fact that taxes on marine insurance were prohibited by this clause and argued instead that changes in commerce clause jurisprudence justified reversal of *Thames & Mersey Marine Ins. Co.* (United States v. International Business Machines Corp., 1996).

The government would probably also be resigned to the same result in regard to taxes on other documents that are essential to exportation. In another case, the Court identified in dicta the kinds of things that, under this clause and in addition to articles that actually are in the course of exportation, must be exempt from taxation: "anything which inherently or by the usages of commerce is embraced in exportation or any of its processes" (William E. Peck & Co. v. Lowe, 1918).

Another attribute of taxes, their discriminatory or nondiscriminatory nature regarding exports, has played a part in some of the cases in which this clause was litigated. *Fairbank* involved a blatantly discriminatory tax. The rate of a tax on bills of lading was one cent per bill that applied to goods that were not to be exported and seventy cents per bill that applied to goods that were to be exported (Fairbank v. United States, 1901). That vast discrepancy, however, played no part in the Court's decision. The Court held that the clause required a complete lack of burden on exports and mentioned that the amount of the tax was irrelevant. If the amount was irrelevant, the amount as compared to the amount of the tax on non-exports was also irrelevant.

A more difficult question is the role that uniformity of taxation plays in deciding whether a tax violates this clause. On the one hand, a tax that applied uniformly to exports and non-exports was upheld, the Court remarking that "[s]ubjecting filled cheese manufactured for the purpose of export to the same tax as all other filled cheese is casting no tax or duty on articles exported, but is only a tax or duty on the manufacturing of articles in order to prepare them for export" (Cornell v. Coyne, 1904). On the other hand, other courts have found uniform taxes to be unconstitutional under this clause. In the case on charter parties, the Court remarked that the fact that the tax applied to all charter parties of a certain tonnage or more did not make it constitutional (United States v. Hvoslef, 1915). Similarly, the tax on baseball equipment that the Court struck down applied to this kind of equipment whether or not it was to be exported (A.G. Spalding & Bros. v. Edwards, 1923). The harbor maintenance tax, which also was held to be unconstitutional, applied to exporters, importers, and local shippers (United States v.

United States Shoe Corporation, 1998). Sorting out these cases is difficult because each of them presents a wide variety of facts in addition to the tax's discriminatory or nondiscriminatory nature.

Fairbank is the only case in which a discriminatory rate applied, and the tax at issue was unconstitutional, but not for this reason (Fairbank v. United States, 1901). However, it seems that obvious discrimination against exports; whether in regard to one of the attributes of the tax, such as the rate, or in regard to taxing only exports, would be unconstitutional. The nondiscriminatory nature of the tax on filled cheese was one factor in the determination that it was constitutional (Cornell v. Coyne, 1904). However, nondiscriminatory taxes were struck down in other cases (United States v. Hvoslef, 1915; A.G. Spalding & Bros. v. Edwards, 1923; United States v. United States Shoe Corporation, 1998). The most logical conclusions that one can draw from this welter of data are that uniformity is a necessary, but not a sufficient, attribute of a tax that will pass muster under this clause and that another factor, or other factors, are more important in determining whether a tax is constitutional.

The other, crucial factor in the cases on Clause 5 is the point in the chain of events leading from manufacture to departure from this country at which the exaction is imposed. However, before explicating this issue, it is necessary to ascertain which ultimate destinations make these events lead to an export, instead of to something else. The common definition of the term "export" is, of course, a shipment to another country. A Court arrived at that meaning, but not by resort to common usage (Dooley v. United States, 1901). Instead, it noted that in an earlier case on the import-export clause the noun "import" was defined as articles imported from foreign countries into the United States (Woodruff v. Parham, 1868). The court then stated that "export" had a "correlative meaning" in this clause. That is, the noun "export" meant goods shipped from this country to another country, and the verb "export" then meant to accomplish this kind of shipment. The Court could also have noted that Clause 6 of § 9 prohibits requiring vessels engaged in interstate shipping to pay duties to either the state from which they leave or to the state at which they arrive. Although that clause does not mention other forms of transportation, there would be considerable overlap between the two clauses if Clause 5 were interpreted as applying to interstate shipments.

A major theme in the case law on Clause 5 is the courts' efforts to "fix a point at which, in view of the purpose of the Constitution, the export must be said to begin" (A.G. Spalding & Bros. v. Edwards, 1923). This is a crucial determination, because "[a]rticles in course of transportation [abroad] cannot be taxed" (A. G. Spalding & Bros. v. Edwards, 1923). Goods that have not left the factory have not begun to be exported and thus are taxable (Turpin v. Burgess, 1886). The Court placed this point in the process earlier than the point at which a tax may constitutionally be imposed, asserting that the exemption "has reference to the imposition of duties on goods by reason or because of their exportation or intended exportation, or whilst they are being exported." The Court also remarked that certain goods that were still at a factory might be destined for export but might not in fact be exported later. To exempt these goods would create a windfall for their owners.

A later Court arrived at the rule set forth in Turpin v. Burgess (1886), but took a different route to get to it (Cornell v. Coyne, 1904). The Court stated that Clause 5 means that

> [n]o burden by way of tax or duty can be cast upon the exportation of articles, and does not mean that articles exported are relieved from the prior ordinary burdens of taxation which rest upon all property similarly situated. The exemption attaches to the export, and not to the article before its exportation.

Like the tax in *Turpin*, the tax in this case was imposed at the factory, and the Court characterized the law that was at issue in the case as "casting no tax or duty on articles exported [but as casting] only a tax or duty on the manufacturing of articles in order to prepare them for export."

The earliest point that was held to be after exportation began, and therefore after a tax could not constitutionally be imposed, was the transfer of goods to a commission merchant (A.G. Spalding & Bros. v. Edwards, 1923). In this case, the commission merchant gave the manufacturer an "export order" that specified the ship that was to carry the merchandise. The title of the document and a reference in it to possible heavy fines imposed by foreign customs houses in the event of errors in weighing or marking clearly indicated that exportation was contemplated. The taxable event was the change of title from the manufacturer to the commission merchant in response to the export order. After obtaining title, the commission merchant obtained a bill of lading, and, still later, the goods were shipped to Venezuela. The Court held that the transfer of title at the time when the export order was given to the manufacturer, in light of the circumstances surrounding it, led inexorably to exportation, and that, therefore, the sale could not constitutionally be taxed. Specifically, transfer of the title "committed the goods to the carrier that was to take them across the sea, for the purpose of export and with the direction to the foreign port upon the goods. The expected and accomplished effect of the act was to start them for that port." The fact that other events had to occur before the ship left did not negate the inevitability of exportation that the transfer of title established.

We have seen that taxes imposed on certain kinds of documents have been found to be unconstitutional under Clause 5, because the owner of the goods had to obtain those documents in order for the exportation to occur. These documents are bills of lading (Fairbank v. United States, 1901), charter parties (United States v. Hvoslef, 1915), and marine insurance (Thames & Mersey Marine Ins. Co. v. United States, 1915). They were obtained after the goods were manufactured and before, in some cases well before, the goods left a location in this country for a location in another country. The bill of lading in *A.G. Spalding & Bros.* was obtained after the taxable event in that case, so obtaining these documents is later in the possible chain of events than the transfer of title. Obtaining these documents should be on the exempt side of the "tax–exempt" continuum, because the documents are sufficiently detailed and specific to indicate that the goods will be exported. For example, the difference between the rate for exports and the rate for non-exports in regard to the tax on bills of lading indicated that a tax administrator could determine from the face of the bill of lading whether the goods to which it applied were to be exported. Similarly, the charter parties in United States v. Hvoslef (1915) on them were negotiated with brokers who arranged for shipment abroad, so the goods that they, too, covered were definitely to be exported. The marine insurance policy would specify on its face the point of destination, so that it would be known for certain at the time whether the goods were to be exported (Thames & Mersey Marine Ins. Co. v. United States, 1915). In all these instances, therefore, it had been decided by the seller that the goods were to be exported. That fact differs from the taxation at the factory of goods, that, a Court had noted, might not actually be exported (Turpin v. Burgess, 1886). Bills of lading, charter parties, and marine insurance are, to borrow a term from one of the cases, "shipping documents," and obtaining them is thus part of the process of exportation (Thames & Mersey Marine Ins. Co. v. United States, 1915).

If the events described above may not constitutionally be taxable events, then later events may not be taxable either. One recent case dealt with an event, in fact with one that occurs very close to the time when the goods left the country, and thus the goods escaped this country's jurisdiction to tax (United States v. United States Shoe Corporation, 1998). This case dealt with a harbor maintenance tax, which was imposed when goods were loaded on a ship bound for a foreign port. In light of the previous cases, the government eschewed the argument that the exaction came too early in the process to fall under the export clause. Well might it have done so. The government argued instead, unsuccessfully, that the exaction was not a tax but a user fee. The cases to this time were perfectly consistent on the issue of drawing, in the chain of events leading to exportation, a line between taxable and exempt events.

One other case deals with the relevance of the timing of the taxable event to the constitutionality under the export clause of taxation (William E. Peck & Co. v. Lowe, 1918). In this case, the Court decided that there was a second dividing line between constitutional taxable events and unconstitutional taxable events, that a taxable event can occur so late that a constitutional tax may be imposed at the time it occurs. At the earlier dividing line, taxability gives way to exemption, and at the later one exemption gives way to taxability. This case on the later dividing line is the income tax case, in which the Court held that the calculation of the tax occurred too late and that so much financial data had accrued by then, that neither the tax nor the portion of it that was attributable to exporting (which could not be computed anyway) was prohibited by Clause 5. In a sense, this case stands solely for the proposition that this clause does not apply to an income tax. However, the Court made much of the fact that the tax was calculated too late, so it is logical to consider the case was also about timing.

One minor issue remains. This is, whether it is necessary to protest a tax in order to preserve one's right to litigate it under Clause 5 (the export clause). In an early case, the issue was a tax on a manifest (a document that lists the cargo, destination, and other information that is usually intended for use by customs agents) (United States v. New York & Cuba Mail S. S. Co., 1906). A manifest is a "shipping document," as the court in *Thomas & Mersey Marine Ins. Co.* used the term. Therefore, if the court adhered to the views of the courts that decided cases involving other shipping documents, the tax would be unconstitutional. The Court did not discuss the merits of the case, however; it stated that the taxpayer had paid the tax "voluntarily and without protest," thereby negating the taxpayer's right to recover the payment. A few years later, a Court held that a statute that was similar to the one at issue in the earlier case and that replaced it explicitly stated that no protest was needed and that Congress probably meant this rule to apply to the later statute (United States v. Hvoslef, 1915). This is a reach, but it brings the case into line with the prevailing modern rule of taxation: that no protest is necessary, particularly when constitutional issues are involved.

The case law on the export clause is impressive for its consistency and its conformity to the policy substratum of the clause. A few anomalies exist: the absolute prohibition on burdening exportation in one case (Fairbank v. United States, 1901) and the requirement of a protest to preserve the right to recovery of taxes paid in another case (United States v. New York & Cuba Mail S.S. Co., 1906). Although the former case has not been explicitly overruled, its value as a precedent has been severely diminished by later cases. Regarding the important issues, the distinction between taxes and other exactions is rational and that distinction is applied to the facts in a rational fashion. One of the Court's options was to interpret the clause literally by holding that it prohibits taxes levied directly upon goods for export and that goods can be taxed only at the time when they are about to leave the country. This would have allowed considerable maneuvering by the government to circumvent the definite boundary between taxable and nontaxable events and thereby to impose taxes. It also would have run counter to the clause's purpose. The courts declined that gambit. Even more impressive is the consistency with which courts have analyzed the various exactions in temporal terms, drawing two firm and logically situated lines at the borders between constitutionally permissible taxes and constitutionally impermissible taxes. In the process of deciding the cases on Clause 5, the Court validated its importance. Certainly if the Court had riddled the export clause with loopholes, even a modest tax increase in revenues from the vast volume of this country's exports would have been fiscally significant.

Clause 6: Preferences to Ports

CLAUSE 6. NO PREFERENCE SHALL BE GIVEN BY ANY REGULATION OF COMMERCE OR REVENUE TO THE PORTS OF ONE STATE OVER THOSE OF ANOTHER; NOR SHALL VESSELS BOUND TO, OR FROM, ONE STATE, BE OBLIGED TO ENTER, CLEAR OR PAY DUTIES IN ANOTHER.

This clause resembles the limit on the taxing power of Congress in Article 1, § 8, Clause 1. After granting the power to tax, that clause provides "all duties, imposts and excises shall be uniform throughout the United States." The requirement of uniformity, as it applies to exactions imposed on goods moving by water into a port in this country, is similar to Clause 6's statement that "[n]o preference shall be given by any Regulation...or Revenue to the Ports of one State over those of another." The latter prohibition would be redundant if Clause 6 applied to entities other than Congress, such as the states, but, as we shall see, that is not the case.

In fact, courts have stated repeatedly, and almost invariably, that Clause 6 applies only to Congress. An exception is two early cases that were consolidated (Smith v. Turner and Norris v. Boston, 1849). In these cases, the Court held that the clause is "binding" on the states. The Court remarked that the purpose of Clause 6 and of Article 1, § 10, which limits the authority of states to lay imposts and duties, was to create uniformity of duties. The Court wrote, "it is inexplicable to me how thirteen or more independent states could tax imports under these provisions" and maintain uniformity. The Court held that the duties imposed by the states were unconstitutional for that reason and also because the states, in imposing them, were usurping the federal power to regulate commerce. These are distinctly minority positions, and the precedential value of these two cases is probably nil.

In another early case, a person who had been fined for operating a warehouse without a license and for charging rates higher than those allowed by law sued Illinois, alleging, among other things, that this state had violated Clause 6 (Munn v. Illinois, 1876). The Court stated that the clause does not apply to states. Ten years later, a Court held the same and cited *Munn* as the authority for its position (Johnson v. Chicago & P. Elevator Co., 1886). That same year, the Court reached the same result by a different method (Morgan v. Louisiana, 1886). The Court in *Morgan* asserted that the clause "is not found among the restrictions of the States, but among those imposed upon the federal government." It is true that Article 1, § 10 lists restrictions that apply to the states, and it is true that, under the case law, Section 9 applies to Congress, but the text of § 9 does not explicitly state that it applies to Congress. Nevertheless, by the end of the nineteenth century, the application of Clause 6 had been definitively limited to Congress. By 1931 courts were merely referring to the limitations on Congress under this clause, without giving reasons why it applies only to Congress (Louisiana Pub. Serv. Comm. v. Texas & N.O.R. Co., 1931).

Clause 6 thus applies to Congress but not to the states. A Court disposed far too brusquely of an interesting argument that the clause applies to actions that Congress permits the states to take (Thompson v. Darden, 1905). Congress had, by statute, permitted the states to require that ships traveling in state's waters have pilots who fulfilled requirements specified by the state. The plaintiff in *Thompson* argued that the requirement was a burden and was therefore a preference for ports that did not impose the requirement. The Court disregarded the argument with the terse remark that many cases (not cited) indicated that Congress had the right to allow the states to impose this requirement. The Court could have made a better answer by pointing out that Congress had not preferred specific ports. However, by authorizing the states to impose this requirement, Congress had made it possible for certain states to become more attractive to shippers by eschewing their right to require pilots and that Congress' connection to that "preference" was too indirect to be a violation of this clause.

Because this clause applies to Congress, it constitutes a limit on Congress' power to regulate commerce under the commerce clause of the Constitution (US Const, Art I, § 8, Clause 3) (see *The Reserved Commerce Power: A Reference Guide to the U.S. Constitution*). As a court considering a challenge under Clause 6 (prohibiting preference to ports) noted, this power is nearly plenary, being limited only by other constitutional provisions (Louisiana Pub. Serv. Comm. v. Texas & N.O.R. Co., 1931). For this proposition, the court cited the classic case on the vast reach of Congress' power over commerce (Gibbons v. Ogden, 1824). The references in the preference clause to revenue and duties also limit Congress' power to tax under Article 1, § 8, Clause 1 and the Sixteenth Amendment (see *The Taxing and Borrowing Powers: A Reference Guide to the U.S. Constitution*).

When the Constitution was framed, marine transport was vital to the economy. Since then, of course, other means of transportation have eroded the importance of that kind of transport. Nevertheless, Clause 6 is, on its face, potentially a powerful constraint on Congress' power. However, the case law has severely diminished this constraint. One important diminution is the principle that in determining whether this clause has been violated, the proper object of attention is not the effect of a statute or action on one port as compared to another but the effect of a statute or action on the ports of one state as compared to the ports of another state. As Part I indicates, this was the Framers' intent. One court stated the prohibition thus: "what is forbidden is, not discrimination between individual ports within the same or different States, but discrimination between States" (Pennsylvania v. Wheeling & Belmont Bridge Co., 1855). To substantiate its view, this court adverted not to the debates at the Constitutional Convention but to a logical analysis, pointing out that if the other possible view of the requirement were adopted Congress would, for example, have to make every port a port of entry if it did so for one port. An even more powerful example is federal appropriations. If this clause prohibited discrimination as to individual ports, an appropriation to one port would have to be accompanied by equivalent appropriations to every port. The determination of equivalency would add another layer of problems. Would an appropriation for dredging at one port require an appropriation for the same purpose at every port? Dredging, by making it possible for larger vessels to use a port, would, at least potentially, increase a port's revenue, which would be an advantage. Granting this advantage to only one port would be giving it a preference. Would the amount of each appropriation have to be equal or would equivalency be determined by means of a formula that reflected the port's size or the amount of its activity (and how would that be measured)? The Court took a wise view of the kind of discrimination that the clause prohibits. After this view became established, courts often merely stated it (Louisiana Pub. Serv. Comm. v. Texas & N.O.R. Co, 1931; Armour Packing Co. v. United States, 1908).

However, in two cases the Court had to decide whether the rule that comparison was to be made state by state must be taken literally. One case involved a statute that forbade, with certain exceptions, the transportation of merchandise between points in the United States, including Alaska, which at the time was a territory, "in any other vessel than a vessel built in and documented under the laws of the United States and owned by persons who are citizens of the United States" (Territory of Alaska v. Troy, 1922). The requirement of ownership by citizens of this country would have excluded ships owned by residents of Alaska and, in the Court's view, would have created a preference for ports of all the states as compared to the ports of Alaska. However, the Court upheld the statute on the ground that Alaska was a territory and that the clause did not forbid preferences for the ports of states as compared to the ports of territories. This made good sense because the residents of territories do not have the complete panoply of rights and privileges that are available to citizens of the United States. The same issue arose, and was decided the same way, in an earlier case regarding Puerto Rico (Downes v. Bidwell, 1901). The Court in this case mentioned that when the treaty that implemented the Louisiana Purchase was debated some persons raised a concern that a provision that admitted French and Spanish ships into the port of New Orleans in exchange for a duty that did not exceed the duty assessed against American ships might violate this clause. The land purchased would initially be a territory, so if the principle that later pertained in the case law on this clause applied to the land that was acquired by the Louisiana Purchase, this provision in the treaty would not have been unconstitutional under Clause 6. The issue of the fate of territories under this clause, although not moot, has clearly diminished since Hawaii and Alaska became states.

The Courts' decision about the basis of the comparison to be used in determining whether an unconstitutional preference has been given has limited this clause's scope. In fact, the bulk of the case law on this clause limits its scope. A principle limit is the commerce power of Congress. In one case, the issue was a failure to obey an injunction that would have stopped the construction of a bridge across the Ohio River (Pennsylvania v. Wheeling & Belmont Bridge Co., 1855). A federal statute had authorized that construction, and the bridge, upon completion, would have stopped travel upstream on the river at Wheeling, thus disadvantaging ports in Pennsylvania. The Court adverted to the commerce clause:

> there are many acts of congress passed in the exercise of this power to regulate commerce providing for a special advantage to the port or ports of one State, and which very advantage may incidentally operate to the prejudice of the ports in a neighboring State, which have never been supposed to conflict with this limitation on its power.

At first glance the Court appears to mean that any exercise of the commerce power is valid notwithstanding this clause. Virtually all potential violations of the clause would involve an exercise of the commerce power. If this is the Court's holding, Clause 6 is virtually, or actually, a nullity. In this statement, the Court supported its position with a vague reference to the contrary view not having been presented.

Fortunately, the Court continued its statement. It made clear that the operative word in the passage just quoted is "incidentally." Its point is that the commerce clause is not trumped by an incidental effect, and it argued that if the contrary view were accepted "upon any such interpretation, the principal object of the framers of the [Constitution] in conferring the [commerce] power would be sacrificed to the subordinate consequences resulting from its exercise." In other words, the Court recognized that two constitutional provisions, Clause 6 and the commerce clause, would occasionally conflict. In these instances, if this clause were vindicated the commerce power would be diminished. Conversely, if the commerce clause were vindicated, this clause would be diminished. In response to that dilemma, the Court implied that the result would be determined by deciding which clause was primarily at play and which was incidentally at play. This could be done in at least two ways. One is to examine the intent of Congress. The other is to determine from the facts whether the advancement of commerce or the disadvantaging of the ports of a state was more significant.

Rigorous application of either method would be difficult, especially because determining Congressional intent is usually difficult. However, if this method is used, it would always be difficult to argue credibly that the main purpose of Congress in enacting a particular piece of legislation was to prefer ports in one state over those in another state. If the second method is used, a delicate weighing of effects would be necessary. The passage about many such acts never having been supposed to violate this clause implies that the case has a subtext: the commerce clause is more significant than Clause 6. The results in the other cases on this clause suggest that this is indeed the view of courts.

One limit is an exception to the clause's constraints for a subset of governmental action. At issue in a case was the construction of a dam on a river that formed the border between two states (South Carolina v. Georgia, 1876). Congress had appropriated money for the dam, so Clause 6 potentially was a problem. The dam had altered the predominant course of river traffic so as to favor one of the states. This constituted a preference for the ports of one state. The ingredients for a successful challenge to the federal action appeared to be present. However, the Court held that the commerce clause gave Congress the power to control navigation on rivers that formed the borders between states. Transportation on them is, by definition, interstate and thus within the commerce clause's reach. Thus, again, the commerce clause trumped Clause 6.

Reasonable ratemaking is another exception to this clause. In one case, the Interstate Commerce Commission had prescribed rates for the transportation of sand, gravel, and other material used to construct roads in a number of southern states (Louisiana Pub. Serv. Comm v. Texas & N.O.R. Co., 1931). These rates included an eight cents per ton add-on cost for material of this kind that was shipped across the Mississippi River. The result was an advantage for Texas ports over Louisiana ports. The Court noted the power of the commerce clause, and it found the rate differential to be reasonable because "[s]ubstantial additions to rates...are necessary to cover extraordinary costs of service." The Court apparently meant that crossing the Mississippi added significantly to the expense of transportation and that the incremental expense should be reflected in higher rates. Louisiana, no doubt due to its determination to aid its own ports, had refused to apply the federal rates. The Court responded that not only were the rates a justifiable regulation of commerce under the commerce clause but also Louisiana's rate structure violated that clause by discriminating against interstate commerce.

Another exception appeared in two cases. A forfeiture for failing to secure the services of a pilot was held not to violate either of Clause 6's provisions (Cooley v. Board of Wardens of Port of Philadelphia, 1851). Pilotage fees are not "duties," so they do not violate the clause's prohibition of this kind of charge, and in this instance the fee did not give a preference to Philadelphia, the defendant in the case. In fact, being a charge, it disadvantaged Philadelphia by "tend[ing] to check its commerce." More than fifty years later, pilotage fees were again an issue

(Thompson v. Darden, 1905). The facts were very similar; the alleged two violations of this clause were the same, and the decision was the same.

The result of another case makes good sense, although its reasoning makes no sense at all (Williams v. United States, 1921). The plaintiff had challenged on a number of grounds, including this clause, a federal law that made it illegal to transport alcoholic beverages into a state where prohibition was in effect. The argument relating to this clause was that the law created a preference for the ports of states where prohibition was not in effect. The Court rejected this argument on the grounds that previous cases had established that constitutional arguments under this clause were frivolous. However, in neither of the cases cited was this clause an issue (Clark Distilling Co. v. Western Maryland Railway Co, 1917; United States v. Hill, 1919). Both cases were about the constitutionality under the commerce clause of regulation of the trade in alcohol beverages. A better argument would have been that the commerce power justified the federal statute and that if a preference for ports resulted it was an incidental effect and therefore did not violate this clause. So the most compelling precedent was Pennsylvania v. Wheeling & Belmont Bridge Co. Thus, although the Court misrepresented the precedents that it cited, its decision that enforcement of prohibition did not violate Clause 6 makes sense.

In addition to the cases in which the commerce clause was held to have more force than does this clause, the other main category of case in which this clause was held not to be dispositive are those in which a governmental action enhanced the importance of an existing factor. In a case involving railroad rates that were fixed by the federal government, the Court wrote that

> [i]t may be true that the regulation of interstate commerce by rail has the effect to give an advantage to commerce wholly by water and to ports which can be reached by means of inland navigation, but these are natural advantages and are not created by statutory law. The fact that regulation, within the acknowledged power of Congress to enact, may affect the ports of one state more than those of another, cannot be construed as a violation of this constitutional provision. (Armour Packing Co. v. United States, 1908)

A similar case was about an order issued by the Interstate Commerce Commission that required certain railroads and certain barge lines to establish joint through routes and to apply to them joint rates that were based on prescribed differentials from the applicable rates for transportation entirely by rail (Alabama G.S.R. Co. v. United States, 1951). The Court's response was similar: "whatever preference there is to New Orleans is the result of geography and not of any action of the Commission." A rational way to conceptualize these two cases and to group them with a third case is to note that they involve governmental decisions that apply generally throughout the pertinent states and that any differential treatment of the ports of these states results not from the governmental actions but from the effect of these actions on existing conditions. The third case is another rate case that was previously examined (Louisiana Pub. Serv. Comm. v. Texas & N.O.R. Co., 1931).

The existing condition that made the difference in this case was the passage of the Mississippi River through Louisiana rather than along its border. The Court remarked that the order making the rates "applied generally throughout the above-mentioned states."

Finally, regarding the limits on the application of the no preference clause, the plaintiff must be harmed by the action of which the plaintiff complains. In two cases, both dealing with the transportation of coal, the cCurt adverted to this principle in deciding against the plaintiff (Avent v. United States, 1924; United States v. P. Koenig Coal Co., 1926). One would expect this result from the generally applicable rules of standing to sue, so it is no surprise to discover it in the context of the preference clause.

In contrast to the many cases in which this clause was found to have only a weak effect, courts have been willing at least to consider its effect in some kinds of cases that would not necessarily be reached by the plain meaning of Clause 6. We have seen a number of cases in which the court held that this clause does not apply to the states but instead applies to Congress. Other Courts were willing to assume that it also applies to federal agencies. This broadening makes sense. In the early days of this country, the power of the executive branch was, of course, minimal. More recently, it has grown, so that any control limited to Congressional actions would be only a piecemeal measure. Moreover, the executive agencies operate under statutes that Congress passed and under regulations that they promulgate themselves but that must have a basis in federal statutes. As one would expect, the agency to which the extension applied was the Interstate Commerce Commission (Louisiana Pub. Serv. Comm. v. Texas & N.O.R. Co., 1931; Alabama G.S.R. Co. v. United States, 1951).

Second, the usual meaning of "port" is a place on an ocean or other large body of water where ships can enter, dock, and exit. However, courts have been willing to consider governmental actions that affect locations on rivers where these three actions may be accomplished (Pennsylvania v. Wheeling & Belmont Bridge Co., 1855; South Carolina v. Georgia, 1876). Again, historical developments made this a wise expansion. In the eighteenth century most of the states had ports on the Atlantic Ocean, and the scarcity of internal improvements made inland movement by water relatively insignificant. However, as new states that were located to the west, and thus had no Atlantic ports, were added to the Union and as internal improvements made river traffic more frequent and important, it became prudent to stretch the meaning of "port" to include ports on rivers. This comports with the clause's purpose of prohibiting the federal government from granting commercial preferences to some states. Moreover, the Court did not stretch the term's meaning beyond all recognition.

It should be noted, however, that in one case the Court, although it dealt very tersely with Clause 6, seemed to be disallowing a different kind of expansion of the meaning of "port" (Edye v. Robertson, 1884). In that case, the plaintiff argued that the imposition of a tax on ship owners who transported persons from other countries to this country violated Clause 6 because the tax was not imposed on the owners of other means of transportation who brought persons from other countries to this country. This argument is somewhat bizarre, so the Court was justified in merely stating that the law applied equally to all ports. Probing beyond the court's response, however, one can imagine the argument that probably was made. It might have been that immigrants entered some "ports," but not all "ports," by non-marine forms of transportation and that the tax therefore discriminated against the latter because all forms of transportation that bore immigrants were taxed in them but not in the other kind of "port." For this argument to make any sense, one would have to define "port" as it is used in Clause 6 as a city that is located on navigable water. This would broaden the reach of this clause to ludicrous proportions because any preference to this kind of city in one state but not in another would violate this clause. The clause, however, to make sense, must regulate cities only as they operate as ports, not in all respects.

Finally, courts declined to dispose of some cases by claiming that the action at issue did not occur at a port but occurred elsewhere and affected ports (Louisiana Pub. Serv. Comm. v. Texas & N.O.R. Co., 1931; Armour Packing Co. v. United States, 1908; Territory of Alaska v. Troy, 1922; Alabama G.S.R. Co. v. United States, 1951). These cases are about a higher rate for trans-Mississipi River shipping, the regulation of railroad rates, requiring pilots who are licensed by this country, and requiring certain railroads and certain barge lines to establish joint through routes. The willingness of courts to consider the third category of cases on their merits and to weigh the contested legislation against the requirements of this clause was certainly proper. Failing to do so would have introduced an exception that has no basis in the clause's text and would be contrary to the intent of the Framers.

Despite the Court's willingness to get to the merits in the three kinds of cases just adumbrated, the result of its doing so is to uphold the constitutionality of the governmental action. Only in two early cases, which were consolidated, has a Court held that there was a violation of this clause (Smith v. Turner and Norris v. Boston, 1849). The reasoning in those cases is tortuous; the prose is turgid; and other courts have consistently rejected the positions espoused in them, particularly the position that this clause applies to states. It is difficult to imagine that these cases are valid precedents. If one dismisses them as anomalies, then the Court has shown no willingness to apply this clause rigorously or to use it as a reason to declare statutes or governmental acts unconstitutional. However, the federal government has shown no interest in creating the kind of direct and intentional preferences that this clause was designed to preclude, and the political process would most likely thwart any such attempts. A blatant attempt to favor directly the ports in one state would have considerable difficulty winning approval by Congress.

Clause 7: No Money to Be Drawn from the Treasury but by Appropriation

CLAUSE 7. NO MONEY SHALL BE DRAWN FROM THE TREASURY, BUT IN CONSEQUENCE OF APPROPRIATIONS MADE BY LAW; AND A REGULAR STATEMENT AND ACCOUNT OF THE RECEIPTS AND EXPENDITURES OF ALL PUBLIC MONEY SHALL BE PUBLISHED FROM TIME TO TIME.

Clause 7 appears to be insignificant, to require merely that the federal government run its fiscal affairs in a businesslike manner. The small number of cases resulting from the clause support that view. However, these cases indicate that the clause implicates the doctrine of the separation of powers, which is, of course, both a bedrock of our system of government and, due to its enigmatic nature, a fecund source of important litigation (see *The Judicial Power and the Separation of Powers: A Reference Guide to the U.S. Constitution*). In particular, in some of the cases on this clause the court was required to determine the relative strength of Congress' power of the purse, as created by Clause 7, and one of the President's enumerated constitutional powers, the right to pardon under Article 2, § 2. These cases on separation of powers, especially the ones that involve presidential authority, indicate that highly significant cases on Clause 7 are possible.

Before turning to the appropriations power, the clause's most important subject, it is worth taking a brief look at the clause's second requirement that regular statements and accounts of receipts and expenditures be published from time to time. This requirement seems even more innocuous than the requirement of spending only by means of appropriations, and the publication of the federal budget and voluminous documents explaining it seems to be more than enough to comply with this requirement. However, just as the executive branch has attempted to circumvent Clause 7's requirement that spending must be based solely on appropriations, it has attempted, and succeeded at, disguising some of its spending. The most notable example is the budget of the Central Intelligence Agency, which is embedded in the Defense Department's budget. Congress has acquiesced in this practice, mainly because certain of its committees have access to this information. A Court, although it did not decide the matter, agreed with the propriety of this acquiescence, commenting in a footnote that "historical analysis of the genesis of cl. 7 suggests it was intended to permit some degree of secrecy of governmental operations" (United States v. Richardson, 1974). In this case, a citizen had attempted to require that the Central Intelligence Agency's budget be made public. He was held not to have standing to sue, which is the likely outcome of citizen suits trying to enforce this part of the clause, but at some point, a Court might reach the merits of a case on this matter. If this happens, the statement in United States v. Richardson will not be a precedent because it was not necessary to the decision in the case.

The Court that declined to decide this suit on the merits noted, but did not decide that, that part of Clause 7 has a reverse side: "it is clear that Congress has plenary power to exact any reporting and accounting it considers appropriate in the public interest." That is, the Court believed that the clause not only obligates Congress to report and account but also it empowers Congress to compel executive branch agencies to do this also. The phrasing of the clause is general enough to support this interpretation.

One can logically begin to analyze the appropriation requirement by attempting to discern its purpose. The most convincing statement that appears in the opinions on Clause 7 is that it is designed "to assure that public funds will be spent according to the letter of the difficult judgments reached by Congress as to the common good and not according to the individual favor of Governmental agents or the individual pleas of litigants" (OPM v. Richmond, 1990). A Court in an earlier case had foreshadowed this statement, writing that allowing expenditures in the absence of appropriations that direct or authorize them "would give the fiscal officers a most dangerous discretion" (Reeside v. Walker, 1850). These statements abet the scholars who have argued that Clause 7 provides significant power to Congress and thus significantly restricts the executive branch. Not surprisingly, those who take the opposite view in the scholarly debate on the clause have argued that its purposes are less weighty, such as an assertion that it is merely procedural. These assertions are not anchored in the case law.

The first issue in regard to Clause 7 is determining the meaning of "money in the treasury" so that it is possible to know the extent of the clause's reach. One case identifies funds that are not in the treasury, which helps in drawing the line between funds to which the clause applies and other funds (Republic Nat. Bank Miami v. United States, 1992). This case indicates that funds held while an in rem proceeding (a proceeding against a thing) determines the owner of the funds are in the hands of the government but not in the treasury and thus not subject to this clause. That is, the United States must own the funds for them to be in the treasury. The Court in this case in effect drew the line that we seek, stating that "[t]he Appropriation Clause governs only the disposition of money that belongs to the United States." This statement can be translated logically into the rule that all funds that belong to the United

States are in the treasury. This makes sense because it avoids a completely literal interpretation: the funds must actually be located in a facility of the Treasury Department. Because money is fungible and because of the complexities of contemporary fund transfers, this would be a ludicrous interpretation.

Another case provided a check on the decision in *Republic National Bank* (Cincinnati Soap Co. v. United States, 1937). Although the opinion in that case includes a number of unconvincing assertions and arguments, it makes sense in regard to the issue of identifying funds that are in the treasury. The funds in *Cincinnati Soap* were a portion of a tax that was to be earmarked for the government of the Philippine Islands. However, in fact, the relevant statute literally decreed that the funds were to be sent to the treasury of this jurisdiction. Thus, the ownership of them by the United States was brief and its termination certain. Nevertheless, the court assumed that these funds were in the U.S. Treasury and could be removed only by means of an appropriation. The United States was a mere conduit, a collection agent for the Philippine Islands. Thus, even a transient ownership interest is enough to place the funds in the treasury for the purposes of this clause. Therefore, any funds that the United States owns are in the treasury and thus subject to this clause.

The next issue is surprising because it would seem that the text of the clause leaves no room for debate and that it could not be an issue. This is the question of whether *in fact* there must be a pertinent appropriation for an expenditure of public funds to be lawful. Two early cases provide examples of courts taking the clause literally. In one case, which we have discussed before, the court held that a surviving spouse had no claim against the treasury, regardless of a judgment in her favor against the Post Office Department, because there was no appropriation to pay her claim (Reeside v. Walker, 1850). Similarly, another Court held that even the President's power to pardon "cannot touch moneys in the treasury of the United States, except expressly authorized by act of Congress" (Knote v. United States, 1877). Of course, this act would include or be an appropriation.

It would seem that these forthright holdings and Clause 7's pellucid clarity would preclude the possibility that a later Court would hold that something less than a literal appropriation would serve. However, it happened. A Court considered a statute that imposed a tax on coconut oil and that specified that the tax revenue derived from oil produced in the Philippine Islands was to be deposited in that jurisdiction's treasury (Cincinnati Soap Co. v. United States, 1937). One of the taxpayers challenged the tax on the grounds that there was no appropriation, only the bare statement just paraphrased, to direct the flow of tax revenue in this way. The Court's response was:

> if the tax, qua tax, be good, as we hold it is, and the purpose specified be one which would sustain a subsequent and separate appropriation made out of the general funds of the Treasury, neither is made invalid by being bound to the other in the same act or legislation.

This tangled prose seems to mean that an appropriation made in a later act would suffice and that even the possibility of such an appropriation would suffice. The fact remains that at the time relevant to the case there was no appropriation that authorized the payment. The clause's very plain meaning requires an appropriation in order to pay money from the treasury. The major argument that the court advanced for its holding that a subsequent appropriation would suffice is an earlier case (Edye v. Robertson, 1884). However, the court in that earlier case noted that "the money thus raised…is appropriated in advance," not that it might theoretically be appropriated in the future.

After having established to its satisfaction that an appropriation directed the flow of revenue, the Court in *Cincinnati Soap* summarily rejected the argument that there was no appropriation, in the process stating its conception of the clause's purpose, which is considerably less convincing than the purpose quoted earlier: "[it] was intended as a restriction upon the disbursing authority of the Executive department, and is without significance here. It means simply that no money can be paid out of the Treasury unless it has been appropriated by an act of Congress." The later part of that quotation is an accurate paraphrase of Clause 7 and it should have demonstrated that, without an appropriation that was effective at the time, the tax revenue could not lawfully have been transferred from the U.S. Treasury to the Philippine Islands' treasury.

Thus, courts have disagreed about the need for an appropriation. Although *Cincinnati Soap* is the most recent case on this subject, it does not explicitly overrule the earlier cases. The decision in the case is illogical and ignores the clause's plain meaning, suggesting that later courts would not accept the possibility that a future appropriation would suffice as compliance with Clause 7's requirement. Even if *Cincinnati Soap* is good law on that point, it must be remembered that its holding cannot logically be extended to apply to the executive branch, as asserted by some participants in the scholarly debate on this clause. It is clear that Congress made a drafting error by stating in narrative form the way in which it wanted part of the tax revenue at issue to be spent, and it neglected to create an appropriation to effect this result. Thus, the intent of Congress was clear, even though its technique was faulty. It would require another leap to arrive at the position that the executive branch can spend federal money without an appropriation that grants permission to do so or without a clear indication that it was Congress' intent, as expressed in enacted legislation that the spending occur, or despite a clear statutory indication that it was Congress' intent that money *not* be spent for a certain purpose.

Another Court later dealt with a situation resembling the one at issue in *Cincinnati Soap* and arrived at the same result but followed a different line of reasoning (Republic Nat. Bank Miami v. United States, 1992). The case was about property that was seized by the government because it was purchased with funds obtained by means of trafficking in drugs. The bank that held a mortgage on the property litigated in an attempt to recover the value of the property. Faced with Clause 7, it argued that there was a relevant appropriation: "[u]pon the entry of judgment for the claimant in any proceeding to condemn or forfeit property seized under any act of Congress, such property shall be returned forthwith to the claimant or his agent" (31 USC 1322 (b) (2)). The Court acknowledged that this statute was not a standard appropriation but concluded "[y]et I have difficulty imagining how an 'appropriation' of funds determined on appeal not to belong to the United States could ever be more specific." Unfortunately, the issue was whether there was an appropriation—and there was none, as the Court's use of quotation marks indicates—not the degree of specificity of the "appropriation."

To understand how far from being an appropriation the statute quoted is one needs to understand the federal budget process, which apparently the Court did not.[16] This process typically has three phases. First, authorizations, which create, amend, or extend programs; are made. Second, appropriations, which provide funds for the authorized programs, are made. More precisely, "[a]n appropriation is a provision of law that provides budget authority for federal agencies to incur obligations." Finally, during the budget process, the third phase, Congress places ceilings on particular expenditures and otherwise more precisely allocates federal revenue. The statement that the court considered to be an appropriation is actually a directive to federal officials. It even falls short of being an authorization, because it does not create or alter a program. It certainly does not allocate funds and is thus not an appropriation by any stretch of the English language as Congress uses it.

The decision in *Republic National Bank* aids persons who seek to justify the executive branch's attempts to gain control of the federal purse strings. One can argue on the basis of this case that anyone who has found any expression of Congress' intent to accomplish something for a particular purpose has thereby found an appropriation and thus has found authority to spend money for this purpose. One would hope that the lack of logic exhibited in the opinion would diminish its value as a precedent.

One could also argue that the main result of the decision and opinion in *Republic National Bank* is to correct drafting errors. That is, Congress clearly wanted payments to be made, but it had not drafted legislation that unequivocally appropriated money to make the payments. A more narrow interpretation of this case is thus possible. It might mean that if Congress *clearly* expresses its will that money be spent for a certain purpose that is enough to satisfy this clause's requirements. If that is the case's meaning, it does not lend much credibility to an argument by the executive branch that a vague and general statutory provision, without a conventional, properly drafted appropriation, is enough to justify expenditures. To make the point with an extreme example, it is not credible to argue that a statutory provision advocating resistance to armed invasion justifies a myriad of fiscal maneuvers to fund resistance to an invasion of another country. However, this has happened in recent years.

Clause 7 requires that the appropriation must be "by law," so it is necessary to determine that phrase's meaning. In one case, the Court considered the limits on paying claims to supporters of the Confederacy even though those limits were included in a joint resolution (Hart v. United States, 1886). That is, the court assumed that joint resolutions were "law." Joint resolutions are not statutes; although this one was codified and although, like statutes, in order to become effective, joint resolutions must be presented to the President under the presentment clause in Article 2, § 7. Joint resolutions should be distinguished from concurrent resolutions, which are not presented to the President and do not have the force of law. It is important to note also, that a restriction on the use of an appropriation, not the appropriation itself, was accomplished by means of the joint resolution. In a more recent case, the Court wrote that "[m]oney may be paid only through an appropriation made by law, in other words, the payment of money from the Treasury must be authorized by statute" (OPM v. Richmond, 1990). This Court was drawing a distinction between statutory law and court-established law. In this instance, the distinction was the doctrine of estoppel, under which a person who has given false information that was reasonably acted upon to the detriment of the person who received it is blocked from imposing a penalty on the other person. The Court did not distinguish statutes from joint resolutions.

Combining the holdings of these two cases, one concludes that an act of Congress is the only kind of law to which Clause 7 refers. The question that then remains is whether a concurrent resolution, which does not require assent by the President or overriding a Presidential veto in order to take effect, is a law for purposes of this clause. That is, the question is whether to follow the assumption made by the Court in *Hart* or the explicit statement made by the Court in *OPM v. Richmond*. The better rule is that only statutes are laws for those purposes. One reason for this assertion is that Article 1, § 7 states that bills may not become "law" unless they are presented to the President for action. That is, the Constitution appears to mean statutes when it refers to "law." As described before, *Cincinnati Soap* confirms this interpretation (Cincinnati Soap Co. v. United States, 1937). In it the Court refers to the kind of law needed to draw funds from the Treasury as an "act of Congress."

"By law" also means that payments may be made only for purposes stated in a statute appropriating funds. In a case about the payment of pension benefits, the Court noted that the appropriation that authorized the general category of payments that the plaintiff was trying to obtain stated that "'[t]he Fund...is appropriated for the payment of...benefits as provided by this subchapter'" (OPM v. Richmond, 1990). It then stated:

> [t]he benefits respondent claims were not "provided by" the relevant provision of the subchapter; rather, they were specifically denied. It follows that Congress has appropriated no

money for the payment of the benefits respondent seeks, and the Constitution prohibits that any money "be drawn from the Treasury" to pay them.

This holding provides no comfort to the executive branch employees and legal scholars who assert that the executive branch may spend funds based on a number of rationales even in the absence of an appropriation explicitly authorizing the payment or even in the face of an appropriation that explicitly prohibits that payment.

Although courts have been equivocal on the force of the requirement that an appropriation is required for spending to be valid, this principle bestows considerable power on Congress. Failing to appropriate is the most obvious way of exercising this power, but it is not likely to lead to litigation. The requirement of standing to sue is one inhibitor of litigation in that situation. Another, more powerful inhibitor is the political question doctrine. In invoking that doctrine, courts ask three questions:

(i) Does the issue involve resolution of questions committed by the text of the Constitution to a coordinate branch of Government? (ii) Would resolution of the question demand that a court move beyond areas of judicial expertise? (iii) Do prudential considerations counsel against judicial intervention? (Goldwater v. Carter, 1979)

Affirmative answers to those questions make it more likely that a Court will decline to decide a case, which usually is tantamount to a decision that the question is better left to the legislative branch.

A more significant use by Congress of its appropriations power is to enact an appropriation that precludes spending for a set of the activities that the appropriation covers. This can be done in two ways. The first way is to remain silent on these activities, creating the inference that money is not authorized to be spent for them. The second way is to state that the funds that the appropriation makes available may not be expended for certain activities. This tactic is likely to join issues and might very well lead to litigation. Because these limits are usually placed on the executive branch, this tactic is also likely to have implications for the separation of powers doctrine. In short, by doing so Congress asserts its authority—sometimes in a confrontational mode—to make policy decisions in an area in which the executive branch either has explicit authority under the Constitution or has claimed authority. A case brought in such a situation would likely have significant issues at stake and might even resolve a constitutional crisis.

Because the use by Congress of its appropriations power to preclude spending has such weighty consequences, it is highly significant whether this power is limited and, if it is, what these limits are. Not surprisingly, these issues have arisen so that judicial decisions on them exist. As Congress becomes more aggressive in limiting executive branch spending, which has recently been the trend, these issues will become even more important.

The most severe possible limit on the appropriations power is restricting it to spending only to accomplish the powers, such as those listed in Article 1, § 8, that the Constitution explicitly grants to Congress. If this were the rule, the appropriations power would not really be a power, and this clause would be procedural, merely stating the means by which Congress may spend funds. Although a Court held an act of Congress unconstitutional for other reasons, it first resolved the issue of whether Clause 7 is merely procedural (United States v. Butler, 1936). On that point, the Court held that "the power of Congress to authorize expenditure of public moneys for public purposes is not limited by the direct grants of legislative power found in the Constitution."

A less restrictive conception of Congress' appropriations power is that it extends to every provision in the Constitution that would justify expenditures. In a poorly reasoned opinion that we have already seen, the Court in *Cincinnati Soap* seemed to arrive at that broader conception: "we inquire first: Is the proposed appropriation to the Philippine Treasury for a constitutional purpose?" (Cincinnati Soap Co. v. United States, 1937). At this point, the Court conveniently omitted that there was no appropriation and that it was considering instead whether an appropriation could conceivably be made later for the purpose at issue. This Court seemed to be looking for something in the Constitution that would validate an appropriation or something in the text that would justify the purpose for which the funds were spent. However, the material that followed indicated that it had another purpose in mind. The Court argued that the United States has "a high moral obligation" to dependencies, such as the Philippine Islands, an obligation that is a debt. This reason neither is to be found in the Constitution's text nor makes any sense. Undeterred, the Court continued: "[h]aving power to raise money for [the] purpose [of paying debts], it of course follows that [that the government] has power to appropriate it to the same object." The "of course" tips the court's hand: it does not follow from the facts; nor does the Court explain the reason why it follows. Moreover, if that chain of "reasoning" is valid, then the taxing power bestowed in Article 1, § 8 subsumes the appropriations power, and Clause 7 is null. However, the Court did help to answer the question of what limits apply to Congress' appropriations power. Its view was that the appropriations power was limited to spending for purposes that had some basis, including a general basis, in the Constitution.

At first glance, another case might indicate an opposite opinion from that of *Cincinnati Soap*. In United States v. Butler (1936) the government argued that the act in question was justified because it was for "general welfare." The Court declined this gambit, holding that the act impinged on the rights that the Tenth Amendment grants to the states. The Court thus examined the act as a whole, stating that the appropriation was a means to effect its purposes. The Court could have held that this clause trumps the Tenth Amendment. It is also important to note that the Court did not hold that *an appropriation* is invalid if it conflicts with part of the

Constitution. Therefore, a more careful reading of this case demonstrates that it does not mean that all other constitutional provisions limit the appropriations power.

The interaction of the appropriations power with explicit grants of power in the Constitution to the executive and judicial branches is a more important issue than is its interaction with parts of the Constitution that do not make such grants. The reasons for this state of affairs are that the doctrine of separation of powers is involved and that litigation is more likely to ensue, and more likely to be very important, than in cases that involve constitutional grants of power to Congress. Fortunately, the opinions on that weightier issue are clearer than the opinion in *Butler*.

A number of cases that arose out of pardons that were granted to persons who had aided the Confederacy in the Civil War, and that thus involved the power of the President to grant pardons under Article 2, § 2, provided the occasion for the court to clarify the appropriation clause's relation to this power in particular and to presidential power in general. In one case, the relevant appropriation provided funds to pay judgments in the Court of Claims but included a proviso (United States v. Klein, 1871). To recover property under the Abandoned and Captured Property Act, the claimant had to demonstrate loyalty to the United States. The proviso in the appropriation was that this loyalty "shall be made by proof of the matters required irrespective of the effect of any executive proclamation, pardon, amnesty, or other act of condonation or oblivion." Moreover, the proviso specified that a pardon was proof of the acts pardoned, that is, disloyalty. Confronted with a pardon, a Court had no choice but to decide that the claimant was disloyal. However, this finding did not dispose of the case. The Court held that the appropriation was unconstitutional because it decreed to courts the effect of a presidential pardon. The proviso stated in effect that "when [a court] ascertains that a certain state of things exists, its jurisdiction is to cease." This indirectly states that Congress had limited this presidential power. It may be argued with some plausibility that the Court also held this, because it added that another effect of the proviso was "to deny to pardons granted by the President the effect which this court had adjudged them to have." The emphasis there, too, is on the proviso's diminution of the Court's authority, but it also pointed out that the President's pardon did not have the effect he intended. It also might be appropriate to generalize by stating that the appropriations power may not impinge on other powers that the Constitution implicitly grants, although making that statement requires making two leaps beyond the Court's statement of its holding. One of them is to apply the holding to statutes that do not direct courts to decide issues in a certain way and the other is to apply the holding to all constitutional provisions. Both of these interpretations of the decision in this case are far too expansive.

Three cases take a view of the appropriation clause's status in relation to the pardoning power that differs from the view taken in *Klein*. However, the facts are significantly different, so those other cases do not overrule *Klein*.

In one of these cases, the Court held that no government official may reimburse a claimant pursuant to a pardon unless there was an appropriation to extract the money from the treasury (Knote v. United States, 1877). In this instance, the potential impediment to paying the claim was not a proviso but the absence of an appropriation. In other words, the appropriations clause means what it says—money may not be paid out of the treasury without an appropriation—and this stands regardless of the pardoning power. Of the relation between the two constitutional provisions, the Court wrote:

> [h]owever large, therefore, may be the power possessed by the President, and however extended its application, there is this limit to it, as there is to all his powers,—it cannot touch moneys in the treasury of the United States, except expressly authorized by act of Congress. The Constitution places this restriction upon the pardoning power.

The constitutional provisions on the President's power to pardon and on Congress' power to appropriate must be harmonized.

The Court in another case distinguished *Klein*, stating that its result depended on the fact that Congress had dictated to the courts the effect of a pardon (Hart v. United States, 1886). It then held that "a creditor of the United States can only be paid in accordance with the provision of the constitution (article 1, 9, subd. 7)...[and] by this joint resolution congress had declared, by law, that this claimant could draw no money from the treasury." Like the statute that was at issue in *Knote*, the statute in *Hart* was addressed not to the courts but to executive branch officials. It did not tell a Court how it must decide a case. Rather, it forbade officers from paying claims to disloyal persons (former Confederates). The proviso in the appropriation stated that a pardon did not prove loyalty, but it allowed the Court to make that determination. This outcome did not diminish the President's power to pardon.

Finally, a claim based on a pardon and faced with an appropriation that specified that only loyal persons had a right to reimbursement came to the court (Austin v. United States, 1894). This appropriation was specifically directed at the claimant. On the same day it was enacted, another statute was enacted that made loyalty a jurisdictional fact; that is, it specified that a claim may be paid only to persons who proved their loyalty. A better alternative would have been to make innocence, which a pardon would have established, jurisdictional. The Court summarized *Knote*, *Klein*, and *Hart*, emphasizing in its account of *Klein* that the problem had been a congressional statement of a rule of decision (a statement of the way in which a court was to interpret the law). In *Austin* the Court held that "[I]n declining to bestow jurisdiction in favor of pardoned offenders, whose claims were barred, congress did not deny its proper constitutional effect to amnesty. To whom the privilege of suit should be accorded was for congress alone to determine." In sum, the Court decided that the proviso in the appropriation accommodated both constitutional provisions, even though it negated an effect that the President assumed his pardon would have.

It is possible to reconcile these four cases. Congress is not required to enact an appropriation in order to allow the President to use the pardoning power to provide funds to a person who has been pardoned. If it does not do so, the President, even though he or she wishes to act on the basis of a power that the Constitution explicitly grants, will be unable to provide funds to this person. Congress may require for payment of a claim proof of a condition that a pardon cannot effect, thereby significantly diminishing the pardon's efficacy. Congress can more easily accomplish that latter result if it enacts an appropriation statute that addresses itself to an executive branch employee rather than to a Court. If Congress does address itself to a Court, it can more easily accomplish its purpose if it frames the proviso in terms of establishing jurisdiction rather than in terms of mandating a particular decision. However, if Congress enacts a proviso in an appropriation that forces a decision on a Court and if that decision nullifies the President's pardoning power, Congress has exceeded its appropriation authority. In sum, Congress can use the appropriations clause to great effect and yet enact appropriation statutes that remain in harmony with the rest of the Constitution, even with those parts that grant power to the executive branch.

We have seen that there are limits to the use of the appropriations power in its relation to the judicial branch of government; for example, an appropriation may not specify a rule of decision to a Court (United States v. Klein, 1871). This limit exists absolutely to prohibit Congress from preventing the court from performing its constitutionally authorized function of adjudicating. It thus lies at the farthest reach of the spectrum of possible inhibitions that Congress, using its appropriations power, can impose on the other two branches of government. In fact, it is beyond the point where constitutional uses of the appropriations power give way to unconstitutional uses. However, this point is located very near one end of the spectrum of possible appropriations.

The reverse side of that coin is that another power that the Constitution authorizes may not negate the appropriations power. To illustrate this principle, one can look to a case previously described in which a surviving spouse had secured a judgment against the Post Office Department (Reeside v. Walker, 1850). Despite the judgment, the Court would not order payment but instead held that the claimant must make a claim to Congress, which, unlike the Court, may draw funds from the treasury by means of enacting an appropriation. At this time there are likely to be appropriations to pay claims, so this decision is not an impediment. However, it illustrates the force that courts attribute to the appropriations power in relation to the judicial branch, because the Court in this case declined to usurp that power. Similarly, in the absence of an appropriation, a Court may not invoke the judicial doctrine of estoppel and then order a payment from the Treasury (OPM v. Richmond, 1990). As the court vividly phrased it, "courts cannot estop the Constitution."

If one begins with the compelling assumption that each provision in the Constitution is to be given effect, it is illogical to invalidate the use of one power, either by making an appropriation or by any other means, to *totally* negate another power. Congress also may not ignore prohibitions in the Constitution that are explicitly directed to it. Short of those two limits, there is nothing in the case law that appears to limit the appropriations power's effect on the executive and judicial branches. Rather, courts have consistently found that this power can be harmonized with other constitutional powers. In fact, one Court made an unequivocal statement of the appropriations power's potency: "[a]ny exercise of a power granted by the Constitution to one of the other branches of Government is limited by a valid reservation of congressional control over funds in the Treasury" (OPM v. Richmond, 1990).

The court in *OPM* also recognized the possibility that executive branch employees would use devious means to nullify the appropriations power (OPM v. Richmond, 1990). That Court asserted that these tactics are unconstitutional:

> [e]xtended to its logical conclusion, operation of estoppel against the Government in the context of payment of money from the Treasury could in fact render the Appropriations Clause a nullity. If agents of the Executive were able, by their unauthorized oral or written statements to citizens, to obligate the Treasury for the payment of funds, the control over public funds that the Clause reposes in Congress in effect could be transferred to the executive. If, for example, the President or executive Branch officials were displeased with a new restriction on benefits imposed by Congress to ease burdens on the fisc (such as the restriction imposed by the statutory change in this case) and sought to evade them, agency officials could advise citizens that the restrictions were inapplicable. Estoppel would give this advice the practical force of law, in violation of the Constitution.

The case law is thus fairly complex and not entirely consistent. At this point, a summary of the major points is useful. Clause 7 applies to all money that the federal government owns; all that money is in the Treasury. Despite one case that assumed that a Congressional joint resolution validly stated conditions for making an appropriation, the dominant view is that the "by law" qualification to the appropriations power means by enacting a statute. In any event, the measure must be passed by both houses of Congress and presented to the President. Courts have been quite flexible in assessing whether a statutory provision is an appropriation. The appropriations power may not totally negate another grant of power made by the Constitution, but the appropriations power must not yield to other grants of power. In fact, exercise of power by the executive and judicial branches is subject to this clause. Moreover, executive branch employees (and, supposedly, judicial branch employees as well) may not use devious means to frustrate the appropriations power in general and Congress' decisions about spending specifically. That is, Congress may add conditions to the authority of the other branches of government to spend federal funds. In a dispute between Congress and the executive branch, if the question is whether a statute is an appropriation and thus allows spending the executive branch has some strong precedents to follow. However, if the question is whether Congress has constitutionally limited the use of funds by adding a proviso to a statute that certainly is an appropriation, Congress has some very strong precedents.

Before leaving the subject of the case law on Clause 7, it is necessary to clear up some matters. Oddly enough, two scholars who argue that the appropriations clause gives extensive power to Congress have summarized *Klein*, a case that was discussed earlier, in a way that undercuts their position. Louis Fisher wrote that, according to *Klein*, Congress "cannot use appropriation bills...to restrict the President's pardon power."[17] Similarly, Kate Stith summarized *Klein* thus: "Congress' power over appropriations does not allow Congress to deny or direct the pardon power."[18] As we have seen, the holding in *Klein* is not that Congress may not use its appropriations power to dilute the President's pardon power but that it may not use that power, by attempting to force a rule of decision (decreeing the way in which courts must decide particular kinds of cases) on the courts, to totally negate the courts' authority to decide cases. Moreover, although both Fisher and Stith briefly mentioned *Hart* and noted that it differed from *Klein*, they did not argue that it indicated the validity of Congress' limiting the pardon power, and neither mentioned the other two cases on pardons that made the same point.

A number of scholars also have attempted to add two cases to the list of precedents that are relevant to determining the extent of the appropriations power. Fisher asserted in the same sentence in which he alluded to *Klein*, that Flast v. Cohen demonstrated that Congress "cannot use the Appropriations power...to establish a national religion" (Flast v. Cohen, 1968). Fisher used both cases to indicate that the appropriations power is not plenary. Another way of making this point is to assert that each provision in the Constitution is subject to every other provision. His second example is certainly not surprising. The First Amendment speaks directly to Congress on this matter: "Congress shall make no law respecting an establishment of religion." Thus, an appropriation, like all other kinds of legislation, is subject to this constraint.

Some scholars also looked to an employment case that involved an appropriation for guidance about the reach of the appropriations power (United States v. Lovett, 1946). Congress had inserted into an appropriations bill a rider stating that a particular appropriation may not be used to pay the salaries of some employees that Congress considered to be "subversive." Stith interpreted the case to mean that "Congress cannot enact bills of attainder through appropriations legislation."[19] Fisher agreed with this interpretation.[20]

The authors of two other articles read *Lovett* even more expansively. Peter Raven-Hansen and William Banks claim that the case can be logically expanded to reach the conclusion that a lower court judge, in a concurrence, stated: Congress may not "trespass upon the Constitutional functions of another branch of the Government."[21] J. Gregory Sidak wrote that "I read *Lovett*—as did Attorney General William P. Rogers in 1960—to mean that Congress may not use the appropriations power to impair the President's ability to perform duties or exercise prerogatives the Constitution imposes on him."[22] Neither article mentions the function or duty upon which the appropriation rider intruded, but let us assume that there is a power of the President that has a basis in the Constitution and that is involved in the continued right of these employees to their jobs.

It does not follow that *Lovett* has the effect that Raven-Hansen, Banks, and Sidak claim. Rather than talking in general about the case and about unspecified powers that it allegedly protects, it is more useful to read the case. The Court wrote:

> [a]ccording to the view we take we need not decide whether Section 304 [of the Urgent Deficiency Appropriations Act of 1943] is an unconstitutional encroachment on executive power or a denial of due process of law, and the section is not challenged on the ground that it violates the First Amendment. Our inquiry is thus confined to whether Section 304 is a bill of attainder.

That is, the Court rejected the government's argument that the case was about only the appropriations power. The reason for the court's view is that "no mere question of compensation procedure or of appropriations was involved, but...it was designed to force the employing agencies to discharge respondents and to bar their ever being hired by any other governmental agency." Thus, the act violated Clause 3 of § 9. Fisher and Stith, not Raven-Hansen, Banks, and Sidak, correctly summarized the case. Moreover, its holding is not in the least surprising or groundbreaking. Every bill of attainder, whether or not it includes an appropriation, is unconstitutional under that clause. That clause, like the establishment clause, is directed explicitly at Congress. Thus, the situation is the same as it was in Cohen v. Flast; Congress may not pass legislation that the Constitution forbids it to pass. To the summary of the case law provided above, one can add the obvious point that the appropriations power, like Congress' general power to legislate, is subject to explicit Constitutional limits that are addressed specifically to Congress. No inferences at all about the reach of the appropriations clause may logically be drawn from *Lovett*, because the court wrote that the case is not about this clause. Certainly, one cannot logically make the kind of inferences made by Sidak that the case demonstrates that the appropriations clause must abjectly and totally yield to every one of the President's powers that is anchored, however tenuously, in the text of the Constitution.

Another way of explaining *Lovett* and of demonstrating that Raven-Hansen, Banks, and Sidak misinterpreted it is to paraphrase the appropriations clause and then to state in similar phrasing Congress' intent in enacting the law that was at issue in that case. Clause 7 says that no money may be drawn from the Treasury except by an appropriation. The accuracy of that literal paraphrase is indisputable. In the law, by means of attaching a rider, Congress decreed that no money may be drawn from the Treasury to pay the salaries of the three federal employees. Congress failed in this matter because the rider violated an explicit constitutional prohibition against the kind of law that Congress had enacted. One cannot credibly argue from this outcome that Congress' power to appropriate, and to limit appropriations, has been diluted. *A fortiori*, one certainly cannot credibly argue that the case's outcome means that the power of the executive branch need not be limited, at least under certain circumstances, by congressional appropriations and that the executive branch may, constitutionally, expend funds that have not been appropriated or may, constitutionally, expend funds for a purpose that Congress has, by enacting a law, denied it the authority to do. Sidak appeared to be trying to use *Lovett* to justify the latter proposition. However, this is not a logical conclusion.

Normally an analysis of a portion of the Constitution would end after all the pertinent cases were discussed. One thinks naturally of a constitutional provision having effect when a court adverts to it in deciding a case. However, this clause is not typical; it illustrates another important function of the Constitution: to induce persons to act in accordance with their understanding of the rights, duties, and prohibitions that, under the Constitution, apply to them. Specifically, Congress, by adding provisos to appropriations, has acted as if it thought that this clause bestows considerable power—the famous "power of the purse"—on it. At the same time, the executive branch has acted as if its exercise of some of the powers granted by the Constitution, most notably the power to control foreign policy, have been inhibited by Congress' overzealous use of the powers that it asserts on account of this clause. The story of that tug of war is part of the story of this clause, although it has not yet caused litigation, but this might happen in the future. Then, Clause 7, as interpreted by a court, will, by resolving a constitutional crisis, be highly significant.

At this point it is useful to understand some of the moves that the executive branch has made in order to avoid ceding all appropriations power to Congress, despite this clause, and the countermoves that Congress has made to assert its authority under this clause.[23] Situations like some of the typical ones that have occurred will probably provide the factual basis for future litigation.

The executive branch's assertion of its power to control appropriations began in President George Washington's administrations. This is not surprising, because the Congress of a new nation of course could not predict very accurately the fiscal needs of the executive branch. As a result, Congress appropriated a small number of block grants instead of a large number of carefully targeted grants. In fact, Alexander Hamilton, the Secretary of the Treasury, drafted the first appropriations bill, which included only four large general appropriations. During Washington's administrations, Congress also failed to object to the executive branch's movement of funds from appropriation to appropriation and enacted appropriations laws after money had been spent and in order to ratify that spending. The latter action was most frequent after an unforeseen emergency had required a rapid, and unfunded, response. Although Hamilton was the primary mover in this necessary (because of the difficulties of launching a government) circumventing of Congress' appropriations power, in an essay, "Explanation," that he published in 1795 he stated that "the *purpose*, the *limit*, and the *fund* of every expenditure should be ascertained by previous law." In other words, he contended that no money may be drawn from the treasury but in consequence of appropriations made by law.

After a time Congress' ability to appropriate more precisely and accurately increased, and it thus regained power over appropriations. Nevertheless, emergencies arose. The outbreak of the Civil War is the most dramatic example. Because Congress was out of session at the time, President Lincoln moved quickly and spent money that had not been appropriated for the war because there had been no war when Congress was last in session. Lincoln later explained his action to Congress and, in the same letter, stated a very broad view of his own powers:

> [i]t became necessary for me to choose whether, using only the existing means, agencies, and processes which Congress had provided, I should let the Government fall at once to ruin or whether, availing myself of the broader powers conferred by the Constitution in cases of insurrection, I would make an effort to save it.[24]

The constitutional text that Lincoln thought gave him broader powers apparently is the portion of Article 2, § 2 that names the President Commander in Chief, although that passage says nothing about broader powers. His other argument, that Congress could not be convened in time, was compelling in 1862, although it would be well short of compelling most other times.

Thus, there were reasonably sound practical reasons for those early examples of seizure of the purse strings by the executive branch, as there were for many other early instances. This is not to say that the actions were constitutional. Moreover, some of the instances that occurred before this century are very difficult, probably impossible, to defend on either constitutional or public policy grounds. One of the more egregious involved the Post Office. The executive branch had begun taking actions that led to "coercive appropriations." That is, it encumbered funds in such a way or under such circumstances that Congress had no choice, or virtually no choice, but to appropriate the funds needed to pay the amounts that were encumbered. The Post Office, in the 1870s, spent all its appropriation for a fiscal year long before the year ended. As a result, Congress had to choose between capitulating to that tactic by appropriating more money for that agency or denying postal service to the nation for the rest of the fiscal year.

More recent examples of the executive branch's spending without clear authorization by means of an appropriation, or even despite a clear prohibition against particular uses of appropriated funds, include its conduct during the episode that came to be known as the Iran-Contra Affair. Congress had passed legislation that was designed to inhibit the executive branch from aiding the Contras, who were attempting to overthrow the Sandinistas and oust them from control of the government of Nicaragua. However, the Central Intelligence Agency used funds from its general appropriation to pay for the mining of Nicaraguan harbors. When this tactic was disclosed, the administration began to solicit from other countries' funds that could be used to support the Contras. Some of the contributors later received increased aid, and one can rationally infer that they were led to believe that this would occur. Louis Fisher, an employee of the Congressional Research Service, stated that his candidate for "a low point in government" was "someone using the pseudonym 'Mr. Kenilworth' (actually assistant Secretary of State Elliott Abrams) [meeting] in a park in London to solicit a contribution from Brunei."[25]

Another recent example of unauthorized spending by the executive branch involved repelling Iraq's invasion of Kuwait in 1990, which eventually became known as Operation Desert Storm. Within about a month after the invasion, there were approximately 100,000 American troops in the area. President George Bush ordered their deployment without an appropriation authorizing it, a fact that should be seen in light of the fact that Congress was in recess, although it could have been convened quickly. At first he paid for the deployment with discretionary funds and did not ask Congress for an appropriation until mid-September. The President also, relying on an old statute that allowed the Secretary of the Treasury to receive and earmark contributions from other countries, also hoped to obtain 15 billion dollars abroad. The administration also used funds in an account for purposes other than those for which they had been appropriated and shifted funds within lump-sum appropriation accounts. Most of these devices were authorized by statutes that were in effect at the beginning of the military buildup.

The executive branch's fiscal maneuvering during Operation Desert Storm illustrates some of the flexibility that it has so that, notwithstanding this clause, it can at least argue with some force that it is not violating the law when it spends without explicit authority from Congress. Whether in each instance it is violating Clause 7 is another matter. Prior general authorization or after-the-fact ratification by Congress cannot transform an unconstitutional action into a constitutional action.

Peter Raven-Hansen and William C. Banks list and explain the major mechanisms available to—or at least used by—the executive branch to spend money without specifically designated Congressional appropriations.

One is the use of lump-sum appropriations. These are appropriations, usually of large sums of money, that are made for very broadly worded purposes. Thus, at least arguably, they validate a large range of expenditures. Making lump-sum appropriations to the Department of Defense is particularly rational and has frequently been done when the country is at war. Another mechanism is to use contingency funds. The inability to predict future fiscal needs is the main reason why Congress has resorted to this kind of appropriation. One example is the Foreign Assistance Act contingency fund, which authorizes spending "in the national interest."[26] It is difficult to imagine a broader purpose. President John F. Kennedy used that appropriation for the initial funding of the Peace Corps, which he had created by executive order. President Reagan used the Central Intelligence Agency's contingency fund to pay in part for the support provided to the Contras. Other kinds of lump-sum appropriations are those that grant authority for emergency spending and those that allow the expenditure of funds received as gifts.

A second mechanism is the use of reprogramming. Reprogramming allows uses of appropriation accounts other than those stated in the appropriation statute. Thus, this mechanism creates flexibility but also thwarts Congress' appropriations power provided under this clause. Some uses, such as diverting funds in response to a situation that everyone agrees is an emergency, are innocent. Others are devious. One of the devious mechanisms is to request an appropriation for a purpose that obviously would be attractive to Congress while knowing that the money obtained by this ruse will be used for another purpose. Usually no statute allows the desired reprogramming, but executive branch agencies and the Congressional committees that have oversight responsibilities over them have worked out agreements that allow the practice, often within agreed-upon limits. As use of this method has proliferated, so have Congressionally imposed limits on that use.

A third mechanism is transfers. Transfers move funds not between programs within an appropriation but from one appropriation to another. Thus, they are actions that have even less foundation in an appropriation made by law than does reprogramming. War in Laos from 1962 to 1969 and in Cambodia in 1970 and bombing of Cambodia in 1973 were financed largely with transfers. The latter instance would have been lawful if it had been reported properly, but the reporting was after the fact. Those three examples were transfers between accounts that were set up for the same agency. Transfers have also been made between agencies. These transfers, too, are subject to statutory constraints.

Even if the executive branch used one of these mechanisms in accordance with every applicable statute, the question of whether the use complies with Clause 7 remains. In these cases money has been transferred out of the treasury according to laws: it is "by law." However, in the clause "by law" modifies "appropriation," not "transfer," in the clause, and the transfer was not "in consequence of an appropriation." It was "in consequence" of an executive branch action, in accordance with or not quite in accordance with a statute, that allowed the executive branch to circumvent this clause's requirements. Congress has acquiesced in some transfers that were made according to statute, and, thus, Congress is unlikely to litigate if its statutory criteria have been fulfilled. If the transfer was not made according to statute, Congress would be more willing to litigate.

Another way to evade this clause's requirements is to spend money that has been contributed by a source other than the federal government. An example is the solicitation of funds from the Sultan of Brunei that has been mentioned. The argument for this practice is that the money never went into the treasury, so that Clause 7 is irrelevant. For example, Raven-Hansen and Banks distinguish between third-party funds that are given in expectation of a return of funds, such as, perhaps, in the case of funds that another country donates, by means of increased foreign aid, and funds that are given without an expectation of a reciprocal transfer.[27] They claim that the former involves the treasury, because after the money stops moving some of it in effect will have come out of the treasury for the desired purpose, but that the latter does not involve the treasury. The difficulty with the distinction is the case law. According to it, the appropriations clause "governs only the disposition of money that belongs to the United States" (Republic Nat. Bank Miami v. United States, 1995). It follows from the fact that the clause governs only that money that it *does* govern that money. Funds that an agent of the executive branch receives for the use of the federal government belong to the United States; the agent has no claim to them, nor does any executive agency as an entity distinct from the federal government. They are "in the Treasury," even though the agent is probably trying to hide them from the Treasury Department. It follows that funds that are received from a third party are subject to this clause.

Up to this point, we have used examples of an acquiescent Congress that has been willing, within limits that it specified, to let the executive branch work its way around the appropriations clause. That has not always been the case. Two important, generally applicable statutes were designed to curb unauthorized spending by the executive branch. In addition, Congress has enacted a number of specific statutes that it intended to have this result.

The first general statute is the Antideficiency Act. In 1820 Congress had become so concerned with coercive spending by the executive branch that it enacted a law that stated "no contract shall hereafter be made by the Secretary of State, or of the Treasury, or of the Department of War, or of the Navy, except under a law authorizing the same, or under an appropriation adequate to its fulfillment" (Act of May 1, 1820, ch.52, § 6, 3 Stat 567, 568). In 1870 the law was rephrased and made applicable to the entire federal government:

> it shall not be lawful for any department of the government to expend in any one fiscal year any sum in excess of appropriations made by Congress for that fiscal year or to involve the government in any contract for future payment of money in excess of appropriations (Act of Jul. 12, 1870, ch. 251, § 7, 16 Stat. 251).

The portion of the current version that is most pertinent to Clause 7 is:

> An officer or employee of the United States Government or of the District of Columbia may not–
>
> (A) make or authorize an expenditure or obligation exceeding an amount available in an appropriation or fund for the expenditure or obligation;
>
> (B) involve either government in a contract or obligation for the payment of money before an appropriation is made unless authorized by law; (31 USC 1341 (a) (1) (A) and (B)).

The second general statute is the Miscellaneous Receipts Statute. It was enacted in 1849 and has not always been generally applicable. Its first version provided that all money "received from customs, from the sales of public lands, and from all miscellaneous sources, for the use of the United States, shall be paid into the treasury of the United States" (9 Stat. 398) The part of the current version that is most relevant to this clause is "Except as provided in section 3718 (b) of this title, an official or agent of the Government receiving money for the Government from any source shall deposit the money in the Treasury as soon as practicable without deduction for any charge or claim" (31 USC 3302 (b)). The general rule specifies that all money that the federal government collects is federal money and is to be placed in the U.S. Treasury. This is a statutory echo of a principle stated recently by the court (Republic Nat. Bank Miami v. United States, 1992). The exception in the Miscellaneous Receipts Statute is for contracts for debt collection.

As Kate Stith pointed out,[28] other statutes create three kinds of exceptions to this rule. These include certain statutes that allow federal agencies to keep and spend collections such as fees. A second exception is for certain revolving funds; these funds begin with an appropriation but sustain themselves by means of revenue generated by the activity funded. A good example is a loan program. The third exception is for certain grants of authority to retain gifts. In regard to national security, the authority to spend money that was received as a gift was particularly generous until Congress, reacting to its overuse on a massive scale in the Iran-Contra affair, imposed very tight restrictions on it.

In addition to these general statutory restrictions that have been law for a long time, Congress, due to its disapproval of certain spending without an appropriation by the executive branch, has recently enacted more specific constraints on that practice.

For example, Congress enacted a number of laws that, by placing restrictions or prohibitions on the use of appropriations, attempted to diminish the United States' military activity during the Vietnam War. The first one, enacted in 1969, limited the use of funds for carrying on the war in Thailand and Laos. In 1973, frustrated that a declaration of policy failed to discontinue the United States' military operations in Cambodia during the Vietnam War, Congress enacted a law that curtailed funding for this purpose (Pub. L. 93-52. § 108). President Nixon, his power considerably weakened by the Watergate Affair, signed this measure. In 1973 and 1974, Congress passed a series of appropriation riders that were intended not merely to restrict the war but to end it.

The next major confrontation between the executive branch and Congress that involved the former spending without an appropriation and the latter enacting laws to counter those moves involved expenditures to aid the Contras in their attempt to displace the Sandinistas in Nicaragua. Congress' first major effort along that line was, early in 1984, enacting a statute to proclaim that it was the sense of Congress not to allow funds for the mining of Nicaraguan harbors. Later that year Congress went further, stating, in the first Boland Amendment, that no funds that were available to the Central Intelligence Agency could be used to attempt to overthrow the Sandinistas. After the administration circumvented this measure, Congress enacted another amendment, Boland II, that forbade any agency that was engaged in intelligence gathering from supporting, directly or indirectly, any military or paramilitary operations in Nicaragua by anyone. The greater detail in Boland II indicates the difficulty of stopping an administration that is intent on funding an activity. Rather than having their desired effect, the Boland Amendments increased the efforts of administration officials to fund the Contras in other ways, most notably by means of gifts.

Congress' efforts to assert its power to appropriate and to place substantive restrictions on the executive branch have not always involved armed conflict. J. Gregory Sidak[29] identified a number of restrictions that were enacted in the 1990 appropriations bills and that related to other subjects. One denied the use of an appropriation to pay the salary of any person who had been nominated for a position that ordinarily required Senate approval but who had not been approved by the Senate (the authority to make recess appointments would otherwise have allowed such a person to serve in office). Another forbade using funds "for the purposes of conducting any studies relating or leading to the possibility of changing from the currently required 'at cost' to a 'market rate' or any other noncost-based method for pricing of hydroelectric power by the six Federal public power authorities." Another rider prevented the Office of Management and Budget from using funds to review any agricultural marketing orders.

Recognizing the strong possibility that these somewhat aggressive governmental practices will eventually lead to very important litigation, a number of legal scholars have published works in which they delineated the power that they think Congress was given by Clause 7 vis-à-vis the President. In fact, the legal scholarship on Clause 7 is rich, although most of it was published recently. The legal scholarship would be even richer if it took more account of the case law. Much of this scholarship was written before 1990, before OPM v. Richmond made the Supreme Court's interpretation of this clause very clear; a careful reading of the four cases on the President's power to pardon would have offered scholars a reasonably good understanding of the Court's interpretation of this clause. However, rather than extensively using the available case law, the scholars have employed historical arguments, assertions about the way that the two branches of government ought to interrelate in regard to the authority to spend, structural analyses of the Constitution, and other means to make their case. Moreover, the debate has often been politicized. For example, J. Gregory Sidak mused about whether those who disagreed with his analysis did not like President Reagan. Because most of these works advocated interpreting the clause to the benefit of either Congress or the President and attempted to refute advocates of the other branch of government, they presaged arguments that will almost certainly be made if major separation of powers cases that involve this clause occur. Because that eventuality appears to be likely, those works are worth careful attention, too. Rather than discussing all the scholarship, it makes more sense to discuss one article that took a very restrictive view of Congress' power under Clause 7 and another article that took a more expansive view.

J. Gregory Sidak, in an article that has already been cited in Part I, defended a very restrictive view of the authority of Congress under this clause, arguing, in effect, for an imperial presidency. Much of his argument is historical in both the sense of tracing the statements of the Framers on this issue and in the sense of chronicling the tug of war between the executive and legislative branches on the issues of who controls spending and to what degree. Some of his arguments were based on his idea of the way in which parts of the Constitution interrelate and cast light on one another. Some of them were based on political theory—his ideas about the ways in which the polity ought to operate. Very few of these arguments were based on the case law.

Sidak maintained that Clause 7 is ambiguous. For example, he points out that "law" may mean the Constitution itself, treaties, common law, or contracts. However, it is not rational to interpret one word at a time. "Law" appears in the context of "appropriation by law," and none of the sources of law that he mentions can appropriate; only Congress can do this. Thus, "by law" has the meaning that the courts have assigned to it: by means of a statute and, perhaps, by means of a joint resolution. Sidak's gambit on this point is designed to enable him to argue that "law" in the clause means the Constitution. The next step in his argument is that Clause 7's placement in Article 1, § 9 indicates that it limits Congress, because all the other clauses in that article do so. However, as we have seen, some of them are not addressed to Congress. Even if the premise with which he starts, that all the clauses in a section of the Constitution must perform the same basic function, made sense, his factual error would invalidate this point.

Sidak assumed that he had demonstrated that the logical way to interpret Clause 7 is to locate it in the scheme of the Constitution. Specifically, he argued that the doctrine of separation of powers is the key to understanding the clause. Although this doctrine does not explicitly appear in the Constitution, it is almost universally agreed that the way in which the governmental powers are parceled out and stated creates this doctrine. Sidak's next point is that the separation between the branches of government is to be absolute: the executive branch is to be "unitary" (only it may execute the laws, and there must be no encroachment on the duties and prerogatives of the President). Sidak asserted that the need for a unitary executive is particularly crucial in regard to issues of national defense. (However, if the executive had been left alone on one national defense issue, the one that led to the Iran-Contra scandal, many persons would wish for a nonunitary executive.) Moreover, Sidak recklessly waved around a double-edged sword. If the executive branch should be unitary, so should the judicial and legislative branches, and the legislative branch's appropriations authority, as established by this clause, should be inviolate. Sidak argued later that the President is entitled, even required, to decline to execute laws that he or she considers to be unconstitutional limits on his or her power. However, under our form of government, the determination of constitutionality is allotted to the judicial branch. Also, making laws is allocated to the legislative branch, and to argue that a President may flout them, as well as to flout his or her constitutional duty to see that the laws are faithfully executed, is to abnegate the doctrine of separation of powers. Thus, the bedrock of Sidak's argument swiftly sinks into a morass. On this point Sidak insinuated that Congress has prohibited the President from exercising his or her prerogatives, but all the historical situations that he cites involve limits on this power, not prohibition of its exercise. The most extreme statement of his position on this issue is "[t]he Constitution does not condition its commands in Article 2 on Congress periodically granting the President permission to act." Clause 7 suggests no such requirement, and Congress has never asserted that the President is its slave. It has merely, from time to time, placed restrictions on the executive branch's spending.

One way to demonstrate the flaws in Sidak's position that the prohibition against legislative intrusion upon the President's duties and prerogatives is absolute is to take it totally seriously and then determine the consequences that would ensue. Sidak maintained that appropriation riders that limited the President in these matters are unconstitutional, so that Congress has no constitutional authority to enact them. However, it also follows that Congress has no authority to appropriate in any way except to make an indefinite appropriation (one that has no monetary upper limit and no time limit in which it is to be expended). To appropriate otherwise is to limit. Indeed, it probably follows from Sidak's absolute position that Congress has no power to appropriate except in block grants, because to specify purposes for which money is to be spent is to limit. Thus, in each session Congress, to satisfy Sidak's rule, would have to make one and only one appropriation to the executive branch. It would have to be an indefinite appropriation for whatever purposes the executive thinks are appropriate. This is an absurd situation that cannot be justified.

Sidak considered the President's duty to execute the laws (US Const, Art II, § 3) to be particularly important and acts that he considered to inhibit it to be particularly egregious examples of Congress' alleged abuse of this clause. However, the appropriation riders that are the most common battleground in regard to this clause are the law; failing to abide by them is failing to execute the law. Sidak actually meant that the President has the power to execute whatever laws he or she wishes to execute and in whatever way he or she wishes to do so. Part of his argument is that the execution of the laws should be unitary. However, the issue is making laws. That is, may Congress make a law, such as an appropriation rider, that must be executed or may the President in effect amend or repeal it on his or her own initiative in order to accomplish a purpose that he or she prefers? If the President may do this, then Congress' authority to make laws is not very valuable.

In his arguments, Sidak occasionally drew back from his absolute position. For example, he wrote that Clause 7 gives Congress "the principal and recurring responsibility for raising public funds and directing their use." This is a bit of a concession, but the clause actually says that no money may be drawn from the Treasury except by means of an appropriation, that is, except by means of congressional action. Congress, therefore, has the sole responsibility for directing the use of public funds. He also asserted that there will be an inevitable electoral check on a President who overreached in exercising his or her alleged spending power. Again we see a double-edged sword. Why does not the same inevitability justify Congress' authority to condition the executive branch's spending? Also, does the availability of electoral retribution make an action constitutional? If so, do we really need courts?

The President, according to Sidak, should also be constrained by three procedural rules. To flout an appropriation rider, the President must be able to point to part of the Constitution's text that states a power or duty that he or she has and that is restricted by the rider; he or she must spend the minimum amount needed "to produce the desired public good"; and he or she must make public his or her actions by publishing a statement of them. Limits to Sidak's absolute position are welcome, but these procedural rules hardly remedy an unconstitutional overreaching.

Kate Stith, in an article that has already been cited, began with the premise that activity in this country is divided between public and private, which seems like an unexceptional analysis. She then asserted that "in specifying the activities on which public funds may be spent, the legislature defines the contours of the federal government." This seems to mean that Congress has the sole authority, under Clause 7, to appropriate money. However, this is the point that she needs to prove, so she seems to be using circular logic.

If Congress is to make appropriations, it needs to control all public funds, and it needs the authority to determine the ways in which they shall be spent. That is, Congress needs the two kinds of authority expressed by Clause 7's plain meaning. Stith expressed the two needs in terms of two principles. One is the Principle of the Public Fisc: all moneys received by the government are public funds. The other is the Principle of Appropriations Control: there may be no expenditure without legislative authorization. Although Stith began by assuming that which she attempted to prove, her second step takes her very close to the positions on these issues that appears in the case law. That is, she seems to have intuited the opinion in OPM v. Richmond, which was issued three years after she published her article.

Unlike Sidak, Stith thought that Clause 7 does not limit Congress but that it orders Congress. That is, the "necessary and proper clause" (US Const, Art 1, § 8, Clause 18) bestows on Congress the power to legislate, and the appropriations clause bestows on Congress the duty to control federal spending by legislating. Another reason for that assertion is that if Congress cedes appropriations power to the President, it weakens its own authority to tax and borrow under Article 1, § 8, Clauses 1 and 2. This follows because these powers must be exercised for purposes that Congress determines and because if the President can exercise coercive spending he or she has usurped some of Congress' power to bring funds into the Treasury: Congress must tax partly for reasons beyond its control. This is an interesting and quite compelling argument. If Congress were to take it seriously, it would more vigorously assert its "power of the purse" against the President.

Stith did recognize limits on Congress' control over appropriations. She made an exception for limits that the Constitution itself expresses, such as the First Amendment. Her analysis is again close to the case law, which recognizes an exception for limits that are directed explicitly at Congress. She also accepted the second limit that appears in the case law—Congress may not totally negate a power that is granted by the Constitution to another branch of government. Unfortunately, she also recognized an enormous exception: one for emergencies. If this were an agreed upon exception, the executive branch would invoke it repeatedly and interpret the appropriations control that Clause 7 grants to be nugatory.

Stith asserted that under the current situation relief for Presidential overreaching in regard to spending would likely not come from the courts, because they would probably decline, either on the basis of the doctrine of standing to sue or on the basis of the political question doctrine, to reach the merits of a case that involved Presidential overreaching. It is, however, far from obvious that a genuine case or controversy cannot be presented and that a court would not touch these issues. For instance, the court in OPM v. Richmond forthrightly took on the issue. In the absence of policing by the courts, Stith suggested that Congress strengthen the General Accounting Office and give it more power to monitor the executive branch's spending.

In short, both Sidak and Stith made some interesting points. Probably more important, they presented an enormous amount of historical information: both writers are extremely well versed in the subject. Stith made far more sense primarily because her position is much closer to the court's interpretation of the clause. However, it is to the case law, not to those two articles, that one needs to look in order to understand the purport of Clause 7. If Congress becomes more aggressive in this area and especially if it becomes litigious, we will have more case law, and thus we will have more illumination of the clause.

Clause 8: Titles and Gifts Prohibited

CLAUSE 8. NO TITLE OF NOBILITY SHALL BE GRANTED BY THE UNITED STATES: AND NO PERSON HOLDING ANY OFFICE OF PROFIT OR TRUST UNDER THEM, SHALL, WITHOUT THE CONSENT OF THE CONGRESS, ACCEPT OF ANY PRESENT, EMOLUMENT, OFFICE, OR TITLE, OF ANY KIND WHATEVER, FROM ANY KING, PRINCE OR FOREIGN STATE.

Oddly enough, despite Clause 8's relative unimportance, one of the prohibitions specified in it is, by means of another constitutional provision, made applicable to the states. Section 10 of Article 1 states, among other things, that "[n]o state shall...grant any title of nobility."

This clause has never been litigated. In fact, because it would be difficult for anyone who wishes to challenge, say, the acceptance of a gift by a public official, to convince a court that he or she has standing to sue, there probably never will be litigation on this clause. However, because the many contacts between officials of this country and officials of other countries ensure that Clause 8's subject matter will frequently be relevant, the clause deserves some examination. The clause also sets the standards for the documents that, in the absence of judicial opinions, guide conduct on the matters that the clause addresses. These documents include ethical codes and administrative conduct manuals.

Analysis of Clause 8 should not be restricted to interpreting, without guidance, the clause's wording. The clause has been interpreted in three kinds of official documents: opinions of the United States Attorney General, opinions of the Office of Legal Counsel in the United States Department of Justice, and opinions of the Comptroller General. Unlike judicial opinions, none of these kinds of document has precedential value. However, if the clause were ever to be the subject of litigation, a court might look at these documents for guidance. Of these kinds of documents, a court would most likely take the opinions of the Attorney General most seriously, so this analysis will deal only with them.

The clause's prohibition against granting titles of nobility is a dead letter. Early in the history of this nation, there would have been a slight chance of these kinds of grants being made. In fact, at that time, a few persons advocated making George Washington in effect a king by granting him lifetime tenure in the office of President unless he was removed for good cause. This arrangement could have been the first step toward establishing a titled nobility. However, this was a distinctly minority opinion, and, after the republic had existed for a few years, granting titles of nobility became inconceivable. Not surprisingly, no opinion of the Attorney General addresses this issue.

However, these opinions do cast some light on the major terms in Clause 8. The opinion that interprets "[c]onsent of the Congress" does so very liberally (40 Ops. Atty. Gen. 513 (1947)). The Attorney General considered the constitutionality of employees of the Weather Bureau being placed on leave without pay and detailed to Eire (Ireland). The Attorney General asserted that a statute allowing the Chief of the Weather Bureau to maintain reporting stations in cooperation with foreign governments indicated the consent of Congress to this arrangement. The Attorney General drew an inference from the statute, jumping from interpreting the statute's plain meaning in regard to cooperation to an assertion that the statute "plainly authorizes the detailing of employees." The inference is considerably overstated but perhaps sustainable. Less convincing is the next inference: that the statute authorized the arrangement's most important details. This inference would be convincing if the persons in question remained U.S. employees and were paid by the U.S. government. Under these circumstances, the Chief would be maintaining weather stations in cooperation with Eire. However, the arrangement in question severed the employees' relations with this country's government. If a court used this opinion as a guide, it would not require instance-by-instance Congressional consent and would be willing to find consent in general statutes. The Attorney General's leniency in this opinion reflects the increasing complexity of relations with other nations.

"Persons" are constrained by that clause. Although in legal contexts that term is sometimes interpreted broadly to include non-human entities such as corporations and units of government, the pertinent Attorney General's opinion defines this term narrowly (24 Ops. Atty. Gen. 117 (1902)). An Attorney General had been asked about gifts that were made to the Navy Department, the Military Academy, the Naval Academy, and a number of individuals. He distinguished among the recipients, stating that the first three entities were part of the government so that the clause was irrelevant to gifts made to them but that the individuals were covered by the clause. Although that part of the opinion is not totally clear, the Attorney General seems to mean that gifts may not, under this clause, be accepted by individuals but they may be accepted by governmental agencies.

If a court were to read the prohibition more broadly, so as to prohibit individuals from accepting presents that were intended for the government, the consequences would be more serious than one might first imagine. First, one needs to think of nonconventional presents—those that are not in the nature of photographs, paintings, and other personal items. An example is a gift of a large amount of cash. As we saw in the analysis of the previous clause, the federal government clandestinely solicited millions of dollars to fund the Nicaraguan Contras in the absence of appropriations by Congress. For example, the Sultan of Brunei gave the U.S. ten million dollars. Although some of the contributions were implicitly connected to a quid pro quo, some were probably pure gifts. If this clause prohibits this kind of behavior, one of the means that the executive branch has exercised to circumvent Clause 7 is precluded by Clause 8. The context in which "present" appears in this clause, however, makes this interpretation unconvincing. Only individuals may receive titles and offices, so it is more likely than not that a court would consider Clause 8 to preclude the acceptance of presents only if the person who ends up in possession of them is an individual. Moreover, aside from the prohibition against granting titles of nobility, the clause appears to be intended to prevent governmental officials from developing divided loyalties as a result of receiving and keeping something of value from another country.

Clause 8 forbids accepting four things—presents, emoluments, offices, and titles—and modifies each with "of any kind whatever," indicating that these things are to be broadly construed. However, Attorneys General have interpreted the four things with varying degrees of rigor. One Attorney General wrote that photographs, which had a minimal value, were presents covered by the clause (24 Opps. Atty. Gen. 17 (1902)). In the nineteenth century, two Attorneys General made formalistic analyses of "emolument" and "office" (6 Ops. Atty. Gen. 409 (1854) and 13 Ops. Atty. Gen. 537 (1871)). According to one of these opinions, a U.S. marshall may not also be a commercial agent of France (6 Ops. Atty. Gen. 409 (1854)). Under the arrangement, the marshall apparently would have literally become an agent of France instead of merely occasionally performing services. A later opinion more firmly drew the distinction, stating that an American minister to another country may serve a third country informally but may not accept an actual commission to do so (13 Ops. Atty. Gen. 537 (1871)). A commission would have created an official relationship, thus making the diplomat the holder of an "office," which Clause 8 forbids. The distinction does not seem particularly compelling.

The other issue about Clause 8 is the foreign entity to which it refers. One opinion stated that the clause's "language has been viewed as particularly directed against every kind of influence by foreign *governments* upon officers of the United States" (24 Ops. Atty. Gen. 117 (1902)). However, the text refers to "prince," which could mean anyone who has that title or, more narrowly, a head of state. The Attorney General in that opinion assumed that the term applied to a titular prince and proceeded to decide on the propriety of this prince's gifts.

If there is a pattern in these four opinions of the Attorney General, it is temporal, not conceptual. That is, the opinions issued in 1854, 1871, and 1902 are fairly rigorous, which reflects the much smaller size of the federal government and the less numerous contacts between its officials and officials of other countries. The opinion that was issued in 1947 resulted from a more flexible approach that suits the vastly increased size of the federal government and the greatly increased frequency of contacts with other countries.

NOTES

1. 3 William Blackstone, *Commentaries on the Laws of England* (1765), I, 129.
2. Martin S. Sheffer, "Presidential Power to Suspend Habeas Corpus: The Taney-Bates Dialogue and *Ex Parte Merryman,*" *Oklahoma City Univ. Law Rev.* 11 (1986) 1.
3. Raoul Berger, "Bills of Attainder: A Study of Amendment by Court," *Cornell Law Rev.* 63 (1978) 356.
4. John C. Hamilton, *History of the Republic of the United States* (1859), 34, quoted in United States v. Brown, 1965.
5. Michael P. Lehmann, "The Bill of Attainder Doctrine: A Survey of the Decisional Law," *Hastings Const. Law Q.* 5 (1978).
6. Lehmann, "Survey," 833–34.
7. Lehmann, "Survey," 961–63.
8. Lehmann, "Survey," 844–45.
9. W.K. Wimsatt and Monroe Beardsley, "The Intentional Fallacy," in *The Verbal Icon: Studies in the Meaning of Poetry* (1954).
10. Lehmann, "Survey," 894.
11. Lehmann, "Survey," 1003.
12. 1 Blackstone, *Commentaries*, 46.
13. Joseph Story, *Commentaries on the Constitution of the United States* (Boston: 1833), 1339.
14. Dante Alighieri, *The Divine Comedy*, Paradiso, XVII, 56–63. Translated by John D. Sinclair.
15. John Milton, "When I Consider How My Light Is Spent."
16. William Holmes Brown, *House Practice: A Guide to the Rules, Precedents and Procedures of the House* (Washington: U.S. Congress, 1996).
17. Louis Fisher, "How Tightly Can Congress Draw the Purse Strings?" *Am. J. of Int. Law* 83 (1989) 762.
18. Kate Stith, "Congress' Power of the Purse," *Yale Law J.* 97 (1988) 1351.
19. Stith, "Congress' Power of the Purse," 1351.
20. Fisher, "The Purse Strings?" *Am. J. of Int. Law* 83 (1989) 762.
21. Peter Raven-Hansen and William Banks, "Pulling the Purse Strings of the Commander in Chief," *Virg. Law Rev.* 80 (1994) 885.
22. J. Gregory Sidak, "The President's Power of the Purse," *Duke Law J.* (1989) 1206–07.

23. The articles already mentioned contain valuable accounts of those moves and countermoves, and they are the basis for the account that follows.

24. Letter to the Senate and House of Representatives, May 26, 1862.

25. "The Appropriations Power and the Necessary and Proper Clause," Wash. Univ. Law Q. 68 (1990) 636. The reference is to a symposium, the participants of which were a government employee and an academic who supported a conception of the appropriations clause that favored Congress and a government employee and an academic who supported a conception of the appropriations clause that favored the executive branch.

26. Pub. L. No. 87–195, § 45, 75 Stat. 434.

27. Peter Raven-Hansen and William C. Banks, "From Vietnam to Desert Shield: The Commander In Chief's Spending Power," *Iowa Law Rev.* 81 (1995) 141.

28. Stith, "Power of the Purse," *Yale Law J.* 97 (1988) 1366–70.

29. Sidak, "The President's Power of the Purse," *Duke Law J.* 1989 (1989) 1208–10.

Conclusion

The eight clauses in Article I, § 9 have little in common. Their subject matter is diverse. Two of them deal with revenue flowing into the federal treasury, specifically with taxation. One of them deals with money flowing out of the federal treasury. Several of them constrain the actions that the federal government may take against its citizens. Looked at from the opposite angle, those provisions create rights for the citizens of our country.

However, the clauses do have a few qualities in common. All of them are directed at the federal government, which is indicated by the appearance in the next section of the Articles of the Constitution, which explicitly is directed at the states, of analogies to some of those clauses, and by their wording. However, only some of them apply to Congress, notwithstanding some of the commentators on this Section. For example, Clause 7 (prohibition against drawing money from the treasury except by means of appropriations) applies principally to the executive branch of government.

The most meaningful pattern in these clauses is that they are underused. Some of the clauses intrinsically have little significance, but others have considerable, but basically unrealized, potential. The courts are partly to blame. Although the case law on Clause 3 (prohibitions against ex post facto laws and bills of attainder) is not consistent, there is a line of cases that assumes these prohibitions to be weak and riddled with exceptions. Congress is also partly to blame. In regard to Clause 7, Congress has worked out a number of makeshift and ad hoc accommodations with the executive branch rather than forcing a constitutional confrontation by litigating.

Bibliographical Essay

Only a few law review articles and no books have been published on Article 1, § 9 of the U.S. Constitution. In fact, no recent law review articles have been published on many of the clauses. However, there is an excellent and exhaustive book-length article on bills of attainder and an interesting scholarly debate on the appropriations clause. Standard treatises on constitutional law and the Congressional Research Service's Budget Office's Annotated Constitution include brief accounts of the case law on the clauses in § 9. Perhaps this book will increase scholarly interest in at least some of these clauses.

On the suspension of the writ of habeas corpus, a note and an article are worth examining. The note, although it is on the writ in general rather than on suspension of the privilege, provides a useful historical survey of the writ in English and American legal history. The article is a study of the case that ensued after President Lincoln suspended the privilege of the writ and of the attack on that decision by Lincoln's Attorney General. Although a few of its interpretations are at least questionable, this article indicates the high stakes that are involved when governmental officials contemplate suspending the privilege. These works are:

Inafuku, Rae F. "Note: Coleman v. Thompson—Sacrificing Fundamental Rights in Deference to the States: The Supreme Court's 1991 Interpretation of the Writ of Habeas Corpus," *Santa Clara Law Review* 34 (1994) 625–61.

Sheffer, Martin S. "Presidential Power to Suspend Habeas Corpus: The Taney-Bates Dialogue and *Ex Parte Merryman*," *Oklahoma City University Law Review* 11, 1 (Spring 1986): 1–30.

The scholarship on bills of attainder includes a very lengthy, superb article by Michael P. Lehmann. He not only includes a helpful historical account of bills of attainder but also meticulously analyzes the prohibitions against this kind of legislation in both Sections 9 and 10 of Article I, the latter being applicable to the states. Whereas, one of Lehmann's points was that the prohibition against bills of attainder should be taken more seriously, Raoul Berger argued for a very narrow view of this prohibition. A law review note on this subject is somewhat valuable but quite old. These works are:

Berger, Raoul, "Bills of Attainder: A Study of Amendment by the Court," *Cornell Law Review* 63, 3 (March 1978): 356–404.

Lehmann, Michael P. "The Bill of Attainder Doctrine: A Survey of the Decisional Law," *Hastings Constitutional Law Quarterly* 5, 4 (Summer 1978) 767–1012.

"The Bounds of Legislative Specification: A Suggested Approach to the Bill of Attainder Clause," *Yale Law Journal* 72 (1962) 330–67.

Of the clauses in this section, Clause 7, the appropriations clause, has generated by far the greatest number of law review articles. If one measures richness by measuring diversity of viewpoints and forthright statement of positions, this clause also has produced the richest array of secondary work. Peter Raven-Hansen and William C. Banks have written two articles that provide much useful background information on the struggles between Congress and Presidents for control of spending on international relations and war and also on the devices used by these branches of government to increase their control over this kind of spending. A symposium that the *Washington University Law Quarterly* published is a good place to begin for anyone who wants to understand the positions taken and arguments employed by the defenders of Congressional prerogatives and the defenders of Presidential prerogatives on control of the purse strings in regard to international and military affairs. One of the participants in that symposium, Louis Fisher, also published an article on the subject. Another symposium and a rather old article by Michael J. Glennon are also worth reading. Persons who wish to examine this issue also should read Kate Stith's article and J. Gregory Sidak's rejoinder to it. Stith defended Congress' power and is more convincing than Sidak. As Part I suggests, both of them are a bit off the mark, and both their positions were undermined by a case that was decided after they published their articles. Nevertheless, they are worth reading. These works are:

Bennett, Charles, Arthur B. Culvehouse, Jr., Geoffrey P. Miller, William Bradford Reynolds, and William Van Alstyne, "The President's Powers as Commander-in-Chief versus Congress' War Powers and Appropriations Powers," *University of Miami Law Review* 43, 1 (September 1988) 17–59.

Fisher, Louis, "How Tightly Can Congress Draw the Purse Strings?" *The American Journal of International Law* 83, 4 (October 1989) 758–66.

Glennon, Michael J., "Strengthening the War Powers Resolution: The Case for Purse-Strings Restrictions," *Minnesota Law Review* 60 1 (November 1975) 1–44.

Meese, Edwin III (Moderator), "The Appropriations Power and the Necessary and Proper Clause," *Washington University Law Quarterly* 68, 3 (1990) 623–57.

Raven-Hansen, Peter, and William C. Banks, "Pulling the Purse Strings of the Commander in Chief," *Virginia Law Review* 80, 4 (May 1994) 834–944.

Raven-Hansen, Peter, and William C. Banks, "From Vietnam to Desert Shield: The Commander in Chief's Spending Power," *Iowa Law Review* 79, 1 (October 1995) 81–147.

Sidak, J. Gregory, "The President's Power of the Purse," *Duke Law Journal* (1989) 1162–1253.

Stith, Kate, "Congress' Power of the Purse," *The Yale Law Journal* 97, 7 (1988) 1346–96.

Table of Cases

A
A.G. Spalding & Bros. v. Edwards, 262 U.S. 66 (1923)
Alabama G.S.R. Co. v. United States, 3490 U.S. 216 (1951)
Armour Packing Co. v. United States, 209 U.S. 56 (1908)
Austin v. United States, 155 U.S. 417 (1894)
Avent v. United States, 266 U.S. 127 (1924)

B
Bryson v. United States, 396 U.S. 64 (1969)
Bugajewitz v. Adams, 228 U.S. 585 (1913)
Burgess v. Salmon, 97 U.S. 381 (1878)

C
Calder v. Bull, 3 U.S. 386 (1798)
Cincinnati Soap Co. v. United States, 301 U.S. 308 (1937)
Clark Distilling Co. v. Western Maryland Railroad Co., 242 U.S. 311 (1917)
Communications Ass'n v. Douds, 339 U.S. 382 (1950)
Communist Party v. Subversive Activities Control Board, 367 U.S. 1 (1961)
Complete Auto Transit v. Brady, 430 U.S. 274 (1977)
Cook v. United States, 138 U.S. 157 (1891)
Cooley v. Board of Wardens of Port of Philadelphia, 53 U.S. 299 (1851)
Cornell v. Coyne, 192 U.S. 418 (1904)
Cummings v. Missouri, 71 U.S. 277 (1867)

D
Dennis v. United States, 384 U.S. 855 (1966)
Department of Revenue of Wash. v. Association of Wash. Stevedoring Cos., 435 U.S. 734 (1978)
De Veau v. Braisted (1960)
Dooley v. United States, 183 U.S. 151 (1901)

Downes v. Bidwell, 182 U.S. 244 (1901)
Dred Scott v. Sandford, 60 U.S. 393 (1856)
Duncan v. Kahanamoku, 327 U.S. 304 (1946)

E

Edye v. Robertson, 112 U.S. 580 (1884)
Ex Parte Bollman, 71 U.S. 2 (1807)
Ex Parte Dorr, 44 U.S. 103 (1845)
Ex Parte Garland, 71 U.S. 333 (1866)
Ex Parte Merryman, 17 Fed. Cas. 144 (1861)
Ex Parte Milligan, 71 U.S. 2 (1866)
Ex Parte Yerger, 75 U.S. 85 (1868)

F

Fairbank v. United States, 181 U.S. 283 (1901)
Fay v. Noia, 372 U.S. 391 (1963)
Felker v. Turpin, 518 U.S. 1051 (1996)
Fisher v. Baker, 203 U.S. 174 (1906)
Flast v. Cohen, 392 U.S. 411 (1968)
Flemming v. Nestor, 363 U.S. 603 (1960)
Fletcher v. Peck, 10 U.S. 87 (1810)

G

Galvan v. Press, 347 U.S. 522 (1954)
Gasquet v. Lapeyre, 242 U.S. 367 (1917)
Gibbons v. Ogden, 9 Wheat. 1 (1824)
Goldwater v. Carter, 444 U.S. 996 (1979)

H

Harisiades v. Shaughnessy, 342 U.S. 580 (1952)
Hart v. United States, 118 U.S. 62 (1886)

J

Johannessen v. United States, 225 U.S. 227 (1912)
Johnson v. Chicago & P. Elevator Co., 119 U.S. 388 (1886)
Jones v. Cunningham, 371 U.S. 236 (1963)

K

Kennedy v. Mendoza-Martinez, 372 U.S. 144 (1963)
Kessler v. Strecker, 301 U.S. 22 (1939)
Knote v. United States, 95 U.S. 149 (1877)

L

Landgraf v. USI Film Products, 511 U.S. 244 (1994)
Lehman v. Carson, 353 U.S. 685 (1957)
Louisiana Pub. Serv. Comm. v. Texas & N.O.R. Co., 284 U.S. 125 (1931)
Luria v. United States, 231 U.S. 9 (1913)
Luther v. Borden, 48 U.S. 1 (1849)

M

Mahler v. Erby, 264 U.S. 32 (1924)
Marcello v. Bonds, 349 U.S. 302 (1955)
Marks v. United States, 237 U.S. 309 (1915)
McNally v. Hill, 293 U.S. 131 (1934)
Michelin Tire Corp. v. Wages, 423 U.S. 276 (1976)
Morgan v. Louisiana, 118 U.S. 455 (1886)
Morgan's L. & T. R. & S. S. C. v. Board of Health, 118 U.S. 455 (1886)
Munn v. Illinois, 94 U.S. 113 (1876)
Murphy v. Ramsey, 114 U.S. 15 (1885)

N

Neeley v. Henkel, 180 U.S. 109 (1901)
Nixon v. Administrator of General Services, 433 U.S. 425 (1966)

O

Ogden v. Saunders, 25 U.S. 213 (1827)
OPM v. Richmond, 496 U.S. 414 (1990)

P

Pace v. Burgess, 92 U.S. 372 (1875)
Pennsylvania v. Wheeling & Belmont Bridge Co., 59 U.S. 421 (1855)
Portley v. Grossman, 444 U.S. 1311 (1980)
Prigg v. Com. of Pennsylvania, 41 U.S. 539 (1842)

R

Reeside v. Walker, 52 U.S. 272 (1850)
Republic Nat. Bank Miami v. United States, 506 U.S. 80 (1992)

S

Selective Service v. Minn. Public Int. Res. Gp., 468 U.S. 841 (1984)
Smith v. Turner and Norris v. Boston, 48 U.S. 283 (1849)
South Carolina v. Georgia, 93 U.S. 4 (1876)
South Carolina v. Katzenbach, 383 U.S. 301 (1966)
State ex rel. Mueller v. Powers, 64 Wis2d 643, 221 NW2d 692 (1974)
Swain v. Pressley, 430 U.S. 372 (1977)

T

Territory of Alaska v. Troy, 258 U.S. 101 (1922)
Thames and Mersey Marine Ins. Co. v. United States, 237 U.S. 19 (1915)
Thompson v. Darden, 198 U.S. 310 (1905)
Trop v. Dulles, 356 U.S. 86 (1958)
Turpin v. Burgess, 117 U.S. 504 (1886)

U

United States v. Brown, 381 U.S. 437 (1965)
United States v. Butler, 297 U.S. 1 (1936)
United States v. Hill, 248 U.S. 420 (1919)
United States v. Hvoslef, 237 U.S. 1 (1915)

United States v. International Business Machines, 517 U.S. 843 (1996)
United States v. Klein, 80 U.S. 128 (1871)
United States v. Lovett, 328 U.S. 303 (1946)
United States v. Maccollom, 426 U.S. 317 (1976)
United States v. New York & Cuba Mail S. S. Co., 200 U.S. 488 (1906)
United States v. P. Koenig Coal Co., 270 U.S. 512 (1926)
United States v. Powers, 307 U.S. 214 (1939)
United States v. Richardson, 418 U.S. 166 (1974)
United States v. Trans-Missouri Freight Ass'n, 166 U.S. 290 (1897)
United States v. United States Shoe Corporation, 523 U.S. 360 (1998)

W

William E. Peck & Co. v. Lowe, 247 U.S. 165 (1918)
Williams v. Fears, 179 U.S. 270 (1900)
Williams v. United States, 255 U.S. 336 (1921)
Woodruff v. Parham, 75 U.S. 123 (1868)

Index

ABOUT THE AUTHOR

JACK STARK is a legislative attorney. He is the editor of this series, Reference Guides to the United States Constitution. He is the author of *The Wisconsin State Constitution* (Greenwood, 1997) and *The Iowa State Constitution* (Greenwood, 1998)

www.ingramcontent.com/pod-product-compliance
Ingram Content Group UK Ltd.
Pitfield, Milton Keynes, MK11 3LW, UK
UKHW021907150926
475560UK00003B/225

9 780313 313523